THE SANS INSTITUTE

ORACLE SECURITY
Step-by-Step

A Survival Guide for Oracle Security

Introduction

One of the great sources of productivity and effectiveness in the community of computer professionals is the willingness of active practitioners to take time to share some of the lessons they have learned and the techniques they have perfected. Much of the sharing takes place through online news groups, web postings, and presentations at technical meetings. Those who take the time to scan the news groups, surf the web, and attend the meetings gain measurably from those interactions.

SANS' Step-by-Step series raises information-sharing to a new level in which experts share techniques they have found to be effective. They integrate the techniques into a step-by-step plan, and then subject the plan in detail to the close scrutiny of other experts. The process continues until consensus has been reached. This is difficult: it asks a large number of people to spend a great deal of time making sure the information is useful and correct.

Security of databases, a frequent topic of discussion both in the media and at security conferences, is becoming more important for security managers and database administrators. The database is an obvious target for external attackers and for internal company abuse. In fact, many Oracle databases and systems can be broken into very easily. This statement is not meant to instill fear, although it should. It is a fact that Oracle databases in general have not been securely installed and maintained. Why is that? While most organizations take security seriously, they do not take database security as seriously as network and Internet security. They should. Companies that use Oracle software and its databases use it to store the most valuable assets that the company possesses — **its data**.

A few words now on what this guide does **not** purport to be. Although this booklet provides valuable insight into the world of securing an Oracle database, it is **not** a textbook on the subject -- textbooks tend to include detailed discussions on how the technology works and background on many related technologies. This guide is written in a cookbook style in order to pass on the experience of many DBAs and Oracle security practitioners. Furthermore, it **cannot** replace in-depth security and Oracle training, which should be undertaken for new Oracle installations. Acting on all of the steps in this guide is **not** a substitute for a sound Oracle database security policy included in an overall corporate security plan. Since security is a continuously evolving field, the security press, web sites and Oracle should be monitored for new vulnerabilities and fixes and patches.

This first edition of this guide covers both Unix and Windows (NT/ 2K and higher) installations of Oracle. Oracle can be installed on many different platforms -- over 70 are supported. While some of the actions and steps in this guide are related to specific operating systems, many are not and can be applied to any Oracle installation.

Introduction

There are three main areas where Oracle security can be jeopardized:

- The default installation parameters that make the database insecure. While it is very difficult for Oracle to create a secure database out of the box, and satisfy customers' needs, Oracle is pro-active on these issues and working towards a more secure default installation.
- Known vulnerabilities found by hackers and crackers, which can be fixed either by applying patches or by implementing workarounds.
- Parameters and settings, those inadvertently set up by the application implementers or the Database Administrator.

This guide can therefore be used in two ways: to secure a new database as it is built, and to secure an existing database. The latter can be harder since existing applications, as well as software and business procedures need to be taken into account.

The text has been divided into phases that cover from general security advice through operating system settings and user access, to the database settings and access controls and right through to the applications that access Oracle. Each phase presents a number of problems and each of these problems defines a step. These steps then include step-by-step instructions for checking for existence of the problem, and describing the exact commands and actions needed to remedy the problem.

Each action includes a matrix describing the operating system that the action applies to as well as the versions of Oracle. The matrix also includes a security severity level, which ranges from 1, the highest, to 5 the lowest. These severity levels are detailed below:

Level	Rating	Description
1	VERY HIGH SECURITY RISK	Check should be made regularly for non-compliance and solution adopted immediately.
2	HIGH SECURITY RISK	Check should be made regularly and solution applied at first scheduled maintenance opportunity.
3	SECURITY RISK	Check periodically for non-compliance and make changes promptly.
4	LOW SECURITY RISK	Check at installation or design / development phase and apply changes if the application / product will allow it.
5	VERY MINOR RISK	Check at installation or design / development phase. Non-compliance could cause a security risk but would not endanger normal systems — solutions should be applied on highly secure systems such as military, health, top secret etc.

Introduction

The appendix includes a cross-reference matrix that lists each action by severity level. It can be useful to apply all the actions to achieve a required level of security. The appendix also cross-references the actions by Operating system and by Oracle version numbers where relevant. Finally the cross-reference details the actions needed to secure a clean default installation.

Application Developers tend to be narrowly focused and as a result can make poor and uninformed decisions regarding security. The actions and problems in Phase Seven allude to this issue, and attempt to guide a development DBA to better assist in the design, development and implementation of secure applications.

This guide is designed for DBAs and security managers: some items are more advanced than others and require more understanding of how Oracle will react to the changes. A junior DBA can carry out most of the actions in this guide, but a senior DBA should be on hand to assist with the advanced items and to guide the junior DBA where necessary. The guide is also of use to the security manager to help him understand the issues inherent in an Oracle database installation and to also help formulate database security policies.

Unless stated otherwise, the SQL tests and checks should be run as the SYS user connecting as SYSDBA. Most tests can be run by any DBA, but some tests require access to tables owned by SYS. All of the operating system checks are run as the root user under Unix and as the Local Administrator on Windows unless otherwise stated.

For those readers who prefer to use GUI tools to administer and monitor their databases, then Oracle Enterprise Manager can be used to perform many of the checks and tasks in this guide. Some of the SQL checks can also be run and scheduled from the OEM and run against many databases from the same console. To make this guide as valuable as possible, details of running tests in OEM have not been provided since this would preclude Oracle customers who choose not to use OEM.

The SANS Institute and the author accept no responsibility for any errors or damage that results from running any of the tests in the guide. The Oracle database is a complex product and some actions can depend on what purpose the database is being used for. Every effort has been made to ensure that the queries and commands do not alter data and work correctly. Where commands or instructions are given to make amendments to the database or to data stored, the DBA should understand how those changes could affect applications running against the database before making the changes. All of the actions in this guide have been tested successfully by the reviewers against many versions of Oracle on differing Operating systems. Given the rapid changes in Oracle technology, however, you may find features that have changed or where we have made mistakes. Please send an email to the author at book@petefinnigan.com.

All of the scripts and SQL samples in this booklet are available from the author's web site at:
http://www.petefinnigan.com/sans/orastepcode.htm

Table of Contents

Introduction		.i
Phase 0	**Planning and Risk Assessment**	.1
Step 0.1	Known Vulnerabilities	.1
Step 0.2	Identify and Record Software Versions and Patch Levels on the System	.2
Step 0.3	Record the Database Configuration	.3
Step 0.4	Record Security Configuration	.3
Step 0.5	Review Database Security Procedures	.3
Step 0.6	Store Copies of the Media Off-Site	.4
Step 0.7	Location of Servers	.4
Step 0.8	Architecture	.5
Phase 1	**Host Operating System Security Issues**	.7
Step 1.1	Define the Owner of the Oracle Software	.7
Step 1.2	Oracle Software File Permissions	.9
Step 1.3	Group Issues	.13
Step 1.4	General File Issues	.14
Step 1.5	Usernames and Passwords in The Process List	.19
Step 1.6	Clear Text Transmission	.21
Step 1.7	SUID and SGID Binaries	.23
Step 1.8	Password and Username Leakage	.24
Step 1.9	Logging and Auditing	.27
Step 1.10	Existence of Control Files	.29
Step 1.11	Trace Files	.30
Step 1.12	Export Files	.33
Step 1.13	Archivelog Files	.34
Step 1.14	External Tables	.37
Step 1.15	Native Compilation of PL/SQL	.38
Step 1.16	Key Files	.39
Step 1.17	Shutting Down Windows Services	.40
Phase 2	**Oracle Authentication**	.41
Step 2.1	Review Log-in Procedures	.41
Step 2.2	Default Accounts	.49
Step 2.3	Secure Application User Accounts	.56
Step 2.4	ORAPWD and the Password File	.62
Step 2.5	Oracle SID's	.63
Step 2.6	Passwords Stored in the Database	.63
Phase 3	**Oracle Access Controls**	**.67**
Step 3.1	Control User Access to Operating System Files	.67
Step 3.2	Reading Lists of Users from the Database	.74
Step 3.3	Making ExtProc More Secure	.76
Step 3.4	Data Access Descriptors	.79
Step 3.5	Access and Use of Oracle Roles	.80
Step 3.6	Reviewing Initialization Parameters	.85
Step 3.7	Objects in System Tablespace	.92
Step 3.8	Excessive System Privileges	.94
Step 3.9	External Users	.108
Step 3.10	Public Packages and Privileges	.111
Step 3.11	Direct Privileges	.116
Step 3.12	Default Tablespaces	.117
Step 3.13	Standard Roles	.119
Step 3.14	The Use of Profiles to Help Prevent Attacks	.122
Step 3.15	Hidden Initialization Parameters	.125
Step 3.16	Object Owners	.126
Step 3.17	Users Quotas	.127
Step 3.18	Naming Conventions	.128
Step 3.19	Triggers Owned by Users	.128
Step 3.20	Access to Critical Views	.130
Step 3.21	Object Creation and Access	.134
Step 3.22	Access to Views	.135
Step 3.23	Control Brute Force Password Attack	.137
Step 3.24	DBA's / Operators Reading System Tables	.138
Step 3.25	Preventing DBA's from Reading Application Data	.138
Step 3.26	Integration and Server to Server Authentication	.139
Step 3.27	Internet Access from the Oracle Database	.139
Step 3.28	Performance Pack Allows Access to SQL	.140

Phase 4	**Auditing**	**141**
Step 4.1	Configure the Storage for Auditing	141
Step 4.2	Audit DML Failures	142
Step 4.3	Set-up Basic Auditing	143
Step 4.4	Basic Auditing Steps	150
Step 4.5	Date / Time Stamps of Objects	152
Step 4.6	Procedures for Reviewing Audit Logs	153
Step 4.7	Row-Level Auditing	153
Step 4.8	Failure to Be Alerted of Suspicious Activity	155
Step 4.9	Failure to Audit the Security Profile	155
Step 4.10	Failure to Audit the Log Files	156

Phase 5 – Networking		**157**
Step 5.1	Listener Configuration	157
Step 5.2	IP Access Restrictions	161
Step 5.3	Listener Password	163
Step 5.4	Listener Banner Information	164
Step 5.5	Oracle Firewall	165
Step 5.6	Security of Client Configuration Files	166
Step 5.7	Database Links	169
Step 5.8	Network File Permissions	174
Step 5.9	Listener Exploits	175
Step 5.10	Remote Access	175
Step 5.11	tnsnames.ora	176
Step 5.12	Intelligent Agent	178
Step 5.13	Transmissions between Oracle Clients and Servers	180

Phase 6	**Availability / Backup / Recovery**	**181**
Step 6.1	Backup and Recovery	181
Step 6.2	Mirroring of Redo and Control Files	184
Step 6.3	Archive Logs	184
Step 6.4	File Locations and Directory Structure	186
Step 6.5	Disk Failures	188
Step 6.6	Disaster Recovery	188

Phase 7	**Application Development**	**191**
Step 7.1	Issues with PL/SQL and Java	191
Step 7.2	Applications that Access the Database	196
Step 7.3	Decommissioning Products / Applications	197
Step 7.4	Adding a New Application	198
Step 7.5	Movers, Leavers and Joiners	198
Step 7.6	Application File Permissions	199
Step 7.7	Development on Production Databases	199
Step 7.8	Ad-Hoc Queries	200
Step 7.9	Development and Test Databases	201
Step 7.10	Application Objects	204
Step 7.11	Resource Limits	205
Step 7.12	Application Authentication	206
Step 7.13	Application Access	207
Step 7.14	Public Synonyms	208
Step 7.15	Application Security	209
Step 7.16	Batch Processes	211
Step 7.17	Restrict Access to SQL*Plus	212
Step 7.18	Encryption of Critical Data	214
Step 7.19	Generated Applications	215
Step 7.20	Change Control Management	216
Step 7.21	Advanced Queues	216
Step 7.22	Tools	217
Step 7.23	Reporting Facilities Have a Different Access Model to Interactive Interfaces	217
Step 7.24	Introduction of Backdoors, Viruses, and Malignant Code by Developers	218
Step 7.25	iSQL*Plus	218
Step 7.26	Oracle Features	222
Step 7.27	Debuggers	223
Step 7.28	Divulging Database Information	224

Phase 8	**Application Servers and the Middle Tier**	**225**
Step 8.1	Oracle Portal	225
Step 8.2	Oracle Wireless Portal	228
Step 8.3	Oracle Web Cache	228
Step 8.4	Oracle iCache (Database Cache)	229
Step 8.5	Apache	230
Step 8.6	Oracle Internet File Server (iFS)	233
Step 8.7	Oracle Reports Server	234
Step 8.8	XML/XSL and the XSQL Servlet	235

A Final Word .243
Appendixes .245
Cross-Reference Check List .247

Phase 0 ~ Planning and Risk Assessment

PHASE 0
Planning and Risk Assessment

This section, the non-technical aspect of Oracle database security, covers physical security, policies and procedures.

Step 0.1 — Known Vulnerabilities

SEVERITY LEVEL
1

O/S VERSION
All

ORACLE VERSIONS
All

PROBLEM: *Oracle, like any other complex software suite, will occasionally reveal security holes. Any vulnerability reported should be addressed as soon as the patch or workaround becomes available*

Stay current with known Oracle vulnerabilities. There are a number of information sources that can help with this, some of which are listed here:

- Oracle's security site at http://otn.oracle.com/deploy/security
- Oracle's customer information site http://metalink.oracle.com also offers security information and patches for supported customers.
- The Bugtraq database at http://www.securityfocus.com/bugtraq/CERT.
- The SANS Institute http://www.sans.org
- The web site of Application Security Inc, http://www.appsecinc.com/ includes a good list of known security exploits.

When security vulnerabilities are found and Oracle releases patches, they should be applied as soon as possible.

Oracle posts security alerts and patches at the following web site, http://otn.oracle.com/deploy/security/alerts.htm
If there is a security patch required which is not available on this site, it could be available via Metalink, http://metalink.oracle.com for which you will require a support contract to download the patch.

You may also wish to consider subscribing to the security mailing lists on the Security Focus web site, particularly the BUGTRAQ and VULNDEV lists.

Oracle also now has a security alert list that can be subscribed to: http://otn.oracle.com/deploy/security/alerts.htm

Application Security, Inc. has an alert mailing list specifically targeted at Oracle vulnerabilities:
http://www.appsecinc.com/resources/mailinglist.html.

This list is provided independent of Oracle so the information disseminated is free of bias.

Note: If you find any Oracle security issues, these should be reported to Oracle through the security team by emailing secalert_us@oracle.com.

Note: Given the complex nature of Oracle software, there is no up-to-date security patch bundle that we can apply to our servers to ensure they are secure. We have to go through each vulnerability, one system at a time.

Phase 0 ~ Planning and Risk Assessment

Step 0.2 — Identify and Record Software Versions and Patch Levels on the System

SEVERITY LEVEL
1

O/S VERSION
All

ORACLE VERSIONS
All

Keep a record of all of the versions of Oracle databases and applications used in your environment, and keep a record of all patch levels installed. This is important in the event of a system being compromised or a serious accident. Knowledge of the software versions in use will help identify which patches need to be installed. In addition, knowledge of the software versions and patch levels installed will make it easier to determine if a new security issue affects your system.

A useful utility that can be used to identify the databases in use on your network is **AppDetective** from Application Security Inc. If Oracle Enterprise Manager (OEM) is installed, then it can be used to *discover* all active databases. A port scanner such as *nmap* can be used to identify ports that could be the Oracle listener. These techniques are only necessary if an organization is not completely aware of all of the databases in its care.

In addition, be sure to record the operating system version and patch levels that are installed, especially patches specific to Oracle.

It is critical to understand the risks of using versions of Oracle that are no longer supported, and for which no new security patches are available. End of correction support generally means (depending on level of perceived need and the customer's insistence) that Oracle will not provide new security bug patches. While this is generally the case, workarounds are available for some issues, and sometimes fixes applied to later versions can be used on older ones.

Patch levels and versions can be found for the main components installed by checking the view v$version. The first three digits show the version and the fourth and fifth digits show the patch level. Although this view only shows the main components, the full list of installed options, versions and patch levels can be found by reading the end of the file *installActions.log* generated during installation and updated when a patch is applied via the Universal Installer. This file can be found in <inventory directory>/logs. Oracle has no on-line means to display or query the patch levels installed.

A good script to extract Oracle versions and patch levels for Unix up to version 8 is *products.sh* in the O'Reilly book *Oracle Scripts* by Brian Lomasky and David C. Kreines.

Example: Some of the listener vulnerabilities in 7.3.4 can be solved by using the listener from Oracle 8.1.7 (See security bulletins 14, 15 and 16 on Oracle's alerts web site).

Phase 0 ~ Planning and Risk Assessment

Step 0.3 — Record the Database Configuration

SEVERITY LEVEL: 2
O/S VERSION: All
ORACLE VERSIONS: All

Consider recording your configuration and settings and storing this data in a suitable storage system such as a source code repository. In the event of any malicious activity, it will allow you to restore your current settings.

Although this is not an exhaustive list, as a minimum, this would mean storing backups of the *init.ora*, *names.ora*, *tnsnames.ora*, *ldap.ora*, *listener.ora*, *snmp.ora*, *ifilecbo.ora* (for Oracle applications) and *sqlnet.ora* or protocol.ora files. The control file should be backed up to trace, and the trace file stored. See *Phase 6* for backup information and *Step 1.10.1* for details of backing up the control file.

In addition, it is important that any operating system configuration files that have been modified by Oracle are also backed up so that they can be easily restored.

Since it is possible for multiple Oracle instances to run on the same operating system host, it is important that this be done on a per-instance basis. It is also a good idea to periodically check that each running instance has the same configuration as the recorded configuration.

There are a variety of ways to store the database configuration and important files, but it is important that a backup is made and the database configuration recorded.

Step 0.4 — Record Security Configuration

SEVERITY LEVEL: 2
O/S VERSION: All
ORACLE VERSIONS: All

As with the database configuration settings, consider recording and storing any configuration settings specific to security so that they can be restored in the event of any malicious activity.

It is also a good idea to establish formal control for these configuration settings, for instance, using a source code repository or a simple MS Excel spreadsheet run on a PC not connected to the network.

The security settings to store depend to a great extent on the site and the reader's judgment. Any settings used from this guide would qualify, such as privileges assigned to roles, roles assigned to users etc.

Note: Here the configuration may be defined by application and middle-tier configuration. Some settings may not have an automated API or configuration file. What may be stored may only be a view of the configuration, and not a repeatable set of scripts.

Step 0.5 — Review Database Security Procedures

SEVERITY LEVEL: 2
O/S VERSION: All
ORACLE VERSIONS: All

A company-wide security policy should already exist in writing and company-wide security guidelines should be developed if they do not exist.

Review any existing security procedures and related documentation paying particular attention to Oracle procedures and details. Improve and add to your company's Oracle security documentation and procedures.

If necessary, write an Oracle security procedure. A very good document describing how to write an Oracle security procedure can be found at the following URL:
http://www.dbatoolbox.com/WP2001/dbamisc/how_to_write.pdf

Phase 0 ~ Planning and Risk Assessment

Step 0.6 — Store Copies of the Media Off-Site

SEVERITY LEVEL: 3
O/S VERSION: All
ORACLE VERSIONS: All

Store copies of all media used to build the Oracle database in a secure location off-site.

Although it is useful to have back-ups stored locally, it is a good idea to also store copies of backups in an off-site location.

Backups should be stored in a secure location and protected from unauthorized use.

In addition to storing Oracle installation media, related software should also be stored in a secure off-site location along with records of important information such as contact names, telephone numbers and support details.

Note: It is good practice to create a business process to control storage of media off site, and to control access to that media, updates to that media as well as use of the media and authorized users in the event of an emergency

Step 0.7 — Location of Servers

SEVERITY LEVEL: 2
O/S VERSION: All
ORACLE VERSIONS: All

Although not strictly database specific, this item is nevertheless very important. The data stored in Oracle databases are usually considered crucial to the organization. The physical location of the server holding the oracle data is important. It should be in a locked and controlled room.

Physical access to the location where servers are located should be controlled, monitored and limited to those individuals who have a legitimate business need to access the location.

There is a good discussion on the issues to consider in controlling physical access to servers at http://www.cert.org/securityimprovement/practices/p074.html.

Clearly as with all systems, it is also important to ensure that consideration has been given to other physical security controls such as fire suppression systems, Uninterruptible Power Supply (UPS) and climate control systems.

Note: There are many good articles on this subject at CERT, SANS and Security Focus.

ORACLE SECURITY Step-by-Step

Phase 0 ~ Planning and Risk Assessment

Step 0.8 Architecture

SEVERITY LEVEL: 3
O/S VERSION: All
ORACLE VERSIONS: All

Database security is critically dependent on the context of the surrounding security architecture. Since there are many diverse application and business requirements, it is difficult to give advice about architecture, but we will try.

Architecture encompasses host operating system security, network segmentation controls, communications security, firewalls and the implementation of critical network services such as naming, directory and authentication services.

Application and database servers should ideally be located on dedicated, protected network segments. Ideally, application and database servers should not be located on the same physical host. This is particularly important for any Internet exposed application server.

As with all systems, an Oracle database server can only be as secure as the implementation of the architecture under which it is running. Therefore, all systems within the architecture must be kept secure. In particular, it is vital to keep up to date with the security issues surrounding the various operating system and applications running on the Oracle server and associated architecture.

Planning and classification of data for security and sensitivity is a good step to take before implementing a Database application.

There are other Step-by-Step guides available in this series, in particular the Step-by-Step guide to secure Solaris, Windows NT and Windows 2000. These can be purchased from the SANS store at http://store.sans.org.

Phase 1 ~ Host Operating System Security Issues

PHASE 1
Host Operating System Security Issues

Step 1.1 — Define the Owner of the Oracle Software

PROBLEM: *The owner of the Oracle software is well known to the blackhat community, and therefore easy to exploit. Since new Oracle vulnerabilities have recently been published, an attacker gaining access to a user list, or even just trying for the Oracle account, would improve his chances of getting in. Because there are a number of well-known exploits involving Oracle software, it is worth disabling the account as well. This can be considered security through obscurity. Obscurity has its place among other methods of securing software. A good article on this can be found at http://www.wideopen.com/story/101.html*

Action 1.1.1

SEVERITY LEVEL: 1
O/S VERSION: All
ORACLE VERSIONS: All

The operating system user account chosen as the owner of the Oracle software should be the account that owns all of the files in the Oracle bin directory. Use operating system commands to check the ownership of the files in $ORACLE_HOME/bin.

Action 1.1.2

SEVERITY LEVEL: 1
O/S VERSION: All
ORACLE VERSIONS: All

Consider locking the oracle O/S account. This can be done as follows on Solaris:

```
$ /usr/sbin/passmgmt <username>
```

Locking and unlocking the account to edit configuration files can be a procedure that is forgotten since users believe it is too awkward. Make sure this procedure is adhered to.

The Oracle services for the database server and the listener, etc all run as a local system account by default on Windows. The services should be run as a separate Oracle software owner user. For more information see *Action 1.2.4*.

Note: Generally speaking: the main problem with Oracle files is that they must be protected. Normal O/S security must be in place. The best approach is for an Oracle Database Server to only be accessible by the root user (Unix) or Administrator (NT/W2K amd higher) and the owner of the Oracle software.

Phase 1 ~ Host Operating System Security Issues

Action 1.1.3

SEVERITY LEVEL: 2
O/S VERSION: All
ORACLE VERSIONS: All

Do not name the owning account of the oracle software *Oracle* since this name is well known and makes it an easy target for hackers.

It is important to set a strong password for this account. The password tends to be set to *oracle*, *oracle7*, *oracle8* etc.

If the account is already named oracle then do not panic, just use the account when necessary, set a secure password or lock the account.

> **Note:** When securing an existing Oracle database, this may involve downtime and re-linking, so try to complete this during a planned system outage. A backup of the database AND of the Oracle binaries should be done before re-linking.
>
> **Note:** Another well known default operating system account is ora<sid> for SAP databases. There is no guarantee that renaming the SAP O/S account would work, and it almost certainly would not be supported by SAP. Please lobby your SAP contact for changes in this area.

Action 1.1.4

SEVERITY LEVEL: 2
O/S VERSION: Unix
ORACLE VERSIONS: All

Limit access to the account that owns the Oracle software through mechanisms such as *sudo*. *Sudo* can be found at http://www.courtesan.com/sudo.

As an alternative, disable remote log-in for the *oracle* account, thereby forcing users to use their own accounts and *su* to the *oracle* account creating a log entry.

Action 1.1.5

SEVERITY LEVEL: 2
O/S VERSION: All
ORACLE VERSIONS: All

Create different users for each piece of Oracle software. Examples:
- *Oraia* for the intelligent agent
- *Orals* for the listener
- *Oradb* for the database

This is one way to secure sensitive files such as *snmp_rw.ora* used by the *dbsnmp* software.

When installing the database software using the universal installer, choose *custom* and install each of the above components as the relevant user, re-starting the installer for each component.

Installing the listener as a separate user is very important since the listener is the outer bastion for the database and is the item that is captured first. Enabling the listener as a separate user, and even on a different server can alleviate a lot of the issues. See *Step 3.3* for more details on securing extproc.

Changing users in an existing installation could incur re-linking. See the note in *Action 1.1.3*.

> **Note:** The above names suggested for users are just that, suggestions. A user of this guide should create his or her own names.

Phase 1 ~ Host Operating System Security Issues

Step 1.2 — Oracle Software File Permissions

PROBLEM: *Incorrect file permissions on some of the Oracle files can cause major security issues.*

Action 1.2.1

SEVERITY LEVEL: 1
O/S VERSION: Unix
ORACLE VERSIONS: All

On Unix systems, ensure that the permissions on ORACLE_HOME/bin are set to 0751 (0755 in 9iR2) or less. Set all other directories in $ORACLE_HOME to 0750 or less.

The exact file permissions can be found in the relevant installation guide for the version of Oracle and the Operating system. The permissions are specified in a table and comply with United States NCSC C2 or European ITSEC E3. This information is included in the *post installations* tasks and in a section called *Verifying database file security*.

For 9i R2 this documentation can be found at
http://technet.oracle.com/docs/products/oracle9i/doc_library/release2/A96167_01/html/post-inst.htm#i1012849.

File permissions can be set tighter than these, but agreement should be sought from Oracle support.

Note: If possible deny users access to a server shell.

Action 1.2.2

SEVERITY LEVEL: 1
O/S VERSION: Unix
ORACLE VERSIONS: All

On Unix systems, ensure that the owner of the Oracle software has an appropriate *umask* value of 022 set. If permissions are not required for others (outside of the OSDBA group) then set the *umask* to 027. The most important feature of setting *umask* is to ensure that no log or trace files are world readable or writable.

Information: *There are two special operating system roles that control database administrator's logins when O/S authentication is used. These are OSDBA and OSOPER. The following privileges are available:*

OSOPER	STARTUP, SHUTDOWN, ALTER DATABASE OPEN/MOUNT, ALTER DATABASE BACKUP, ARCHIVE LOG and RECOVER and also the RESTRICTED SESSION privilege.
OSDBA	Has all system privileges WITH ADMIN and also contains the OSOPER role and allows CREATE DATABASE and time based recovery.

These two roles can only be granted to a user at the operating system level. When a user logs on as administrator, and REMOTE_LOGIN_PASSWORD_FILE=NONE Oracle first attempts to use the role OSDBA, and if this is not possible, then OSOPER is used. If it is not possible to enable either role, then the connection is not allowed. During installation these two O/S roles are "mapped" to O/S groups. They can be mapped to the same group as necessary.

Phase 1 ~ Host Operating System Security Issues

Action 1.2.3

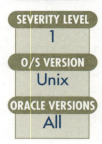

SEVERITY LEVEL
1

O/S VERSION
Unix

ORACLE VERSIONS
All

On Unix systems, ensure that the owner, group and modes of the Oracle files created upon installation are set to allow minimum privilege.

Run the following under Unix (note the group and owner are for illustration only, the correct intended group and owner should be substituted):

$chgrp –R oinstall $ORACLE_HOME

$chown –R oracle $ORACLE_HOME

Particular attention needs to be paid to ownership and group membership when cloning a database. A good source of information is **Note 141096.1 on Metalink**. To automate this process, a group can be created that allows files for similar databases to be read and copied but not altered.

The $ORACLE_HOME/rdbms/admin directory should be protected, especially *catalog.sql* and *catproc.sql* and any of the other scripts called from these. Trojans can easily be planted for the DBA to execute after any upgrade. Backups of these files should be kept. Of particular note is the fact that some of the scripts in this directory contain usernames and passwords.

The reader should refer to the platform-specific installation instructions for the Oracle software. These guides include specific instructions to meet ITSEC E3 configuration.

Note: Running the above commands will lose any SUID bits that were set. See Action 1.7.1 for details of the SUID binaries.

Phase 1 ~ Host Operating System Security Issues

Action 1.2.4

SEVERITY LEVEL
1

O/S VERSION
Windows

ORACLE VERSIONS
All

Take the following steps to address Oracle file permission issues on Windows environments.

- If Oracle is installed on a Windows server, then the file system used must be *NTFS* since using *FAT/FAT32* file systems provides no file system security. If Oracle has been installed on a *FAT/FAT32* file system, then the server should be rebuilt to use *NTFS*. It is possible to convert file systems to *NTFS* on Windows. If Windows XP is used, convert the file system to use *logical volumes*.
- Create a user to own the Oracle software. **Do not call the user *oracle***.
- The user used to install Oracle should be a local user and not a domain user.
- Create an operating system group to be the OSDBA group. **Do not call it *ORA_DBA***.
- Make the group added above part of the admin group.
- Stop other administrators accessing the files owned by the Oracle software owner.
- All files under the ORACLE_BASE and ORACLE_HOME directories **should not allow** permissions to the *everyone* group.
- If the datafiles are placed in another directory, then apply the same permissions to these files.
- Ensure that Windows file permissions are set for files to inherit the permissions of their directory.

If the Windows box is specifically a server, and users will not be using tools such as *SQL*Plus* locally, then set the permissions on the Oracle drives and directories to ORA_DBA=full. ORA_DBA should be the only group accessing the files. If users locally access tools such as *SQL*Plus*, then specific access can be granted to those tools.

See the following note from Oracle on securing Windows for Oracle: DocID 95592.1 Windows NT 4.0 Administrative Security Structures.

Note: A Trojan horse is a piece of code installed by a hacker so that an unsuspecting administrator or user runs it for him at a later date. An example could be installing a simple ALTER USER statement into an application or script so that the writer of this can change the SYS password easily later.

Note: By default under Windows, the ORA_DBA group is created and the only default member is the Local Administrator.

Phase 1 ~ Host Operating System Security Issues

Action 1.2.5

SEVERITY LEVEL: 1
O/S VERSION: Unix
ORACLE VERSIONS: All

During the installation, it is also necessary to make sure you are using a temporary directory that is locked down: using /tmp is insecure, anyone can write to it. Securing the installation is done by setting the environment variables: TMPDIR or TMP_DIR to a suitably secure location. The variable TEMP should also be set. TMPDIR is used by operating system programs such as "ld" or "ar" and TEMP is used by Oracle. Create a separate directory as follows (the example is *ksh*):

```
$ mkdir /u01/tmp
$ TEMP=/u01/tmp; export TEMP
$ TMPDIR=/u01/tmp; export TMPDIR
```

Note: While anyone can write to /tmp, the sticky bit ensures that no one other than the owner and root can remove a given file, at least on Unix. Using the correct umask should prevent attackers from seeing temporary files.

Action 1.2.6

SEVERITY LEVEL: 1
O/S VERSION: Windows
ORACLE VERSIONS: All

Action 1.2.4 opens up a couple of other vulnerabilities, e.g. privilege escalation (aside from the fact the 'Everyone' can simply remove the database). Remove everyone access privileges from ORACLE_HOME and ORACLE_BASE.

On Windows 2000 / Oracle 8.1.7 the default permission sets are as follows:

- Owner : Local Administrators
- Group; Everyone - Full Control permissions to Oracle root directory and all sub directories.

Note: Installation of Oracle software or just rebuilding the binaries should be performed on a server that is definitely not connected to the Internet, and ideally on a server that is standalone and has no users on it.

Note: While installing 9i, one of the things noticed was that the Universal Installer doesn't create any Windows Access Control Lists (ACL's) on an Oracle Windows install, and suggests a default location of c:\oracle (or d:\ or whatever). It creates a Windows group, but this is for 'integrated' Windows access to the database (i.e. use your Windows account to login to the database.) It doesn't create an account to 'own' the Oracle binaries or configuration files. Unfortunately, the Oracle install then inherits the permissions from the c:\ drive, which by default is Everyone\Full Control.

Phase 1 ~ Host Operating System Security Issues

Step 1.3 Group Issues

PROBLEM: *Oracle on Unix uses a specific group to administer the Oracle software. This group is usually called dba, but it doesn't have to be this name. This group is used to check if a user is allowed privileged access to start and stop the database. If any users have access to this group, then they can get privileged access to the database without further authentication.*

Action 1.3.1

SEVERITY LEVEL 1
O/S VERSION Unix & Windows
ORACLE VERSIONS All

On Unix systems, review membership of the OSDBA group *(Note: Historically this group is called dba)* in the */etc/group* file. The Unix group defined as OSDBA should only contain the user who is the owner of the Oracle software, and should **not** contain the root account. If any other users are in this group remove them. Issue the following:

```
$ grep -i dba /etc/group
dba::100:oracle
$
```

Note: Oracle recommends that separate groups be created for OSDBA and OSOPER (see the platform dependent installation guides) and that a separate group be created to own the installation.

On Windows, review membership of the group ORA_DBA.

The feature that allows members of the DBA group to connect using "connect internal" or "connect / as sysdba" can be disabled by setting SQLNET.AUTHENTICATION_SERVICES=(NONE) in the sqlnet.ora file.

Note: The "connect internal" feature has been removed from Oracle 9i, so only the "as sysdba" feature needs to be considered

Action 1.3.2

SEVERITY LEVEL 1
O/S VERSION Unix
ORACLE VERSIONS All

On Unix systems, ensure that the oracle account is not a member of the root group. Use the following command:

```
$ grep -i root /etc/group
root::0:root
bin::2:root,bin,daemon
sys::3:root,bin,sys,adm
adm::4:root,adm,daemon
uucp::5:root,uucp
mail::6:root
tty::7:root,tty,adm
lp::8:root,lp,adm
nuucp::9:root,nuucp
daemon::12:root,daemon
$
```

Phase 1 ~ Host Operating System Security Issues

Action 1.3.3

SEVERITY LEVEL: 1
O/S VERSION: Unix
ORACLE VERSIONS: All

On Unix systems, do not name the primary group used by the owner of the Oracle software *dba*, since this name is well known and naming it dba makes it an easy target.

Also beware that any user gaining access to the server can read /etc/group and /etc/passwd and try to establish who owns the Oracle software and what groups are used. Not choosing the default names will deter a casual attacker.

Note: SAP and other major third party applications will break if this group is not named dba. The SAP installation, for instance, checks for specific usernames and groups.

Action 1.3.4

SEVERITY LEVEL: 1
O/S VERSION: Windows
ORACLE VERSIONS: All

On Windows systems, take the following steps to address this issue:

- Do **not** use the name ORA_DBA for the O/S group that maps to the OSDBA role. This group can only be changed to ORA_<sid>_DBA as the name ORA_DBA or ORA_<sid>_DBA is hard coded into the network code by Oracle. The same issue applies to ORA_OPER as well on Windows.
- Only grant ORA_DBA (or equivalent) to database administrators. Do not include O/S administrators in the ORA_DBA group. Make sure all files are exclusively owned by the ORA_DBA group.

Note: Please see the SANS step-by-step guides for securing Windows NT and Windows 2000 from the SANS store at http://store.sans.org/. These guides include standards for creating users and groups under Windows.

Step 1.4 — General File Issues

PROBLEM: *Oracle uses numerous programs and files and can generate a lot of files depending on the configuration. One type of file generated regularly is the trace file. Quite often these can be generated with public read permissions by setting an un-documented parameter. Permissions can be changed by the DBA or worse still, the files can be moved to a directory where they could be read by any other user, such as the /tmp directory on a Unix server. A lot of structural information can be retrieved from these files about the function of an application. It's also possible to read clear-text passwords. See a posting the author made to the PenTest mailing list at securityfocus - http://lists.jammed.com/pen-test/2001/08/0138.html.*

Phase 1 ~ Host Operating System Security Issues

Action 1.4.1

SEVERITY LEVEL 3
O/S VERSION All
ORACLE VERSIONS All

Check regularly for trace files on the system and the permissions of those files. If trace files are found, then the first step is to move them to a central location, i.e. user_dump_dest. The second step is to ensure that the permissions of such trace files do not allow anyone other than the owner of the Oracle software to read them and gain valuable information about the database.

The undocumented parameter is _trace_files_public. This can be found using the SQL in *Action 3.6.15*. It is not possible to set the un-documented parameters using the ALTER SESSION syntax, so there is only an issue if this parameter has been set in the initialization file *init.ora*.

Trace files have a naming convention that is different on each operating system. The general convention is <sid>_<pid>.trc. Trace files are stored in three locations, udump, bdump and cdump. These can be found as follows:

```
SQL> select name,value
  2  from v$parameter
  3  where name like '%dump_dest';

NAME
-----------------------------------------------------------
VALUE
-----------------------------------------------------------
background_dump_dest
/db001/appp/oracle/product/8.1.7/admin/PETE/bdump
user_dump_dest
/db001/appp/oracle/product/8.1.7/admin/PETE/udump
core_dump_dest
/db001/appp/oracle/product/8.1.7/admin/PETE/cdump
SQL>
```

Make the udump and bdump and cdump directories in Unix un-traversable by world.
Set the permissions to either 0700 or 0600.

> **Note:** Avoid multiple databases on a shared server using the same directories for trace files and for archive log files. If one database has problems with disk space, then all databases sharing directories will.

Phase 1 ~ Host Operating System Security Issues

Action 1.4.2

SEVERITY LEVEL: 3
O/S VERSION: All
ORACLE VERSIONS: All

The *tkprof* utility is useful to read trace files.
This utility should be removed from production environments.

Action 1.4.3

SEVERITY LEVEL: 1
O/S VERSION: All
ORACLE VERSIONS: All

Confirm the permissions of the actual datafiles. If the Oracle processes are run as the "owner" of the Oracle software, then the datafiles can be set to read/write only for the "owner". If, on the other hand, a user in the OSDBA group is used, then the datafiles need to be read/write for owner and OSDBA group. An example is shown below:

```
$ ps -ef | grep pmon
  oracle     412      1   0 12:05:55 ?           0:02 ora_pmon_PETE
$
$ ls -al
total 1397572
drwxrwxr-x   2 oracle     oinstall         512 Jun 17 21:43 .
drwxrwxr-x   3 oracle     oinstall         512 Jun 17 21:33 ..
-rw-rw----   1 oracle     oinstall    56627200 Aug  8 12:30 indx01.dbf
-rw-rw----   1 oracle     oinstall   541069312 Aug  8 13:01 rbs01.dbf
-rw-rw----   1 oracle     oinstall     8392704 Aug  8 12:30 tools01.dbf
-rw-rw----   1 oracle     oinstall   109056000 Aug  8 12:30 users01.dbf
$
```

To change to read / write only for the owner, type the following:

```
$ cd <datafile directory>
$ chmod -R 600 *
```

Or for read / write for owner and group, type the following:

```
$ cd <datafile directory>
$ chmod 660 *
```

Owner and group should own all datafiles, trace files and admin files and their directories. No "group" or "other" permissions except for setgid should be set at all. This is 2700 (for set group) and 0600 for files.

9iR2 on Windows restricts the data file permissions to that of the local Administrators group and the SYSTEM user.

Phase 1 ~ Host Operating System Security Issues

Action 1.4.4

SEVERITY LEVEL: 3
O/S VERSION: All
ORACLE VERSIONS: All

Log file monitoring and administration could be split into three actions:
- Duplicate the log files. Log files should be duplicated to a remote server for additional security.
- Rotate the log files.
- Use a tool to monitor for strange behavior or errors in the log files.

See also *Action 1.9.2*. This includes reference to a free tool from Oracle to monitor log files.

Some log monitoring products that are available include OracleTool, HP Openview, swatch, logcheck and home-grown scripts. Use email or SMS for alerts.

Action 1.4.5

SEVERITY LEVEL: 2
O/S VERSION: All
ORACLE VERSIONS: All

Check for temporary files or development files in areas used by DBA's such as /tmp, /, $ORACLE_HOME, /var, /var/tmp, home directory etc. These files could contain sensitive information and should be removed.

For Windows Temp files, check the following locations:

On Windows 2000 Versions:

`C:\Documents and Settings\<USERNAME>\Local Settings\Temp`

And

`C:\WINNT\Temp`

On Windows NT Versions:

`C:\Temp`

And

`C:\WINNT\TempFolder.<NAME_OF_FOLDER_CREATED>`

Phase 1 ~ Host Operating System Security Issues

Action 1.4.6

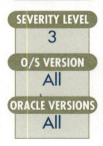

SEVERITY LEVEL 3
O/S VERSION All
ORACLE VERSIONS All

Check for creation of trace files from Oracle Networking, the database, 9iAS, CMAN and many more. These files contain sensitive information and should be secured or removed and backed up.

See also *Step 1.4.1* for details of the server trace files. Also see *Step 1.9.2* for details of a free tool for viewing and reviewing Oracle generated log files.

The trace files can be found using the following command:

An example command is:

```
# find $ORACLE_HOME -name "*.trc" -exec ls -al {} \; -print
-rw-rw----    1 oracle    oinstall         47 Jun 10 20:29 /db001/app/oracle/product/rdbms/log/ora_3281.trc
/db001/app/oracle/product/rdbms/log/ora_3281.trc
-rw-r-----    1 oracle    oinstall         47 Jun 11 10:27 /db001/app/oracle/product/rdbms/log/ora_771.trc
/db001/app/oracle/product/rdbms/log/ora_771.trc
-rw-r-----    1 oracle    oinstall         47 Jun 11 10:33 /db001/app/oracle/product/rdbms/log/ora_626.trc
/db001/app/oracle/product/rdbms/log/ora_626.trc
-rw-r-----    1 oracle    oinstall         47 Jun 14 10:28 /db001/app/oracle/product/rdbms/log/ora_624.trc
/db001/app/oracle/product/rdbms/log/ora_624.trc
-rw-r-----    1 oracle    oinstall         47 Sep  5 15:02 /db001/app/oracle/product/rdbms/log/ora_641.trc
/db001/app/oracle/product/rdbms/log/ora_641.trc
-rw-r-----    1 oracle    oinstall         47 Aug 31 14:06 /db001/app/oracle/product/rdbms/log/ora_639.trc
/db001/app/oracle/product/rdbms/log/ora_639.trc
-rw-r-----    1 oracle    oinstall         47 Jun 20 10:24 /db001/app/oracle/product/rdbms/log/ora_638.trc
/db001/app/oracle/product/rdbms/log/ora_638.trc
-rw-r-----    1 oracle    oinstall         47 Sep  6 23:32 /db001/app/oracle/product/rdbms/log/ora_640.trc
/db001/app/oracle/product/rdbms/log/ora_640.trc
-rw-r-----    1 oracle    oinstall         47 Aug 29 17:32 /db001/app/oracle/product/rdbms/log/ora_642.trc
/db001/app/oracle/product/rdbms/log/ora_642.trc
```

Action 1.4.7

SEVERITY LEVEL 3
O/S VERSION All
ORACLE VERSIONS All

If you have problems with Oracle software, you must sometimes create Remote Data Access (RDA) files for Oracle support (see Metalink for detailed information). These files contain clear text passwords (e.g. snmp_rw.ora) and other sensitive information. These files should be removed if not needed, and controlled with care.

Phase 1 ~ Host Operating System Security Issues

Action 1.4.8

When Oracle is installed to use raw devices, the permissions of devices / disks / volumes should have minimum permissions set so that they can be mounted and accessible only by the Oracle database and backup software. Raw and block devices should be audited. Volume managers such as Veritas VxVM have their own permissions and owner / group embedded in the metadata. This information should also be audited.

Step 1.5 — Usernames and Passwords in The Process List

PROBLEM: *Shell scripts or C programs are often used with an Oracle application, or for administration such as backups. These scripts need to log into the database as a relevant user. Passing the username and password on the command line means user-names and passwords can be seen with a simple "ps" listing.*

Action 1.5.1

See also Step 1.8

Use a script or manually use the "*ps*" command regularly to check for anyone using or running scripts that display Oracle usernames and passwords. If any usernames or passwords are found, then take action to remove them. There are a lot of techniques to do this: one suggestion is to use Oracles C program *hide.c* available from metalink. Two good notes from metalink describing this issue are:

- Note:136480.1: "How do you hide username/password in ps on 8i?" (via shell-Script).
- Note:1009091.6: "How do you hide username/password in ps?" (via hide.c).

Another alternative is to use the less well known /nolog option of SQL*Plus then hardcode the username and password (not recommended) in the SQL script. For example create an SQL script as follows:

```
connect scott/tiger
select sysdate from dual;
exit;
```

Then at the shell command prompt run

```
sqlplus /nolog @x.sql
```

Using "*/nolog*" will show "*sqlplus /nolog*" in the process list and not the username and password.

Phase 1 ~ Host Operating System Security Issues

The same idea can be achieved using a shell script and an environment variable. The following shows an example:

```ksh
#!/bin/ksh
export UP=scott/tiger
export SCRIPT=script.sql
{ echo ${UP}; cat ${SCRIPT};} | sqlplus
exit
#
```

This will only show *sqlplus* in the process listing. Another method would be to put the username and password into a protected file and read them into an environment variable at run time.

Using a SSH gateway solution could also be an option. A good source of information is the O'Reilly book *SSH, The Secure Shell: The definitive guide*. This book covers SSH and SSH gateways.

Note: Hide may not work on all platforms. Operating systems derived from System V store the arguments in an area that cannot be modified so "ps" will always show original values. Hide is written to trick these versions of Unix by padding 3000 '/' chars into argv[0]. See Metalink Note: 1009091.6.

Action 1.5.2

SEVERITY LEVEL: 2
O/S VERSION: Unix
ORACLE VERSIONS: All

Restrict the "*ps*" command at the operating system level to prevent casual identification of process listings including usernames and passwords.

Action 1.5.3

SEVERITY LEVEL: 2
O/S VERSION: Unix
ORACLE VERSIONS: All

Search through shell history files and remove any oracle usernames and passwords. Although shell history is useful if the site needs to be particularly secure, then do not allow users to create history files.

Restricting the history file is not practical, but a couple of things can be done to reduce the chance of passwords and usernames being found from history files:

- Add *cron* entries for each user to remove their history files daily or even more frequently if necessary, for example, 0 2 * * * rm ~/.hist* to remove the history file at 2am.
- Set the environment variable HISTSIZE for each user in .profile to 10. This will only keep the last 10 commands rather than the default of 128.

Phase 1 ~ Host Operating System Security Issues

Step 1.6 — Clear Text Transmission

PROBLEM: *Oracle uses its own proprietary protocol called Transparent Network Substrate (TNS). It is common for data and information to be sent to the database server in clear text. This data can be read and used by an attacker utilizing a simple packet sniffer. (Note: TNS runs on top of TCP/IP)*

Action 1.6.1

SEVERITY LEVEL: 3
O/S VERSION: All
ORACLE VERSIONS: All

Use a packet sniffer to see if sensitive information is being sent in clear text from applications to the database.

IPSec can be used to provide secure IP communications. See http://www.ietf.org/html.charters/ipsec-charter.html for the IPSec charter and details of the ssh sentinel. IPSec software can be found at http://www.ipsec.com

See *Action 1.6.3* and *1.6.4* for details of encrypting password exchanges.

Using the "support" level of SQL*Net tracing also reveals the packet contents. This avoids the need to install a packet filter. Ensure that if this method is used, that resources are monitored since tracing at this level uses a lot of CPU and file system resources.

Trace can be enabled on the client by setting the following parameters in the *sqlnet.ora* file:

TRACE_FILE_CLIENT: Defaults to sqlnet.trc, can be set to any value.

TRACE_DIRECTORY_CLIENT: Defaults to $ORACLE_HOME/network/admin and on Windows $ORACLE_HOME\net80\trace. It can be set to any directory.

TRACE_LEVEL_CLIENT: Defaults to OFF, Possible values include USER, ADMIN and SUPPORT. The value SUPPORT gives the maximum amount of information.

TRACE_UNIQUE_CLIENT: Default is OFF; leaving the default will result in the trace file being overwritten each time. Setting the variable to ON appends the process ID to the trace file name.

Tracing of Net8 can also be performed on the server. The parameters TRACE_FILE_SERVER, TRACE_DIRECTORY_SERVER and TRACE_LEVEL_SERVER can be set in the server *sqlnet.ora* file and have the same meanings as the client parameters. It is also possible to set trace for the listener by setting the parameters TRACE_DIRECTORY_{listener_name}, TRACE_FILE_{listener_name} and TRACE_LEVEL_{listener_name} in the *listener.ora* FILE. Again these parameters work the same as those for the client.

> **Note:** It is worth noting that the password exchange is encrypted by default. Whether or not to encrypt everything with the Oracle Advanced Security is a decision based on the architecture used — i.e., who could get there to sniff, what is the form of the 'network' — two cables into a switch in a rack, or on every desk in the corporation? What would be the payoff to sniff the data?

Action 1.6.2

SEVERITY LEVEL: 3
O/S VERSION: All
ORACLE VERSIONS: All

By using Oracle Advanced Security, encryption of data over networks can be performed. This is supported in version 2.2 of SQL*Net and higher (note: *the name of SQL*Net was changed to Net8 and subsequently to Oracle Net*)

A good reference for the Oracle Advanced Security can be found by reading the documentation available at:

http://download-west.oracle.com/otndoc/oracle9i/901_doc/network.901/a90150/toc.htm

Action 1.6.3

SEVERITY LEVEL: 1
O/S VERSION: All
ORACLE VERSIONS: All

To prevent users from accidentally revealing their passwords, the DBA can set the *environment variable* ORA_ENCRYPT_LOGIN on the server. Also set DBLINK_ENCRYPT_LOGIN parameter to **TRUE** in the server initialization file, *init.ora*.

> **Note:** Passwords are encrypted by default in 7.3 and up. Also, passwords could not be encrypted in Version 7.1 and down, which have been de-supported. ORA_ENCRYPT_LOGIN is set to FALSE by default in Oracle 7.3.4 and up.

Action 1.6.4

SEVERITY LEVEL: 1
O/S VERSION: All
ORACLE VERSIONS: All

The ORA_ENCRYPT_LOGIN environment variable also needs to be set by the client in order for the connection **not** to transmit the password in *clear* text. For server-to-server connections (i.e. distributed queries), set DBLINK_ENCRYPT_LOGIN.

Oracle always encrypts a password when a connection attempt to a server is made. If the connection fails and audit is turned on, then an audit log record is created. Oracle then checks the appropriate variable. If the variable is set to FALSE then another attempt is made to connect using an unencrypted password. If successful, then the failed entry in the audit log is replaced with the successful connection.

To stop an attacker forcing an unencrypted second connection attempt, set these variables to TRUE.

> **Note:** The parameter DBLINK_ENCRYPT_LOGIN is no longer available in 9iR2 since the default behavior now is to not attempt the second connection in clear text.

> **Note:** Older versions of the database client could not encrypt the login process. If these are still used, then the only option is to use Oracle Advanced Security or upgrade.

Phase 1 ~ Host Operating System Security Issues

Action 1.6.5

SEVERITY LEVEL: 1
O/S VERSION: All
ORACLE VERSIONS: All

The OCI JDBC client stack is similar to a typical Net*8 client stack. The thin JDBC driver on the other hand has similar components but is implemented differently and completely in Java. It uses Java sockets to connect directly to the database. It implements its own version of the two-task communications protocol (TTC), which communicates over an emulation of Oracle Net using TCP/IP. The thin driver does not require Oracle software on the client. The thin driver is self-contained and can be run from inside a Java Applet in a browser.

The JDBC thin driver transmits clear text error messages and also the username in clear text. If the username is found on the server, an encrypted password is sent from the client to the server.

Beware that usernames and the password encrypted on the client could be intercepted and possibly used.

If access is allowed via a Java thin driver, ensure that minimum permissions are granted to those users.

Step 1.7 — SUID and SGID Binaries

PROBLEM: *Oracle versions earlier than 8.1.7 used a lot of SUID and SGID binaries, some of which were SUID root. There are a number of reported exploits against most of them that allow shell access or escalation of privileges.*

Action 1.7.1

SEVERITY LEVEL: 3
O/S VERSION: Unix
ORACLE VERSIONS: All

All of the SUID and set group files can be found with the following command:

```
$ find $ORACLE_HOME -type f \( -perm -2000 -o -perm -4000 \) -print
/db001/appp/oracle/product/8.1.7/bin/dbsnmp
/db001/appp/oracle/product/8.1.7/bin/oracle
/db001/appp/oracle/product/8.1.7/bin/oracle0
/db001/appp/oracle/product/8.1.7/dbs/orapwPETE
$
```

The list of SUID and SGID binaries has changed radically between each version of Oracle. In earlier versions, there were many SUID binaries, which is no longer the case in later versions. In general, the SUID bits can be removed from the binaries, or the binary removed if the functionality is not required. After and including Oracle 8i, only 2 SUID binaries are shipped *Oracle* and *dbsnmp*. A good list of these files can be found in Chapter 4 of the *Oracle Security Handbook* by Marlene Theriault and Aaron Newman.

Beware that the post installation script *root.sh* will reset any UID bits on binaries, especially the root SUID bit on *dbsnmp*.

Note: Some of the common vulnerabilities against Oracle databases involve buffer overruns. If the overrun is stack based and not heap based, this can be protected against if the O/S supports non-executable stacks. On Solaris, for instance, add the line "set noexec_user_stack=1" in the /etc/system file to make the stack non-executable.

Phase 1 ~ Host Operating System Security Issues

Action 1.7.2

SEVERITY LEVEL: 3
O/S VERSION: Unix
ORACLE VERSIONS: All

Check that no un-authorized SUID binaries have been added to the Oracle tree. Use the output of *Action 1.7.1* and store in a secure location. Periodically check the difference with *diff* between the output of the current check and a known good output. The use of a tool like *tripwire* would be advantageous.

Step 1.8 — Password and Username Leakage

PROBLEM: *Without resort to known exploits, one of the few ways into an Oracle database is to obtain a username and password. This is sometimes easier than it looks. Usernames and passwords may be exposed by careless use of environment variables to store them to make scripts easier to run or make "cron" jobs more automatic. Worse still, usernames and passwords may be embedded in scripts. Some organizations also create their own authentication and replicate in full or part some of Oracle's function.*

Another mechanism by which username and password leakage can occur is when they are passed on the command line (for instance to a script) since this means they can be seen with a simple process listing.

Action 1.8.1

SEVERITY LEVEL: 3
O/S VERSION: All
ORACLE VERSIONS: All

Check all users' environment variables and particularly DBA and schema owners for usernames and passwords used to access applications and batch programs.

Phase 1 ~ Host Operating System Security Issues

Action 1.8.2

SEVERITY LEVEL: 2
O/S VERSION: All
ORACLE VERSIONS: All

Check the whole machine for scripts that have usernames and passwords embedded in them. Use a simple find command on Unix and search file in Explorer on Windows. Any files that have passwords in them should be investigated, and the need for passwords to be stored should be understood.

The passwords should be either removed, encrypted, or if it is not possible to remove or encrypt the passwords, ensure that the permissions on the scripts are set to stop anyone but the owner reading or writing the script files.

It is important before conducting this review to understand the architecture of the Oracle software that is installed.

A simple script to simply search for "connect" statements and for the use of *sqlplus* is as follows:

```
#!/bin/bash
find $ORACLE_HOME -name "*" -print | while read filename
do
      echo "Filename is "$filename >> user.lis
      egrep -i 'connect|sqlplus' $filename >> user.lis 2> /dev/null
done
```

This can be expanded to search for other signs of user-names and passwords and also to process the huge amount of data returned with this command.

Action 1.8.3

SEVERITY LEVEL: 2
O/S VERSION: Unix
ORACLE VERSIONS: All

Check *cron* jobs for usernames and passwords embedded within them. If found, then implement a suitable alternative that does not need passwords to be stored on the server.

An example would be to invoke SQL*Plus as follows:

```
sqlplus " / as sysdba" <f:\test.sql >f:\test.log
```

or

```
svrmgrl "connect / as sysdba" <d:\ohirstart.sql >d: \ohirstart.log
```

Both of these examples are for Windows and operating system authentication is being used.

Some suggestions follow:

- The database username and password could be stored in an encrypted file. The values could be read into an environment variable in a shell script. Utilities that could be used include enigma, crypt and bdes.
- A simpler solution could involve again storing the username and password in a file, and protecting the file with 0400 permissions as follows:

```
export PASS=`grep username /u01/app/oracle/.passwd | cut -f 2`
$ORACLE_HOME/bin/sqlplus $PASS @/u01/app/oracle/dostuff.sql >>$ORACLE_HOME/logs/dostuff.log <<EOF
EOF
```

Phase 1 ~ Host Operating System Security Issues

Action 1.8.4

SEVERITY LEVEL
2

O/S VERSION
All

ORACLE VERSIONS
All

Check the client machine for usernames and passwords stored in application configuration files. It is quite common for application writers to store usernames and passwords in clear text in a simple configuration file. These files are often readable by all.

Note: Oracle has an undocumented parameter to the ALTER USER command that allows a DBA to become any other user. If any DBA account is captured, this command can be used to "become" any other user in the database. This functionality was used in export / import in earlier versions and is replaced now with the BECOME USER command. The "become user" command can only be used to change users from within import and export. The "values" command can be used in SQL*Plus. It is possible to use "become user" behavior from OCI, see Action 3.8.17.

Action 1.8.5

SEVERITY LEVEL
2

O/S VERSION
All

ORACLE VERSIONS
All

The database creation assistant creates scripts that can be run to create a database. These scripts contain username/password combinations and are readable by any user on Windows. On Unix, the file permissions allow any user to read these files.

After the database has been created, remove the scripts either completely or save to a source repository first. Regularly check for scripts in the $ORACLE_HOME area that contain "CREATE DATABASE" and ascertain if they are the generated scripts, and take action as above. There is a need to check regularly since anyone can run the database creation assistant *dbassist* and create these files.

Use the Universal Installer and remove the database creation utilities from production servers.

Phase 1 ~ Host Operating System Security Issues

Step 1.9 — Logging and Auditing

PROBLEM: *Some actions performed within Oracle cannot be detected even with comprehensive auditing configured within the Oracle database. If an attacker or disgruntled employee were to access configuration files or run binaries directly to enter the database, these attempts would not be logged.*

Action 1.9.1

SEVERITY LEVEL: 2
O/S VERSION: All
ORACLE VERSIONS: All

Consider using operating system level auditing for critical use of Oracle where it can be audited from the operating system.

Some operating systems do not support user processes dumping to the audit trail. The use of a tool like *tripwire* can be made on /etc/passwd, /etc/group, Oracle configuration files and the Oracle installation directory. Also consider the use of *swatch* to monitor the log files generated.

See http://www.tripwire.com for details of *tripwire* and *swatch* can be downloaded from http://www.cert.org/security-improvement/implementations/i042.01.html.
A good discussion on the use of *swatch* is http://www.enteract.com/~lspitz/swatch.html.

Action 1.9.2

SEVERITY LEVEL: 2
O/S VERSION: All
ORACLE VERSIONS: All

It is a good idea to write Oracle log information to the SYSLOG file on Unix systems, and/or write Oracle logging information to remote log hosts. Log files should be rotated on a regular basis. Pertinent logging information can be monitored using tools such as *swatch*, *logcheck*, etc, and emailed to the relevant individuals for immediate action.

A simple command as follows could be used to view a log file such as the alert log, and email the administrator when specific errors occur.

```
nohup tail -f thelog | nohup nawk '/SomeString/ {system("mailx -sCheckLogNow youremail < /dev/null")}' &
```

If possible, spool the alert log file as it is written and use the *syslog* functionality to send the alert log to another machine for safekeeping and analysis. The logger shell command can be used to write to Syslog as follows:

```
$ /usr/ucb/logger -p local0.notice "Some error message"
```

Describing how to configure *syslog* is beyond the scope of this guide. A good source of information can be found in *Essential System Administration* by Aeleen Frisch published by O'Reilly.

An interesting paper has just been published by Oracle detailing 7 utilities for Oracle 9iAS. This is available from http://otn.oracle.com/products/ias/ias_utilities.html. The interactive log file viewer could be used as a basis for monitoring log files. The tool includes a substantial set of data files that list most log files generated by Oracle. The tools are extendable and free.

The above tool lists most Oracle log files, but a simple starting point could be to simply process and store the *alert.log* and the *listener.log*.

> **Note:** On NT server 4 and higher, the Event Viewer was intended to be a central repository for application logs but it is not always used by application vendors. Instead, Oracle relies on log files. The problem is that Oracle can have dozens of log files that have to be checked. These include the database alert log file, trace files, core dumps when Web sessions disconnect abruptly, net8 log files and log files for every Oracle-related Windows service.
>
> NT Server 4 (and higher) by default has auditing turned off. Security is not covered in the MCSE 4 certification exams or courses. Installation of Oracle on Windows does not "fix" this, nor does it set any audit flags against important Oracle software files that should not be accessible to the world.

Phase 1 ~ Host Operating System Security Issues

Action 1.9.3

SEVERITY LEVEL: 2
O/S VERSION: Unix
ORACLE VERSIONS: All

Consider using integrity protection tools such as *Tripwire* to allow the integrity of important binary and configuration files to be checked. Other new tools such as *samhain* and *AIDE* are also well worth using in this situation. For these tools use the following URL's:

http://samhain.sourceforge.net/surround.html?main_q.html&2

http://www.cs.tut.fi/~rammer/aide.html

Home grown solutions can be implemented using free copies of the MD5 or SHA-1 hashing algorithms.

Action 1.9.4

SEVERITY LEVEL: 3
O/S VERSION: All
ORACLE VERSIONS: All

Consider the use of host-based Intrusion Detection Systems on the server(s) hosting the Oracle database.

Action 1.9.5

SEVERITY LEVEL: 2
O/S VERSION: All
ORACLE VERSIONS: All

Review the "expected" processes regularly with a tool such as "lsof" on Unix. On Windows see the following URL:

http://www.sysinternals.com/ntw2k/freeware/pstools.shtml

Phase 1 ~ Host Operating System Security Issues

Step 1.10 — Existence of Control Files

PROBLEM: *The control file is a binary configuration file that controls access to data files among other things. If the file is writable by anyone other than Oracle, it can be altered or removed and cause problems with the running of the database.*

Action 1.10.1

SEVERITY LEVEL: 2
O/S VERSION: All
ORACLE VERSIONS: All

Ensure that the control files exist and in a directory pointed at by Oracle and only the owner of the Oracle software can read and write them. If the control files do not exist, Oracle is corrupt and will not start.

The following SQL will show the control file locations:

```
SQL> col name for a50
SQL> select name
  2  from v$controlfile;

NAME
--------------------------------------------------
/db002/oradata/PETE/oradata/PETE/control01.ctl
/db003/oradata/PETE/oradata/PETE/control02.ctl
/db004/oradata/PETE/oradata/PETE/control03.ctl

SQL>
```

For resilience, there should be at least three copies of the control file so that if one becomes corrupted, it can be easily recovered. The command:

```
ALTER SYSTEM BACKUP CONTROL FILE TO TRACE;
```

will create a trace file with the control file creation details in it. A good metalink note: 1012929.6 "How to Recreate the Control file" admirably describes the process.

If control files are incorrect, set correct values in the *init.ora* file. The control file must also be saved to the correct directory while the database is shut down. The correct permissions must then be set on the file and the database restarted.

Phase 1 ~ Host Operating System Security Issues

Step 1.11 — Trace Files

PROBLEM: *Trace files can be created by many different methods within an Oracle database and also by many different users. Most of the SGA (System Global Area) structures and datafile contents can be dumped to trace files. Any user who has the privilege ALTER SESSION can do this, so it is wise to restrict this privilege.*

Action 1.11.1

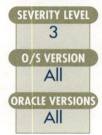

Check for trace files and identify if any non-DBA is creating trace files that are not authorized.

A simple report can be written that will identify new trace or core dump trace files added to the *udump*, *bdump* or *cdump* directory. The O/S username is displayed in some of the trace files so users creating some of the trace files can be identified.

```
#!/bin/bash
find $ORACLE_HOME -name "*.trc" -print | while read filename
do
        echo "Filename is "$filename >> trc.lis
        egrep -i 'Image' $filename >> trc.lis 2> /dev/null
done
```

This will list trace files and find any O/S usernames where they are available.

Action 1.11.2

Check the contents of trace files and identify any user who is dumping Oracle internal structures or parts of the SGA. If a user can dump the library cache and then read the trace file, it is possible to steal passwords. A simple check is to use the find command above in *Action 1.11.1* and add the string "identified by" to the *egrep* call.

Phase 1 ~ Host Operating System Security Issues

Action 1.11.3

SEVERITY LEVEL: 1
O/S VERSION: All
ORACLE VERSIONS: All

Ensure that no database user has the privileges ALTER SYSTEM or ALTER SESSION. ALTER SYSTEM, among other things, allows a database user to change the trace and dump directories on-line. ALTER SESSION can be used to dump internal database structures to trace files. The following SQL demonstrates how an attacker could take advantage of this privilege:

In session 1...

```
SQL> create user tester identified by tester;
User created.
SQL> grant create session to tester;
Grant succeeded.
SQL> grant alter system to tester;
Grant succeeded.
SQL> connect tester/<password>
Connected.
SQL> alter system enable restricted session;
System altered.
SQL>
```

In a session 2 try the following.

```
Microsoft Windows 2000 [Version 5.00.2195]
(C) Copyright 1985-2000 Microsoft Corp.

C:\>sqlplus dbsnmp/dbsnmp

SQL*Plus: Release 8.1.5.0.0 - Production on Thu Jul 11 21:42:19 2002

(c) Copyright 1999 Oracle Corporation.  All rights reserved.

ERROR:
ORA-01035: ORACLE only available to users with RESTRICTED SESSION privilege

Enter user-name:
```

The above shows how easy it is for a hacker to stop all other users from accessing the database.

Phase 1 ~ Host Operating System Security Issues

Use the following SQL to establish which users have these privileges.

```
SQL> select grantee,privilege
  2  from dba_sys_privs
  3  where privilege in ('ALTER SYSTEM','ALTER SESSION');

GRANTEE                         PRIVILEGE
------------------------------  ----------------------------------------
CONNECT                         ALTER SESSION
DBA                             ALTER SESSION
DBA                             ALTER SYSTEM
MDSYS                           ALTER SESSION
MDSYS                           ALTER SYSTEM
RECOVERY_CATALOG_OWNER          ALTER SESSION

6 rows selected.

SQL>
```

Any users or roles that have these privileges should be reviewed, and the privileges revoked if not necessary. This can be done as follows:

```
SQL> revoke alter system from mdsys;

Revoke succeeded.

SQL>
```

Alternatives to allowing developers / or users to kill their own sessions could be to allow access to the *orakill* utility, or if under Unix and shell access is available on the server, for the developer to use *kill –9*. To kill sessions on a Windows platform, use kill.exe from the NT resource kit. In addition, a package could be created that exposes only the kill functionality of the ALTER SYSTEM command.

The *orakill* utility can be used as follows:

```
Select spid,osuser,s.program
from v$session s, v$process p
where p.addr=s.paddr;

select name from v$database;
```

orakill <sid> <thread>

Where the *sid* is found in v$database and the thread is the *spid* column found above. To kill resilient sessions on Windows NT4, use *kill.exe* from the NT Resource kit and under Windows 2000 use the *ptree* utility.

Note: If multiple languages are supported within the database, then unfortunately the user will need to set the national Language Set (NLS) using ALTER SESSION. This could be worked around by writing an authid PL/SQL package to expose this functionality. If the database does not use National Language Support (NLS), then it is perfectly reasonable to remove ALTER SESSION privileges from all users.

ORACLE SECURITY Step-by-Step

Phase 1 ~ Host Operating System Security Issues

Step 1.12 Export Files

PROBLEM: *Export files are used by the DBA and others to extract data (either all of a database or just a table or anything in between) in a proprietary format that can then be used to re-load the data into the same database later or into another database. These files,* **if carelessly left on a machine and not protected from other users**, *can allow an attacker to steal the files and insert the data into their own database, or to read the file and steal details of your schema's structure or database link passwords, or a list of users and their password hashes. These could be easily installed into another database and connection attempts brute forced.*

Action 1.12.1

SEVERITY LEVEL: 1
O/S VERSION: All
ORACLE VERSIONS: All

Check for export files on the machine and identify any that are readable or writable by users other than the Oracle user or those in the OSDBA group, and either remove the file or change the permissions. Stray export files allow either stealing of usernames and hashes, or stealing schema structure or application data from the export file. These can be found as follows:

```
# find $ORACLE_HOME -name "*" -print | while read filename
do
     egrep -i 'EXPORT' $filename >> exp.lis 2> /dev/null
done
```

This command will search out all files and then check if the word EXPORT appears in the file. Export files have the word EXPORT in the header.

It is worth noting that free tools such as DataBee from http://www.databee.com allow the structure of a database to be extracted from a full export file that has been done with rows=n.

Note: Once the user has an export file, he can import it into another database even if he does not know the account password used to create the export file. Oracle checks the connection information for the recipient database, not against the information in the export file. A full import will not change the password for the SYSTEM or SYS accounts if the import is done by SYS. If the import is done by SYSTEM or another DBA then the SYS and SYSTEM passwords will change

Note: Ensure that there is a recorded process in place to backup to tape the export files and to remove them from the machine's file systems. These files can be used to steal data from the database. An export file could also be changed by a hacker with a binary editor. If the export is full, a password hash could be altered to allow the attacker access to the database at a later date.

Action 1.12.2

SEVERITY LEVEL: 1
O/S VERSION: All
ORACLE VERSIONS: All

If a full export is performed against the production database with the intent of populating a test or development database, this can lead to security issues with production passwords and database link passwords.

After a full export of this nature, it is important to change all imported user passwords so that development and test staff are not given production passwords or so that the hashes could not be available for anyone to brute force an account. All database links should be either removed or passwords changed.

Phase 1 ~ Host Operating System Security Issues

Step 1.13 Archivelog Files

PROBLEM: *When a database is in ARCHIVELOG mode, it generates archivelog files. These can be written to one or more directories. These files should also be backed up either to another drive on line or ideally to tape or other storage type and removed from the machine as soon as practicable. If an attacker steals these files, they can be dumped to trace file in any other database of the same version and the data extracted.*

Action 1.13.1

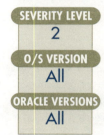

SEVERITY LEVEL: 2
O/S VERSION: All
ORACLE VERSIONS: All

First identify if the database is in archivelog mode by querying the column log_mode in the system view v$database.

```
SQL> select log_mode
  2   from v$database;

LOG_MODE
------------
NOARCHIVELOG

SQL>
```

Find all of the log files on the machine, look in v$parameter for all destinations by querying for parameters which are used for log files. Ensure that any archive log files in existence cannot be read by anyone other than the owner of the Oracle software. The parameters can be found as follows:

```
SQL> col name for a35
SQL> col value for a35
SQL> select name,value
  2   from v$parameter
  3   where name like '%arch%';
```

Note: We should differentiate between requirements for OLTP versus data warehouse environments verses decision support, etc – these have very different recovery strategies, e.g. data warehouse would generally not require archivelog mode set to true.

Phase 1 ~ Host Operating System Security Issues

```
NAME                                VALUE
----------------------------------  ----------------------------------
log_archive_start                   FALSE
log_archive_dest
log_archive_duplex_dest
log_archive_dest_1
log_archive_dest_2
log_archive_dest_3
log_archive_dest_4
log_archive_dest_5
log_archive_dest_state_1            enable
log_archive_dest_state_2            enable
log_archive_dest_state_3            enable
log_archive_dest_state_4            enable
log_archive_dest_state_5            enable
log_archive_max_processes           1
log_archive_min_succeed_dest        1
standby_archive_dest                ?/dbs/arch
log_archive_trace                   0
log_archive_format                  %t_%s.dbf

18 rows selected.

SQL>
```

> **Note:** The parameters LOG_ARCHIVE_DEST and LOG_ARCHIVE_DUPLEX_DEST have been deprecated in 8i and 9i EE and replaced by LOG_ARCHIVE_DEST_n

Phase 1 ~ Host Operating System Security Issues

Action 1.13.2

SEVERITY LEVEL: 2
O/S VERSION: All
ORACLE VERSIONS: All

All of the archive logs should be purged to disk. Most sites leave archive logs on disk for several days to ensure that they get several copies to tape. The following commands can be used:

```
find /u01/arc -name 'arc*' -mtime +3 -exec rm {} \;
find /u01/arc -name 'arc*' -mtime +4 -exec compress {} \;
```

Utilizing RMAN script techniques will remove archivelogs and backups on disk automatically. It scans the backups and archivelogs for corruption before backing up.

Example:

```
replace script 'INC1_backup'
{
delete backup completed before 'SYSDATE-7' device type disk;
backup incremental level 1 cumulative database tag inc_level_1 format
'/u03/rman_%U.bus';
backup archivelog all;
delete archivelog until time 'SYSDATE-7';
}
```

For Windows a freeware utility called *delold* can be downloaded from http://www.savilltech.com/delold. Simple batch scripts can be written with this tool and can be run from the command line such as:

```
delold c:\archive\*.* /-c /q /n:7
```

A Microsoft utility called *forfiles* can also be used. Finally a tool set such as *cygwin* can be used so that Unix commands can be run on Windows.

Warning! Ensure there is enough disk space for the archive log files. Otherwise a denial of service attack could be mounted and the database stopped.

> **Note:** Ensure that there is a recorded process in place to backup to tape the archivelog files and to remove them from the machine's file systems. These files can be used to steal data from the database.

Step 1.14 External Tables

PROBLEM: *External tables provide a way for Oracle to create a table based on an O/S file. This means that if an attacker can alter the file, the data that is returned can be altered. An attacker can even use this functionality with the correct permissions to access O/S files.*

Action 1.14.1

SEVERITY LEVEL: 2
O/S VERSION: All
ORACLE VERSIONS: 9i

There are a number of issues to consider with external tables: the permissions of the underlying file systems used, the locations of directories, and permissions of directory objects installed in the database.

In 9i, the concept of external tables forces the location of these underlying files and so-called directories to be protected — or hackers could alter these files changing the outcome of selecting from external tables.

External tables are currently read only, and there is no support for DML so they are less of a risk than normal data tables and certainly less of a risk than UTL_FILE. External tables appear to be located in the *system* tablespace, but the data is in fact kept in external O/S files. There are two new views to monitor external tables: DBA_EXTERNAL_TABLES and DBA_EXTERNAL_TABLE_LOCATIONS. These are relatively self-explanatory. Use the former to find the tables and the latter to find the file, i.e.:

```
SQL> select location
  2  from dba_external_tables
  3  where table_name='TEST_TABLE';

LOCATION
--------------------------------------------------------
test_date.csv
```

Audit the file and directory permissions of the underlying file to ensure that only the user needing external tables can access it. Audit the database DIRECTORY object used for its permissions. Ensure that only the users who should have access to the table have read and write access granted on the directory object.

There are two reasonably serious bugs for 9i: #1678633 relates to failure to audit a directory object for write, and #1679704 relates to the audit trail for external objects not being recorded.

Remember that in 9i, any public directory objects will allow a user (with other correct privileges) to create an external table and read O/S files.

Step 1.15 Native Compilation of PL/SQL

PROBLEM: *Native compilation allows access to a C compiler from within the database, and also provides another mechanism for attackers to steal data.*

Overview

In 9i, it is possible to compile a PL/SQL procedure to a shared object in a given location in a file system. A hacker with access to this location could change the procedure or at least wrap it and steal the arguments and possible results.

The following metalink note describes native compilation:

Note.151224.1 Ext/Pub PL/SQL Native Compilation in Oracle9i

The native compilation process takes the PL/SQL code and converts it to C code, and then compiles and links that C code into shared libraries. Even *wrapped* PL/SQL packages can be compiled. Three things need to be set before compilation can take place. A C compiler also needs to be present.

```
$ sqlplus system/<password>

SQL> alter system set plsql_native_make_file_name=
       '/home/pete/plsql/sample_makefile.mk';

System altered.

SQL> alter system set plsql_native_make_utility='/usr/ccs/bin/make';

System altered.

SQL> alter system set plsql_native_library_dir=
       '/home/pete/plsql';

System altered.
```

Then as the user who will compile:

```
SQL> connect pete/<password>

Connected.

SQL> alter session set plsql_compiler_flags='NATIVE';

Session altered.
```

Then the package or PL/SQL can be compiled

The system parameters can be added to the *init.ora* file or to the SPFILE.

It is also possible to abuse this process and execute other binary files.

Phase 1 ~ Host Operating System Security Issues

Action 1.15.1

SEVERITY LEVEL: 1
O/S VERSION: All
ORACLE VERSIONS: 9i

Disable access to this feature if it is not needed. If it is needed, then restrict access to only those developers building native code and protect the file systems used.

Since there are no specific native compiler privileges, then to restrict the use of this feature a check is needed in v$parameter for the plsql_% parameters. If they are set, then remove them from the initialization file. To restrict a user from compiling native PL/SQL if these parameters are set, the ALTER SESSION privilege should be revoked. It is also important that no general users have ALTER SYSTEM privileges.

Note: There is no conceivable reason why this feature should be left enabled on a production system.

Step 1.16 Key Files

SEVERITY LEVEL: 3
O/S VERSION: All
ORACLE VERSIONS: All

This section provides a list of the key files used by Oracle:

File	Comments
OPWDsid.ora	Contains current SYS-Hashkey (if remote_login_password_file = SHARED [not the default]. Default in 8.1.7 and higher is remote_login_password_file=EXCLUSIVE
Snmp_rw.ora	Contains Intelligent Agent passwords
Backups *.dmp	Full backups contains Oracle hashkeys
Htaccess	Apache passwords
Wdbsvr.app	Contains mod_plsql passwords
Webcache.xml	Contains weakly encrypted passwords
Listener.ora	Contains the listener password either encrypted or in clear text.
spfileSID.ora	Can be read for init.ora parameters
Database creation scripts	Usually in $ORACLE_HOME/admin/SID/create. This set of files created by the tool *dbasst* contains usernames and passwords.

The security manager and database administrator should be aware of the critical files in an Oracle distribution and should take the relevant steps to protect them. All of the files are discussed in various sections of this guide.

Step 1.17 — Shutting Down Windows Services

PROBLEM: *Under Windows, it is possible to shut down a password-protected listener from a remote (Windows) site.*

Action 1.17.1

SEVERITY LEVEL: 3
O/S VERSION: Windows
ORACLE VERSIONS: All

Under Windows, it is possible to shut down a password-protected listener from a remote site with special tools (sc from NT Resource Kit, psservice from SYSINTERNAL (http://www.sysinternals.com/ntw2k/freeware/psservice.shtml) or Windows Admin Tool: Hyena) if the rights are not properly set.

The NT Resource kit tool sc allows a remote service to be shutdown if the correct account is available. The tool from *sysinternals* allows the service to be shutdown without the correct account available. Protect the services by running them under secure accounts.

Note: Password protecting the listener is discussed in Step 5.3

PHASE 2
Oracle Authentication

Step 2.1 Review Log-in Procedures

PROBLEM: *Application users are normally issued their own usernames and passwords. Often, users in the same area share accounts because they have forgotten their own passwords and are reluctant to have it rectified, or because users in a particular area want anonymity so they all agree to log in under one account. Alternatively, an inquisitive user may look over a support technician's shoulder and note his password, and later use it to browse the system.*

These are two examples, and there are many more. The objective of this section is to consider what people may be doing with others' accounts.

QUESTION: *Is there a user account with all privileges?*

ANSWER: *Yes, the SYS account has all available privileges, always. On some platforms, certain default users such as MDSYS or FINANCE are granted ALL PRIVILEGES.*

QUESTION: *Is there an audit record created when someone uses a user with all privileges?*

ANSWER: *Not by default!*

QUESTION: *Who has access to these users' accounts?*

ANSWER: *Anyone with the password!*

Action 2.1.1

SEVERITY LEVEL 3
O/S VERSION All
ORACLE VERSIONS All

Check regularly "who is active" in the database: which Oracle accounts are running. A simple report can be run from *cron* on Unix or on Windows and the results emailed to the administrator. This can be run once per hour. The following SQL shows the users who are logged in and whether they are active:

```
set lines 132
col username for a10
col unam for a8
col status for a8
col spid for a9
col sid for 9999
col serial# for 999999
col program for a25
col terminal for a20

select   proc.username,
         sess.username unam,
         sess.status,
         proc.spid,
         sess.sid,
         sess.serial#,
         proc.program,
         proc.terminal
from     v$process proc,
         v$session sess
where    proc.addr=sess.paddr
/
```

Phase 2 ~ Oracle Authentication

Running the query shows:

```
USERNAME    UNAM STATUS   SPID   SID  SERIAL#  PROGRAM                       TERMINAL
----------  ---- -------  ------ ---- -------  ----------------------------  --------------------
oracle           ACTIVE   332    1    1        oracle@saturn (PMON)          UNKNOWN
oracle           ACTIVE   334    2    1        oracle@saturn (DBW0)          UNKNOWN
oracle           ACTIVE   336    3    1        oracle@saturn (LGWR)          UNKNOWN
oracle           ACTIVE   338    4    1        oracle@saturn (CKPT)          UNKNOWN
oracle           ACTIVE   340    5    1        oracle@saturn (SMON)          UNKNOWN
oracle           ACTIVE   342    6    1        oracle@saturn (RECO)          UNKNOWN
oracle           ACTIVE   344    7    37       oracle@saturn (SNP0)          UNKNOWN
oracle           ACTIVE   346    8    37       oracle@saturn (SNP1)          UNKNOWN
oracle           ACTIVE   348    9    37       oracle@saturn (SNP2)          UNKNOWN
oracle           ACTIVE   350    10   37       oracle@saturn (SNP3)          UNKNOWN
oracle      SYS  ACTIVE   400    11   47       oracle@saturn (TNS V1-V3)     console

11 rows selected.

SQL>
```

The problem is at first a case of *investigation*. A more detailed picture of **when** and **who** uses the database can be achieved by using Oracle's audit features.

It is trivial to change the application and block out this behavior, but sometimes it is better to understand what is being done first and then educate the users.

Further investigation into **who** is logging in and **from where** can be done using audit or using log on triggers (later versions), see *Phase 4* for details. Look for users who are sharing logins and passwords (example would be where 5-6 members of the same department use the same login.) or users who have a login they should not have (example: a DBA's login being used in the accounts department).

(RADIUS compliant) can be used for higher levels of assurance, e.g. thumbprints, smart cards.

Simple things can be done like setting the number of times an account can be used concurrently. Restrict or just monitor where DBA accounts are used. Profiles can be used to prevent some of the issues, see *Action 2.1.3*.

Phase 2 ~ Oracle Authentication

Action 2.1.2

SEVERITY LEVEL: 3
O/S VERSION: All
ORACLE VERSIONS: All

All users should be allocated their own login ID rather than an application that uses one ID to access the database, and then having the application managing users itself. While some applications require this method, it has problems:

- Generally passwords for the *one* user are hard coded or known by most staff. This makes circumvention easy.
- Application user encryption and management are generally weaker.
- Applications store these pseudo usernames and password in Oracle tables.

Fixing existing applications authentication and user management is not easy. The only option is to lobby the supplier to improve its applications security. Ensure that it is at least difficult or impossible to bypass the application security — this is probably not possible!

Many web based applications use one or a small number of database accounts, and thousands of users access using these accounts. Oracle label security could also be considered in this case. See *Action 4.7.2*.

Action 2.1.3

SEVERITY LEVEL: 2
O/S VERSION: All
ORACLE VERSIONS: 8, 8i & 9i

User passwords should be changed on a regular basis. The passwords should be checked to ensure that they are not weak, and that passwords are not re-used. Opinion differs as to whether it is a good idea to change a password regularly. Some argue it is better to ensure users have strong passwords and change less regularly so that the passwords do not get written down. Some ideas follow:

- If a password has to be written down to remember, then store it encrypted in an organizer, **not** on a *sticky*.
- Create a password from a sentence, e.g. Pete Finnigan writes a book about security => PFwabas1.
- Test password strength. Visit http://cnlab.ch/pwcheck for example.

In general, I would recommend that all the password management features be enabled in the DEFAULT profile. This can be done as follows:

```
SQL> alter profile default
  2    limit failed_login_attempts 5
  3    password_life_time 60
  4    password_reuse_max 20
  5    password_reuse_time unlimited
  7    password_lock_time 1
  8    password_grace_time 3;

Profile altered.

SQL> select profile,resource_name,limit
  2    from dba_profiles
  3    where resource_type='PASSWORD';
SQL> /
```

Note: The password management features are not enabled by default in an Oracle database.

Phase 2 ~ Oracle Authentication

```
PROFILE         RESOURCE_NAME                    LIMIT
------------    --------------------------       --------------------
DEFAULT         FAILED_LOGIN_ATTEMPTS            5
LIMIT_USERS     FAILED_LOGIN_ATTEMPTS            DEFAULT
DEFAULT         PASSWORD_LIFE_TIME               60
LIMIT_USERS     PASSWORD_LIFE_TIME               DEFAULT
DEFAULT         PASSWORD_REUSE_TIME              UNLIMITED
LIMIT_USERS     PASSWORD_REUSE_TIME              DEFAULT
DEFAULT         PASSWORD_REUSE_MAX               20
LIMIT_USERS     PASSWORD_REUSE_MAX               DEFAULT
DEFAULT         PASSWORD_VERIFY_FUNCTION         UNLIMITED
LIMIT_USERS     PASSWORD_VERIFY_FUNCTION         DEFAULT
DEFAULT         PASSWORD_LOCK_TIME               1
LIMIT_USERS     PASSWORD_LOCK_TIME               DEFAULT
DEFAULT         PASSWORD_GRACE_TIME              3
LIMIT_USERS     PASSWORD_GRACE_TIME              DEFAULT

14 rows selected.

SQL>
```

The final feature to be enabled is the password verification function. Oracle allows a DBA written PL/SQL function to be called every time a user attempts to change passwords. The function must have the format:

routine_name (
userid_parameter IN VARCHAR(30),
password_parameter IN VARCHAR (30),
old_password_parameter IN VARCHAR (30)
)
RETURN BOOLEAN

A sample function is included in the file $ORACLE_HOME/rdbms/admin/utlpwdmg.sql. This function can be installed or modified and installed. Either write a new function using the format specified above to encompass the entire password restrictions required, or modify the sample provided by Oracle to add additional functionality.

> **Note:** Running the script $ORACLE_HOME/rdbms/admin/utlpwdmg.sql will install the verification function but will also alter the DEFAULT profile and turn on all of the password management features. If you do not want Oracles default values, then simply comment out the ALERT PROFILE statement in this file.

Phase 2 ~ Oracle Authentication

The password verification function must be owned and installed by the SYS user and you must do "connect sys/<password> as sysdba" first to install it.

As a minimum, installing the sample function provided by Oracle is recommended. This function checks that the password satisfies length requirements and that the password is not the username.

This can be done as follows:

```
$ cp $ORACLE_HOME/rdbms/admin/utlpwdmg.sql ./passwd.sql
```

Comment out the alter profile statement at the end of this file. Then:

```
SQL> connect sys/<password> as sysdba
Connected.
SQL> @passwd

Function created.

SQL> alter profile default
  2   limit password_verify_function verify_function;

Profile altered.

SQL>
```

Action 2.1.4

SEVERITY LEVEL: 2
O/S VERSION: All
ORACLE VERSIONS: All

Establish a computer use policy that prohibits "shared" accounts and penalties for using them, and train employees on the dangers of using shared accounts.

In the database consider setting initialization parameters to limit the number of sessions per users.

This can be done in a couple of ways. Change the DEFAULT profile to include a restriction on the number of sessions per user

```
SQL> select profile,limit
  2   from dba_profiles
  3   where resource_name='SESSIONS_PER_USER';

PROFILE                          LIMIT
------------------------------   ------------------------------
DEFAULT                          UNLIMITED

SQL> alter profile default
  2   limit sessions_per_user 1;

Profile altered.
```

Note: Many applications use single Oracle account and therefore need multiple concurrent sessions, e.g. SAP application.

Note: All unspecified limits for a new profile take on the values of the DEFAULT profile. Any user who is not explicitly assigned a profile will conform to all of the limits of the DEFAULT profile.

Phase 2 ~ Oracle Authentication

```
SQL> select profile,limit
  2   from dba_profiles
  3   where resource_name='SESSIONS_PER_USER';

PROFILE                          LIMIT
-------------------------------- --------------------------------
DEFAULT                          1

SQL>
```

Or create a new profile with these settings and then assign that profile to the users who need to be restricted.

```
SQL> create profile limit_users
  2   limit sessions_per_user 1;

Profile created.

SQL> select profile,limit
  2   from dba_profiles
  3   where resource_name='SESSIONS_PER_USER';

PROFILE                          LIMIT
-------------------------------- --------------------------------
DEFAULT                          UNLIMITED
LIMIT_USERS                      1

SQL> create user pete identified by pete profile limit_users;

User created.

SQL>
```

This can also be monitored in OEM with session info.

Phase 2 ~ Oracle Authentication

Action 2.1.5

SEVERITY LEVEL
2

O/S VERSION
All

ORACLE VERSIONS
All

Oracle provides *proxy* authentication in Oracle8i and later. Up until 9iR2, this is only available by using OCI. In 9iR2, this is also available through JDBC.

Proxy authentication can help reduce the "single login" problem. This method allows a trusted user to become other users without knowing their password.

There is a good chapter in Tom Kytes book *Expert One-on-One Oracle*, which describes proxy authentication and auditing. The example given in the book creates a simple SQL*Plus from one of the demo programs.

The basic steps are as follows:

Create tables as APP_OWNER, then revoke create session privileges.

- Grant suitable privileges to END_USERxxx
- Create user APP_LOGIN with create session privilege
- Alter user END_USERxxx grant connect through APP_LOGIN;
- Grant access on APP_OWNER's data to END_USERxxx.
- APP_LOGIN can log in but do nothing to the data.
- END_USERS can log in and change the data but are identifiable.

End-users attaching to the database can otherwise be made to connect through an application module that has logged in as APP_LOGIN. The user APP_LOGIN then becomes the end user for the purposes of accessing the database.

The only 'public' password is APP_LOGIN, but it has no privilege to access the data.

ORACLE SECURITY Step-by-Step

Phase 2 ~ Oracle Authentication

Step 2.2 Default Accounts

PROBLEM: *There are a large number of possible default accounts that can be installed as part of an Oracle installation. The current count is about 120 for Oracle itself, but with some of the common applications, this can easily rise to over 180. Of course, 120 default accounts are not created in every installation. There are usually about 10 or so to start, but as the options accumulate, the numbers rise steadily. The danger here is that a DBA may neglect to change the passwords on these accounts, or may neglect to remove them when they are no longer needed. These accounts provide the easiest way for an attacker to enter your system.*

Note: Attention has been paid to default accounts in 9i and the dbca tool now prompts the user to either lock/unlock accounts. All accounts except SYS, SYSTEM, DBSNMP and SCOTT are locked by default. The universal installer also prompts to the users to set the SYS and SYSTEM passwords.

Action 2.2.1

SEVERITY LEVEL: 1
O/S VERSION: All
ORACLE VERSIONS: All

Using SQL*Plus identify any default accounts installed in the database. Check if any of those default accounts still have the known default passwords.

A list of default users and their passwords and a simple shell script to check with can be obtained from the author's web site at http://www.petefinnigan.com/sans/orastepcode.htm This list is a simple space separated list of the form:

```
ADAMS WOOD
ADLDEMO ADLDEMO
ADMIN JETSPEED
ANDY SWORDFISH
APPLSYS FND
APPLYSYSPUB PUB
```

The list contains over 170 users and passwords and will be updated as new usernames and passwords are found. This list can be used to generate a simple SQL program of the form:

```
connect ADAMS/WOOD
select user||' has a default password of (WOOD)' from sys.dual;
connect ADLDEMO/ADLDEMO
select user||' has a default password of (ADLDEMO)' from sys.dual;
```

This can be automated on Unix as follows with a simple script for Linux:

```
#!/bin/bash
rm -f sql.out
cat user.txt | while read username password
do
     echo "connect $username/$password"
     echo "select user||' has a default password of ($password)' from sys.dual;"
done > sql.out
echo "exit" >> sql.out
cat sql.out | sqlplus -s /nolog | grep "has a default" >>s.lis
```

Phase 2 ~ Oracle Authentication

Sample output is shown here:

```
AURORA$ORB$UNAUTHENTICATED has a default password of (INVALID)
CTXSYS has a default password of (CTXSYS)
DBSNMP has a default password of (DBSNMP)
MDSYS has a default password of (MDSYS)
ORDPLUGINS has a default password of (ORDPLUGINS)
ORDSYS has a default password of (ORDSYS)
OUTLN has a default password of (OUTLN)
SYS has a default password of (CHANGE_ON_INSTALL)
SYSTEM has a default password of (MANAGER)
TRACESVR has a default password of (TRACE)
```

If any default users still exist, then a decision needs to be made on whether they should be removed or not.

If any default users still exist and the password is still the default, then as a minimum, the password has to be changed or the account should be locked. The accounts can be locked as follows:

```
SQL> connect sys/<password> as sysdba
Connected.
SQL> alter user dbsnmp account lock;
User altered.

SQL> connect dbsnmp/<password>
ERROR:
ORA-28000: the account is locked

Warning: You are no longer connected to ORACLE.
```

SQL> connect dbsnmp/<password>
Connected.

SQL> alter user dbsnmp identified by values '!impossible!';

User altered.

SQL> connect dbsnmp/!impossible!
ERROR:
```
ORA-01017: invalid username/password; logon denied

SQL>
```

Note: Some default accounts are not provided by Oracle but by some third party applications such as SAP. These default user accounts cannot be changed easily since it is necessary to follow a set procedure provided by the manufacturer. Some manufacturers also hard code the username and passwords into the applications and into database table, so changing the default accounts can cause an application to work incorrectly.

To change some of the default account password on Oracle Applications, the reader should consult the following Metalink notes: 140457.1, 135819.1, 139936.1, and 160337.1

Note: It is only possible to lock accounts in Oracle 8 and later. In earlier versions, it is necessary to lock the account (if it needs to be retained) by setting an invalid password as follows:

Phase 2 ~ Oracle Authentication

Any of the accounts that are not required can be dropped as follows:

```
SQL> drop user pete cascade;

User dropped.

SQL>
```

Passwords can be changed as follows:

```
SQL> alter user pete identified by pete;

User altered.
SQL>
```

Or by using the password function:

```
SQL> connect sys/<password> as sysdba
Connected.
SQL> password dbsnmp
Changing password for dbsnmp
Password changed
SQL>
```

Note: If the older syntax is used instead of the password function then the password strength checking mechanism is still invoked.

Action 2.2.2

SEVERITY LEVEL
1

O/S VERSION
All

ORACLE VERSIONS
All

It is also necessary to install all of the password management features for the default accounts. The details of how to do this for the DEFAULT profile, or to add a new profile are covered in *Action 2.1.3* above so they will not be repeated here.

Phase 2 ~ Oracle Authentication

Action 2.2.3

SEVERITY LEVEL: 2
O/S VERSION: All
ORACLE VERSIONS: 8i & below

Using SQL*Plus, attempt to log into Oracle as the alias Internal with the default password *oracle*. If login is successful, change this password as described above. This test should be performed as a user who is not in the password file and therefore does not have the SYSDBA privilege.

```
SQL> connect internal
Enter password:
Connected.
SQL>
```

If the password of SYS has been changed, then this will be the password for *internal*.

Note: Internal is not a user but an alias used to connect to the SYS schema and used for the privileged actions such as stopping and starting a database. This syntax has been deprecated in Oracle 8 and removed altogether in Oracle 9i. The new syntax is CONNECT / AS SYSDBA.

Action 2.2.4

SEVERITY LEVEL: 2
O/S VERSION: All
ORACLE VERSIONS: All

There are a number of other non-database default users with default passwords that should be checked. Simply login to these applications and use these default passwords. A small sample follows:

Username	Password	Application
Administrator	Administrator	Webcache
User id cn=orcladmin	Welcome	Internet Directory Service
Sysman	oem_temp	OEM

Note: The password for the sysman user in OEM is set by default to oem_temp. When first logging into OEM as sysman, the user is prompted to change this default password, and this should be done.

Action 2.2.5

SEVERITY LEVEL: 1
O/S VERSION: All
ORACLE VERSIONS: All

Explicitly ensure the SYS account password is changed from its default of change_on_install.

The password of the SYS account should be at least 12 characters long and contain at least two numeric characters and at least 2 punctuation characters. The SYS password should be changed every 30 days on production systems.

The SYS account should be locked and only used when absolutely necessary. A database administrator can log on as the SYS user by using the AS SYSDBA clause. This logs the administrator on as SYS, but the audit trail shows their real database account name. SYSTEM should never be used for day-to-day administration, so it should also be locked.

Note: In general the existence of default accounts within a production database can be minimized by not building the database with the database assistant tool provided by Oracle, but by creating the database by hand.

ORACLE SECURITY Step-by-Step

Phase 2 ~ Oracle Authentication

Action 2.2.6

SEVERITY LEVEL: 1
O/S VERSION: All
ORACLE VERSIONS: All

Explicitly ensure the system account password is changed from its default of manager.

The password of the SYSTEM account should be at least 12 characters long and contain at least two numeric characters and at least 2 punctuation characters. The SYSTEM password should be changed every 30 days on production systems.

This task will be time consuming in an organization that has many databases since the system password will need to be changed in the database, Enterprise Manager and any scripts.

Action 2.2.7

SEVERITY LEVEL: 2
O/S VERSION: All
ORACLE VERSIONS: All

Initiate a business process to audit all databases and Oracle applications for default passwords on a frequent process.

It is important to note that there are differences in default accounts created between platforms and also between versions of Oracle, and some differences in the use of those default accounts. Before locking a default account or dropping it, it is important to understand the use of the account.

For example: If Oracle ConText (formally Intermedia) is used, then the user ctxsys, who owns the database objects needed for Intermedia functionality should not be removed.

Action 2.2.8

SEVERITY LEVEL: 2
O/S VERSION: All
ORACLE VERSIONS: All

Disable the remote login password file in the initialization file init<SID>.ora. All accounts in these files are easily brute forcible since there is no password lockout feature for these accounts. The parameter REMOTE_LOGIN_PASSWORDFILE should be set to NONE. This is the default value prior to 8.1.7. In 8.1.7 and above, the default value is EXCLUSIVE. This means that Oracle behaves as though there is no remote password file so that no privileged connections are allowed over non-secure connections.

Add the line below to the init<SID>.ora file.

```
REMOTE_LOGIN_PASSWORDFILE=NONE
```

If OEM is used for remote administration, then this parameter cannot be set, since doing so would stop any connections "as sysdba" and would therefore prohibit start up/shut down.

See also Action 3.6.13 for details of the parameter remote_os_authent.

Phase 2 ~ Oracle Authentication

Action 2.2.9

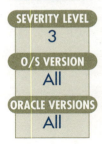

SEVERITY LEVEL
3

O/S VERSION
All

ORACLE VERSIONS
All

Some of the default accounts when created are assigned default tablespaces of SYSTEM and temporary tablespaces of SYSTEM. These should be checked:

```
SQL> select username,default_tablespace,temporary_tablespace
  2   from dba_users;

USERNAME                           DEFAULT_TA  TEMPORARY_
------------------------------     ----------  ----------
SYS                                SYSTEM      TEMP
SYSTEM                             TOOLS       TEMP
TRACESVR                           SYSTEM      SYSTEM
OUTLN                              SYSTEM      SYSTEM
DBSNMP                             SYSTEM      SYSTEM
ORDSYS                             SYSTEM      SYSTEM
AURORA$JIS$UTILITY$                SYSTEM      SYSTEM
OSE$HTTP$ADMIN                     SYSTEM      SYSTEM
AURORA$ORB$UNAUTHENTICATED         SYSTEM      SYSTEM
ORDPLUGINS                         SYSTEM      SYSTEM
MDSYS                              SYSTEM      SYSTEM

11 rows selected.

SQL>
```

And can be changed as follows:

```
SQL> alter user dbsnmp default tablespace tools
  2   temporary tablespace temp;

User altered.

SQL>
```

Any users who have a default tablespace of SYSTEM could be used to start a denial of service attack. Ensure all users have a quota assigned against all tablespaces, including SYSTEM to reduce the possibility of a denial of service attack. See also *Step 3.17*.

Phase 2 ~ Oracle Authentication

Action 2.2.10

SEVERITY LEVEL: 1
O/S VERSION: All
ORACLE VERSIONS: All

A lot of the default users and their passwords installed into an Oracle database are done so from Oracle supplied alter scripts available in various directories in the $ORACLE_HOME area.

If any default account is still needed and the password has been changed, it is important that the relevant alter script is located and the default password is changed in the script. Doing so is a security risk, so change the password to an input variable so that the person running the scripts will need to supply the password. Beware Oracle support may not support you if you change the alter scripts, so it might be better to supply your own script to run after the Oracle ones to change any default account passwords.

The alter scripts could be run anytime patches or upgrades are applied.

Action 2.2.10

SEVERITY LEVEL: 1
O/S VERSION: All
ORACLE VERSIONS: All

Like the default users supplied with various versions of Oracle, it is also possible to find some default roles supplied with Oracle that also have known default passwords. There are only a few known passwords at the time of writing so these are listed here:

Role Name	Password
ORD_SERVER	ODS
WKADMIN	WKADMIN
WKUSER	WKUSER

Check for these default passwords by running the following command as any user who has been granted these roles (This can be found by checking the view dba_role_privs):

```
SQL> SET ROLE <ROLE NAME> IDENTIFIED BY <ROLE PASSWORD>;
```

As with default users, if any of these roles still have their default passwords, they should be changed or the role dropped if it is not needed.

Step 2.3 — Secure Application User Accounts

PROBLEM: *It is commonly known that the easiest way into an Oracle database is to use one of the default accounts with known passwords that are documented in many places. There are other ways as well. It's a well-known fact that organizations use naming conventions for accounts. It's not difficult to get employee names using phone books, conference attendee lists, etc. For example, e-mail address conventions often suggest, or are the same as, usernames. Additionally, employees may choose very weak passwords, making simple mistakes like setting the password to the username or using dictionary words.*

Action 2.3.1

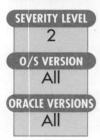

SEVERITY LEVEL: 2
O/S VERSION: All
ORACLE VERSIONS: All

If the password verification mechanism is not in place, then a simple check for users where the password is the same as the username can be done. This is best checked by generating a list of users account names by selecting them from the system DBA view dba_users, and generating a simple SQL script to test them.

See also *Step 2.1*.

Here is a sample piece of SQL to show how this can be done:

```
set head off
set feed off
set verify off
set termout off

spool use.run

col user_id newline
col show_it newline

select  'spool use.lis' from sys.dual;
select  'connect '||username||'/'||username user_id,
        'select ''connected as ''||user||'' with password ''||user from sys.dual;'
show_it
from    dba_users;
select  'spool off' from sys.dual;

spool off

set head on
set feed on
set verify on
set termout on
```

Phase 2 ~ Oracle Authentication

```
@@use.run
```

The output is captured in the file *out.lis*. This can be passed through grep on Unix and the output looks like:

```
connected as OUTLN with password OUTLN
connected as DBSNMP with password DBSNMP
connected as ORDSYS with password ORDSYS
connected as ORDPLUGINS with password ORDPLUGINS
connected as MDSYS with password MDSYS
connected as CTXSYS with password CTXSYS
connected as PETE with password PETE
```

Action 2.3.2

SEVERITY LEVEL: 2
O/S VERSION: All
ORACLE VERSIONS: All

Checking existing Oracle user accounts for weak passwords can be very useful but currently the methods to do this are quite limited. Oracle keeps the proprietary password algorithm secret. It is still possible to run password crackers against Oracle user accounts and passwords.

Some commercial tools include a *true* Oracle password dictionary cracker. Application Security Inc's AppDetective product and ISS include a cracker in their tools. Crackers probably exist in the *blackhat* community so it is worth the DBA making some efforts in this direction. See the following URL for *AppDetective*:

http://www.appsecinc.com/products/appdetective/oracle

A simple ALTER USER command can be used to check dictionary passwords against the stored password. The steps could include the following:

- Insert the dictionary words into the database to be checked or into a remote database if the check is to be done off-line.
- If it is not possible to alter password of the user being checked, then create a new user to use for the check. Oracle just concatenates the username/ password so taking a subset of the username and pre-pending the rest of it to the password guess can be done. This is demonstrated below.

```
SQL> create user pete identified by c#rr0t;

User created.

SQL> create user pet identified by ec#rr0t;

User created.

SQL> select username,password
  2  from dba_users
  3  where username like 'PET%';
```

Phase 2 ~ Oracle Authentication

```
USERNAME                        PASSWORD
------------------------------  ------------------------------
PET                             21625954072349E0
PETE                            21625954072349E0
SQL>
```

The above example shows that the same hash is generated for the same username/password concatenation. Therefore it is possible to create another user with one less character in the name (or however many characters are necessary to create a unique name) and append dictionary words. Note that if the password contains digits and the new password starts with a digit, then the above will fail. Logic is needed to ensure this is not the case.

- Create a new profile with no password features in it and assign this role to your test user.
- Simply loop through all of the dictionary words and alter the password with an alter user command and compare the hash with that of the user being checked.

This method is not ideal but can result in 700 passwords per minute on a reasonable PC.

The details of exactly how to write a cracker are left to the reader. A simple "alter user" based cracker is available from http://home.earthlink.net/~adamshalon/oracle_password_cracker

It is useful to install the password verification function as well as all of the password features as described in *Action 2.1.3*.

Action 2.3.3

SEVERITY LEVEL: 3
O/S VERSION: All
ORACLE VERSIONS: All

Check for dormant accounts in the database, lock after a specified number of days and then remove. This can be done by turning on audit and monitoring the records generated by running the following command:

```
SQL> audit create session whenever successful;
Audit succeeded.

SQL>
```

Create a simple report to parse the audit trail and lock accounts not accessed after a set number of days, and after a further set number of days, the accounts could be removed. The following SQL could be used:

```
SQL> select distinct (u.username)
  2   from dba_users u
  3   where not exists (select 'x'
  4   from dba_audit_trail a
  5   where a.username=u.username
  6   and a.logoff_time>sysdate-30
  7   );

AURORA$ORB$UNAUTHENTICATED
CTXSYS
DATA_ALIGNMENT_CHECKER
DBSNMP
MDSYS
ORDPLUGINS
ORDSYS
OUTLN
SYSTEM
TRACESVR

10 rows selected.

SQL>
```

Details of how to lock an account or drop it are shown in *Action 2.2.1*.

> **Note:** If an account is created and CREATE SESSION is granted to the account instead of the CONNECT role, and then someone attempts to brute force the account, then nothing would show up in the audit trail if we audited CONNECT and not CREATE SESSION. This is because audit would audit the use of the CONNECT ROLE, not a connection attempt.

Phase 2 ~ Oracle Authentication

Action 2.3.4

SEVERITY LEVEL: 5
O/S VERSION: All
ORACLE VERSIONS: All

Check out what user information is stored in the database. While in some respects this data is sometimes useful, it could also be used by an attacker to build a profile of employees.

An initial starting point for an investigation like this is to understand the schemas present in the database and which users own objects.

The Oracle internal tables hold little information except usernames and external names if set up. It is possible to combine employees email address, web site information and any other sources with the information in the view

ALL_USERS and learn something about who they are and what they do.

Solution: Revoke access to the system view ALL_USERS.

At the application level, it is usual for applications to store user's first names, last names, phone numbers and many other items.

If this information is necessary, then revoke access to these tables from all users unless they need to edit them. Also audit access to those tables with "AUDIT SELECT ON <TABLE_NAME>".

Action 2.3.5

SEVERITY LEVEL: 5
O/S VERSION: All
ORACLE VERSIONS: All

Use a naming convention for user accounts and administrator accounts that is not based on the user's name or other easily guessed parameters. One example: employee number (6 digits in our case) with either leading or trailing alpha characters.

This will make it harder for an attacker to guess user's accounts to try and log onto the database. Conversely, there is also a chance that the user will write down the username if it is not easy to remember.

Action 2.3.6

SEVERITY LEVEL: 4
O/S VERSION: All
ORACLE VERSIONS: 9i & above

Use LDAP or other external authorization to remove the need for database passwords.

A good metalink document describing the use of LDAP is Note: 135696.1 "The Oracle Net - LDAP FAQ".

Action 2.3.7

SEVERITY LEVEL: 2
O/S VERSION: All
ORACLE VERSIONS: All

List out all users in the database and using company records, identify these accounts with individuals. If accounts cannot be *linked* to an individual or an Oracle feature or application, then these accounts should be initially locked. If no further information is forthcoming after a set period of time, then the account should be archived and removed. A list of users can be obtained as follows:

```
SQL> select username
  2   from all_users;

USERNAME
------------------------------
SYS
SYSTEM
TRACESVR
OUTLN
DBSNMP
ORDSYS
AURORA$JIS$UTILITY$
OSE$HTTP$ADMIN
AURORA$ORB$UNAUTHENTICATED
ORDPLUGINS
MDSYS
PETE
PET
LIB
TESTIT

15 rows selected.

SQL>
```

Phase 2 ~ Oracle Authentication

Step 2.4 — ORAPWD and the Password File

PROBLEM: *Oracle provides a password file to keep track of database users who have been given permission to perform database administration activities. This file contains password hashes for the SYS user and INTERNAL and also any user granted the roles SYSDBA or SYSOPER (Note: 50507.1: "SYSDBA and SYSOPER Privileges in Oracle" describes these roles. This file if not protected can be altered to change the SYS password hash to a known value.*

Action 2.4.1

SEVERITY LEVEL: 3
O/S VERSION: All
ORACLE VERSIONS: All

The password file is stored in $ORACLE_HOME/dbs/orapw <SID> on Unix and will have the following permissions as default:

```
-rwSr-----   1 oracle   oinstall    1536 Jun 25 15:48 orapwPETE
```

There is no reason to enable the default SUID bit on this file. Therefore this should be removed and the permissions set to

```
-rw-r-----   1 oracle   oinstall    1536 Jun 25 15:48 orapwPETE
```

If SYSDBA and SYSOPER access is not required remotely, then set the remote_login_passwordfile parameter in the *init.ora* file to *none* as described in *Action 2.2.8*.

On Windows, the best way to secure this file is to set the permissions to read and write for administrators and the owner of the Oracle software only. The file is located in $ORACLE_HOME\database\PWD<SID>.ora and by default; it has SYSTEM/Administrators/Full Control and Authenticated Users/Read permissions. Set the file to be accessible only by ORA_DBA.

If the password file is needed and it is not secure, then it is easy to replace the second hash key with a hex-editor with 4DE42795E66117AE (=SYS) and do:

```
SQL> connect sys as sysdba
Enter password:                    -- SYS
Connected.

SQL> create user hacker1 identified by hacker1;
SQL> grant dba to hacker1
```

Note: The RMAN (Recovery Manager) utility does not definitely require a password file, but most metalink notes suggest that one is created. So beware if RMAN is used

Note: It is also important to lock down the password file very hard because of known environment variable hacks that allow access as SYS.

Also remember it is not a problem for root or Administrator to become a DBA account.

Phase 2 ~ Oracle Authentication

Step 2.5 — Oracle SID's

PROBLEM: *If a hacker finds a way to view one of a company's systems, and knows about common Oracle based applications, he can quickly identify if those applications are there and attempt access. This is because quite a lot of applications are always installed in the same way: Same SID, same Application account names, same account passwords. Some vendors are basically sloppy.*

Action 2.5.1

SEVERITY LEVEL: 4
O/S VERSION: All
ORACLE VERSIONS: All

When installing a third party application, change the SID or service name from the defaults. Change the application user names and default passwords. If the application has to use these values because they are hard coded, then *ask the vendor for a solution*.

Step 2.6 — Passwords Stored in the Database

PROBLEM: *Some common third party applications store encrypted and clear text passwords in the database since they forego the Oracle authentication for users and implement it themselves. This makes the hacker's task easy because obtaining these passwords gives them a way in.*

Action 2.6.1

SEVERITY LEVEL: 3
O/S VERSION: All
ORACLE VERSIONS: All

Application writers often create their own authentication, and this sometimes involves storing passwords and usernames in the database itself. The passwords can be encrypted (often weakly) or be in clear text.

The DBA needs to be aware of this and look for usernames and passwords, and identify the risk based on the results returned. A simple query such as the one that follows, although not exhaustive, will start the process.

Phase 2 ~ Oracle Authentication

```
SQL> connect system/<password>
Connected.
SQL> col object for a30
SQL> col typ for a30
SQL> col owner for a10
SQL> select object_name object,
  2   object_type typ,
  3   owner owner
  4  from dba_objects
  5  where owner<>'SYS'
  6  and ((object_name like '%USER%'
  7  and object_name not like 'USER_%')  8  or object_name like '%USR%'
  9  or object_name like '%PASSWD%'
 10  or object_name like '%PWD%'
 11  or object_name like '%PASS%')
 12  and object_type in('VIEW','TABLE')
 13  union
 14  select table_name object,
 15   column_name type,
 16   owner owner
 17  from  dba_tab_columns
 18  where owner<>'SYS'
 19  and (column_name like '%USER%'
 20  or column_name like '%USR%'
 21  or column_name like '%PASSWD%'
 22  or column_name like '%PWD%'
 23  or column_name like '%PASS%')
SQL> /
```

Phase 2 ~ Oracle Authentication

```
AQ$DEF$_AQCALL              DEQ_USER_ID            SYSTEM
AQ$DEF$_AQCALL              ENQ_USER_ID            SYSTEM
AQ$DEF$_AQCALL              USER_DATA              SYSTEM
AQ$DEF$_AQERROR             DEQ_USER_ID            SYSTEM
AQ$DEF$_AQERROR             ENQ_USER_ID            SYSTEM
AQ$DEF$_AQERROR             USER_DATA              SYSTEM
CTX_USER_INDEXES            VIEW                   CTXSYS
CTX_USER_INDEX_ERRORS       VIEW                   CTXSYS

8 rows selected.

SQL>
```

The above example does not show any rogue tables because there is no third-party software on my system.

If tables are identified that store usernames and / or passwords, then access to these should be revoked from all users except the user that changes the data or authenticates access. Ideally this should be done through a package procedure. If passwords are stored in clear text, then *please encourage the vendor to make changes to make it safer.*

PHASE 3
Oracle Access Controls

Step 3.1 — Control User Access to Operating System Files

PROBLEM: Oracle provides a PL/SQL package to allow access to Operating System files. This package is owned by the user SYS and is called UTL_FILE. It is quite restrictive in that there are no facilities to list directories or delete files, but its facilities allow access to Oracle-owned files and other files whose permissions permit access. This is quite useful to an attacker: with the wrong privileges in the database and incorrect settings, it is possible to dump Oracle's internal memory structures and read the contents from trace files using this package.

Action 3.1.1

SEVERITY LEVEL: 3
O/S VERSION: All
ORACLE VERSIONS: All

The initialization parameter utl_file_dir controls which directories can be accessed by the package utl_file. This package can read and write text files in any directory it can access where it has the relevant file permissions. If this parameter is set incorrectly, then users can access files and directories that they should not.

Read the value of utl_file_dir from the view v$parameter as follows:

```
SQL> select name,value
  2  from v$parameter
  3  where name = 'utl_file_dir';

NAME
-----------------------------------------------------------------
VALUE
-----------------------------------------------------------------
-------
utl_file_dir

SQL>
```

Note: Although it is not possible to delete a file using UTL_FILE, it is still possible to delete the contents of a file by opening an existing file for write, then closing the file without writing to it. This will truncate the file.

Phase 3 ~ Oracle Access Controls

The worst-case scenario would be that this value is set to "*", which means read any directory on the system. Another bad case would be if it were set to the same value as the trace directory. The trace directory can be found by reading the parameter user_dump_dest from the view v$parameter as follows:

```
SQL> select name,value
  2    from v$parameter
  3    where nane='user_dump_dest';

NAME
---------------------------------------------------------------

VALUE
---------------------------------------------------------------
user_dump_dest
/db001/appp/oracle/product/8.1.7/admin/PETE/udump

SQL>
```

Note: Avoid multiple databases on a shared server using the same utl_file_dir locations. Doing so would allow code to be written to read / write files in each other databases.

Set utl_file_dir to the directories needed by the application and ensure that it is not set to the following:

Setting	Reason to not use the setting
"*"	This allows access to any files to read or write that can be accessed by the owner of the Oracle software
Any of the trace directories	Allowing access to trace files would mean that critical information could be read such as clear text passwords from the SGA
"/tmp"	Commonplace for DBA's to leave alter scripts, export files backups etc
"/"	The same as /tmp
"."	This would allow access to the current directory of the process executing utl_file on behalf of the Oracle software owner.
Any of the datafile locations	Potentially data files could be accessed and corrupted or lost.
"\"	Not a valid directory; could be interpreted as a shell escape.
Core_dump_dest	This directory can be located by querying v$parameter. It stores core dump trace files.

Note: The Oracle log miner functionality requires the utl_file_dir parameter to be set.

Phase 3 ~ Oracle Access Controls

If the UTL_FILE package is not needed, then revoke access to it from PUBLIC and then grant access to the users directly:

```
SQL> select grantee,privilege
  2  from dba_tab_privs
  3  where table_name='UTL_FILE';

GRANTEE                         PRIVILEGE
------------------------------- -------------------------------
PUBLIC                          EXECUTE

SQL> revoke execute on utl_file from public;
Revoke succeeded.
SQL>
```

Note: From Oracle 9iR2, it is possible to write files to the operating system using UTL_FILE without setting the UTL_FILE_DIR parameter. This parameter is now obsolete. See metalink Note.196939.1 "Ext/Pub UTL_FILE_DIR init.ora parameter obsolete from 9.2". **This is a security risk!** In 9iR2 the privilege CREATE (ANY) DIRECTORY is now also needed. One advantage to the new change is that instance re-starts are not required to write to a different directory.

Action 3.1.2

SEVERITY LEVEL: 3
O/S VERSION: All
ORACLE VERSIONS: 8, 8i

The supplied package DBMS_BACKUP_RESTORE provides many file system functions. These facilities include copying files, altering control files, accessing devices and deleting files.

This package is very dangerous in the wrong hands.

Check which users have access to it as follows:

```
SQL> select privilege,grantee
  2  from dba_tab_privs
  3  where table_name='DBMS_BACKUP_RESTORE';

no rows selected

SQL>
```

Note: By default execute on this package is not granted to anyone.

If any users have access to this package, then revoke that access if it is not necessary.

Action 3.1.3

SEVERITY LEVEL: 2
O/S VERSION: All
ORACLE VERSIONS: 8 & above

Oracle provides methods to access the O/S and many O/S features from Java. Accessing the O/S from Java involves a number of steps. First, Java permissions need to be granted to the users who will own the Java classes. The classes then need to be loaded into the database to access the O/S. Finally, a PL/SQL wrapper function/procedure needs to be created to access the Java. A good example of how to do this is shown in Tom Kytes' book *Expert One-on-One Oracle*.

The minimum privileges required are the following:

- CREATE SESSION so that the user can connect to the database;
- Java permissions to access the file or program needed; Java permissions to generate output from Java;
- CREATE PROCEDURE to create the code in the database.

Very little permission is needed to access the O/S from Java. It is worth checking the Java permissions granted and also if CREATE PROCEDURE is granted. Otherwise developers and users alike can access the O/S.

This query shows how to check the Java permissions granted:

```
SQL> select grantee,kind,type_name,type_schema,name,action
  2  from dba_java_policy
  3  where grantee not like 'JAVA%'
  4 and grantee<>'SYS'
SQL> /

GRANTE KIND       TYPE_NAME             TYPE_SCH NAME            ACTION
------ ---------- --------------------- -------- --------------- ---------------
PETE   GRANT      java.io.FilePermissi  SYS      /usr/bin/ls     execute
                  on

PETE   GRANT      java.lang.RuntimePer  SYS      *               writeFileDescri
                  mission                                            ptor


PUBLIC GRANT      java.lang.RuntimePer  SYS      createSecurityM
                  mission                            anager

PUBLIC GRANT      java.lang.RuntimePer  SYS      exitVM
                  mission

GRANTE KIND       TYPE_NAME             TYPE_SCH NAME            ACTION
------ ---------- --------------------- -------- --------------- ---------------
...
14 rows selected.

SQL>
```

Any permission granted within Java should be monitored and those users that do not need these permissions should have them revoked. This is done through the Java package DBMS_JAVA as follows:

```
SQL>begin
  2    dbms_java.revoke_permission('PETE',
  3    'java.io.FilePermission',
  4    '/usr/bin/ls','execute');
  5  end;
SQL> /

PL/SQL procedure successfully completed.

SQL>
```

Note: In earlier versions of Java supplied by Oracle, if you had permission to do anything, you generally had permission to do everything. Later versions have applied a finer grained access control to assist security.

If Java is not needed in the production database, then it can be removed by running an Oracle supplied script. To check that Java has been installed, run the following query:

```
SELECT Count(1)
FROM dba_objects
WHERE object_type Like '%JAVA%';
```

This should return more than 4000 records if Java has been installed. To remove Java from the database run the script $ORACLE_HOME/javavm/install/rmjvm.sql.

Action 3.1.4

SEVERITY LEVEL: 2
O/S VERSION: All
ORACLE VERSIONS: 8 & above

How do Java, PL/SQL, SQL and external procedures call each other? The Database administrator and Security administrator should be aware of the ways it is possible to call out from the database, as well as how to make calls to the database. If access is granted to write Java, **beware**: there are other ways to access outside of the database.

To have Java call SQL and PL/SQL, use the embedded JDBC driver in the database Java VM or the embedded SQLJ translator. To call a Java method from PL/SQL or SQL, it is necessary to publish a "call descriptor" in PL/SQL. The call descriptor maps PL/SQL to Java data types and parameter modes. To invoke a Java method from SQL and PL/SQL, the call descriptor is invoked as though it were PL/SQL and the call is routed directly to the Java VM without adding overhead.

- Java can invoke native C via two methods: external procedures and CORBA callouts.
  - The Java VM can use Oracle's external procedure mechanism. Using OCI or Pro*C, it is possible to call back to the same Java transaction from the external C procedure.
  - The Java program can also use the data-base's CORBA callout facilities to invoke C. The main difference between the two methods is the data types shared between the two methods of communication. With external procedures, communication is via SQL data types, and in CORBA, communication is via IDL data types.

Action 3.1.5

SEVERITY LEVEL
3

O/S VERSION
All

ORACLE VERSIONS
8, 8i, 9i

The Oracle ConText (formally Intermedia) functionality allows access to external files. These files are treated as BFILE objects and can be indexed using some advanced features to allow directories of files to be indexed and catalogued. A user called CTXSYS owns the functionality. The packages provided allow access to the Operating system and to files to index them. This functionality could be abused.

If Oracle ConText (formally Intermedia) is not required, then remove the user CTXSYS and all of the objects owned by this user as follows:

```
SQL> drop user ctxsys cascade;
User dropped.
SQL>
```

If Oracle ConText (formally Intermedia) is required, then some steps need to be taken to secure its use. This functionality is used in Oracle Applications. The account CTXSYS can be locked without removing any of the usefulness of its features.

```
SQL> alter user ctxsys account lock;
User altered.
SQL>
```

Access to all of the CTXSYS owned packages and tables should be revoked from PUBLIC, and then granted back only to the users that need the functionality.

The following query will give the objects owned by CTXSYS and reveal who has privileges on them:

```
SQL> col grantee for a15
SQL> col privilege for a20
SQL> col table_name for a30
SQL> select grantee,privilege,table_name
  2  from dba_tab_privs
  3  where owner='CTXSYS';

PUBLIC          EXECUTE             CONTAINS
PUBLIC          EXECUTE             CONTEXT
PUBLIC          SELECT              CTX_CLASSES
PUBLIC          EXECUTE             CTX_CONTAINS
CTXAPP          EXECUTE             CTX_DDL
PUBLIC          EXECUTE             CTX_DOC
...
```

Phase 3 ~ Oracle Access Controls

```
PUBLIC          EXECUTE                 DRISCORE
CTXAPP          EXECUTE                 DRITHSL
PUBLIC          EXECUTE                 SCORE
PUBLIC          EXECUTE                 TEXTINDEXMETHODS
PUBLIC          EXECUTE                 TEXTOPTSTATS

46 rows selected.

SQL>
```

The same principles and thoughts can be applied to other default users such as MDSYS and WKSYS.

Action 3.1.6

SEVERITY LEVEL: 2
O/S VERSION: All
ORACLE VERSIONS: 7 & above

Oracle provides a little known access library for Oracle clients called OO4O *(Oracle Objects For OLE)*. This is a wrapper around OCI *(Oracle Call Interface)* and can be used by VB, VC++, MS Excel and Word and others to access an Oracle database. It is provided with the Oracle client software. An ActiveX control ORADC is also provided as an OLE wrapper around OO4O.

While this in itself is not a direct security risk, there are known security holes in this library. It allows casual users to access the database from desktop applications when other ODBC based sources have been removed.

Solution: Remove the DLL that is loaded in C:\oracle\ora81\bin\oradc.ocx and remove the OO4O directory from the Oracle client installation. Remove the type library in c:\oracle\ora81\bin\oip8.tbl. Lock the Oracle client directories.

Note: Because of the proliferation of Oracle client software CDs, this step is probably a waste of time since anyone can get an Oracle 8 client CD and load it. It is therefore the responsibility of the network / desktop administrators to secure the clients from unwanted software.

Step 3.2 — Reading Lists of Users from the Database

PROBLEM: *An attacker could gain access to a database by accessing a particular user account. While this is an issue in itself, the attacker may gain access to additional users within the database. This is done easily by querying the SYS-owned view ALL_USERS.*

Action 3.2.1

SEVERITY LEVEL: 3
O/S VERSION: All
ORACLE VERSIONS: All

Check and remove access to the SYS owned view ALL_USERS as follows:

```
SQL> select grantee, privilege
  2    from dba_tab_privs
  3    where table_name='ALL_USERS';

GRANTE PRIVILEGE
------ ----------------------------------------
PUBLIC SELECT

SQL> revoke select on all_users from public;

Revoke succeeded.

SQL>
```

Access to this view allows a hacker to build a list of user-names so that a brute force attack could be attempted.

Note: Access to this view could be necessary for some third party applications to function correctly. Revoking access to the view could cause issues with these applications, so it should be done with care.

Action 3.2.2

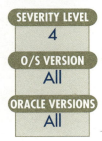

SEVERITY LEVEL: 4
O/S VERSION: All
ORACLE VERSIONS: All

Taking the action described in *Action 3.2.1* a bit further leads to revoking access to any of the PUBLIC views starting with ALL_

These can be viewed as follows:

```
SQL> select grantee,privilege,table_name
  2    from dba_tab_privs
  3    where table_name like 'ALL_%';
SQL>
GRANTE PRIVILEGE                                        TABLE_NAME
------ ------------------------------------------------ --------------------------------
PUBLIC SELECT                                           ALL_CATALOG
PUBLIC SELECT                                           ALL_CLUSTERS
PUBLIC SELECT                                           ALL_COL_COMMENTS
PUBLIC SELECT                                           ALL_COL_PRIVS
PUBLIC SELECT                                           ALL_COL_PRIVS_MADE
PUBLIC SELECT                                           ALL_COL_PRIVS_RECD
PUBLIC SELECT                                           ALL_DB_LINKS
PUBLIC SELECT                                           ALL_INDEXES
PUBLIC SELECT                                           ALL_IND_COLUMNS
....
```

There are over 150 records returned on Oracle 8.1.7 and 336 in 9i. The list should be reviewed and all PUBLIC access revoked unless it is necessary for applications to function correctly.

Phase 3 ~ Oracle Access Controls

Step 3.3 — Making ExtProc More Secure

PROBLEM: *The External Procedure architecture provides a way for users of PL/SQL to call out to C code or Java code enabling Oracle to be extended. It is possible to execute locally any C function available in any C library on the machine. It is also possible to execute any C function in any library remotely.*

Action 3.3.1

SEVERITY LEVEL: 2
O/S VERSION: All
ORACLE VERSIONS: 8, 8i, 9i

The ExtProc functionality allows external C and Java functions to be called from within PL/SQL allowing the functionality to be extended. This means that it is very easy to access any O/S commands by creating an external procedure that accesses the C system() function. This can be demonstrated below with this code:

```
create or replace library shell_test
as
    '/lib/libc-2.1.3.so';
/

create or replace package shell is
procedure exec(command in char);
end shell;
/

create or replace package body shell is
procedure exec(command in char)
 is external
 name "system"
 library shell_test
 language c;
end shell;
/
```

Note: Prior to Oracle 8.1.6, Oracle ConText (formally Intermedia) requires the Extproc functionality. Some features of Oracle 9i ConText also again require Extproc functionality.

Phase 3 ~ Oracle Access Controls

Running this package and testing gives:

```
SQL> create user pete identified by pete;
User created.
SQL> grant create session,create procedure,create library to pete;
Grant succeeded.
SQL> connect pete/<password>
Connected.
SQL> @lis
Library created.


Package created.


Package body created.
SQL> exec shell.exec('ls');
8iStarterKit     test      dir_1
PL/SQL procedure successfully completed.
SQL> spool off
```

If the *extproc* functionality is not required, then

- Remove the entries for ExtProc from the ADDRESS_LIST and the SID_DESC sections of the *listener.ora* file in $ORACLE_HOME/network/admin.
- Also remove the EXTPROC entry from the *tnsnames.ora* file in the same location.
- Delete the *extproc* binary from the $ORACLE_HOME/bin directory.
- Revoke the CREATE (ANY) LIBRARY privilege from any users that don't need it.

Note: To create a library in your own schema, you need the CREATE LIBRARY privilege. To create a library in another user's schema, you need CREATE ANY LIBRARY.

If the *extproc* processing is needed, then the listener process needs to be secured. This is possible by doing the following:

- Create a separate user who has no permissions like the Unix user *nobody*.
- Remove the extproc entries from the main *listener.ora* file and *tnsnames.ora* files in $ORACLE_HOME/network/admin

Phase 3 ~ Oracle Access Controls

- Create a new *listener.ora* and *tnsnames.ora* files with only entries for the Extproc process and point at these with the TNS_ADMIN environment variable.
- Start a second listener on a different port than the main database listener for the Extproc.

For Oracle 9iR2, the metalink note 198523.1 describes the process in detail for accessing external libraries. The default setting is to allow DLL's to be only loaded from the bin directory $ORACLE_HOME/bin. The list of DLL's can be set in an environment variable called EXTPROC_DLLS on the server, but the preferred method is to add the ENVS parameter to the *listener.ora* file. The recommended setting is to use the ONLY syntax so that only explicit DLL's can be loaded. In Oracle 9iR2, check the value of the ENVS parameter and if it is not set to ONLY, then set it to ONLY and list the explicit DLL's that are allowed. An example from the note is

```
ENVS="EXTPROC_DLLS=ONLY:/home/xyz/mylib.so:/home/abc/urlib.so,
LD_LIBRARY_PATH=/private/xpm/lib:/private/mylibs,
MYPATH=/usr/ucb:/usr/local/packages,APL_ENV_FILE=/apl/conf/env.txt"
```

It is also possible to start the extproc listener on a different machine using a TCP connection in 9i using the REMOTE_LISTENER parameter described in Note: Doc ID: 153376.1 - "Init.ora Parameter REMOTE_LISTENER" Reference Note on metalink.

Note: A default installation of Oracle 9iAS also creates a tnsnames.ora file containing EXTPROC entries.

Note: In Oracle 9iR2 and later, Oracle will only load DLL's from the $ORACLE_HOME/bin directory.

Phase 3 ~ Oracle Access Controls

Step 3.4 — Data Access Descriptors

PROBLEM: *Oracle now provides a wealth of three-tier applications that can and do access the database. The most popular of these is through Oracle's own Application Servers. Users who access the database invariably do so through a Web server, and a proxy connection is made on their behalf to the database. Users are connected using Data Access Descriptors (DAD's), which may be subject to remote access due to an authentication flaw.*

Action 3.4.1

SEVERITY LEVEL: 4
O/S VERSION: All
ORACLE VERSIONS: 9iAs

The Data Access Descriptors are one way of connecting to an Oracle database remotely. There are others — J2EE stack, RMI, CORBA — among other possible ways to connect.

The DAD's are administered via a web page. These users are also stored in the PORTAL30_SSO schema. The actual DAD's are stored in a file on the O/S usually in $ORACLE_HOME\iSuite\Apache\modplsql\wdbsvr.env. This file contains the usernames and passwords used to connect to the database.

DAD's can be set up and administered via a configuration web page that is usually available to anyone who can logon. Disable this web page and also disable the user administration web pages.

HTTPS and SSL are not usually configured by default. Oracle supplies a demo certificate that is the same in every installation. To obtain a real certificate, then a fee must be paid to companies such as Verisign. There are other companies. Alternatively sophisticated administrators can create their own certificates.

Single-sign on is present by default, but depends on the Java option. Some sites may be using SSO anyway. MetaLink note 158949.1 mentions how to set up the DAD configuration page without dependency on the portal database, and how to secure it from Apache instead of SSO.

The documentation for 9iASr2 is at
http://otn.oracle.com/docs/products/ias/doc_library/90200doc_otn/manage.htm
The Oracle 9iAS Security Guide is available at
http://otn.oracle.com/docs/products/ias/doc_library/90200doc_otn/core.902/a90146/toc.htm
Certificates are discussed in Chapter 3. The FAQ for Apache-SSL is a decent place to look for information on server certificates:
http://www.apache-ssl.org/#FAQ

> **Note:** The following metalink notes can help in securing the PL/SQL gateway administration pages:
>
> How to secure the PL/SQL Gateway Admin Pages
> Type: Note Doc ID: 108661.1
>
> Using Apache configuration to tighten mod_plsql security
> Type: Note Doc ID: 135681.1

Step 3.5 — Access and Use of Oracle Roles

PROBLEM: *Oracle provides the concept of roles to control access to objects within the database. The use of roles, while offering some advantages, can also lead to security issues. Some default roles allow access that should not be given to all users, and a hierarchy of roles that becomes too deep may allow privileges to pass to users unseen.*

Action 3.5.1

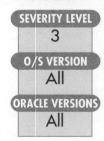

Ensure that only DBA role (or a suitable alternative to the DBA role) holds the SELECT_CATALOG_ROLE, EXECUTE_CATALOG_ROLE and DELETE_CATALOG_ROLE. This is checked with the following query.

```
SQL> select grantee,granted_role
  2  from dba_role_privs
  3  where granted_role in ('SELECT_CATALOG_ROLE','EXECUTE_CATALOG_ROLE','DELETE
_CATALOG_ROLE');

GRANTEE                        GRANTED_ROLE
------------------------------ ------------------------------
DBA                            DELETE_CATALOG_ROLE
DBA                            EXECUTE_CATALOG_ROLE
DBA                            SELECT_CATALOG_ROLE
EXP_FULL_DATABASE              EXECUTE_CATALOG_ROLE
EXP_FULL_DATABASE              SELECT_CATALOG_ROLE
IMP_FULL_DATABASE              EXECUTE_CATALOG_ROLE
IMP_FULL_DATABASE              SELECT_CATALOG_ROLE
OEM_MONITOR                    SELECT_CATALOG_ROLE
SYS                            DELETE_CATALOG_ROLE
SYS                            EXECUTE_CATALOG_ROLE
SYS                            SELECT_CATALOG_ROLE

11 rows selected.

SQL>
```

Revoke the catalog roles from those roles and users that do not need them. This is done with

```
SQL> revoke select_catalog_role from oem_monitor;

Revoke succeeded.

SQL>
```

> **Note:** Some third-party applications require the SELECT_CATALOG role to access dictionary views and will not function if this role is disabled. In addition, if this role is revoked, then OEM will not work. It is possible to revoke some privileges from this role to allow OEM to function.

> **Note:** Another problem with Oracle roles is that neither revoking a role from a user, nor dropping a role entirely affects a user session before it disconnects. Revoking a privilege from a role, however, does cause users who received it through that role to lose it immediately (i.e., at their next queries). If the situation is dire, the session can be killed with ALTER SYSTEM KILL SESSION or at the O/S level in Unix with kill -9.

> **Note:** Enforce least privilege principle and only add permissions for the objects and tables that individual users need to database roles.

Action 3.5.2

SEVERITY LEVEL: 3
O/S VERSION: All
ORACLE VERSIONS: All

The DBA views mainly used to manage roles are described below:

View	Description
DBA_ROLES	Lists all roles and if passwords are required.
DBA_SYS_PRIVS	Lists system privileges granted to roles and users
DBA_ROLE_PRIVS	Lists roles granted to users and other roles
ROLE_ROLE_PRIVS	Lists roles granted to roles.

Access to these DBA views gives a complete picture of the structure of roles in the database. The access to these views should be restricted. This can be checked as follows:

```
SQL> select grantee,privilege,table_name
  2  from dba_tab_privs
  3  where table_name in ('DBA_ROLES','DBA_SYS_PRIVS',
  4  'DBA_ROLE_PRIVS','ROLE_ROLE_PRIVS');

GRANTEE                         PRIVILEGE         TABLE_NAME
------------------------------  ---------------   ------------------------------
PUBLIC                          SELECT            ROLE_ROLE_PRIVS
SELECT_CATALOG_ROLE             SELECT            DBA_ROLES
SELECT_CATALOG_ROLE             SELECT            DBA_ROLE_PRIVS
SELECT_CATALOG_ROLE             SELECT            DBA_SYS_PRIVS

SQL>
```

There are USER_% versions of the above views as well that list the same information but per user. These user views include USER_TAB_PRIVS, USER_ROLE_PRIVS etc.

Action 3.5.3

SEVERITY LEVEL: 4
O/S VERSION: All
ORACLE VERSIONS: All

Any roles created for use by the admin personnel including the built-in admin roles should be password protected. All of the roles in the database can be viewed and then passwords added as follows:

```
SQL> select *
  2  from dba_roles
  3  ;

ROLE                             PASSWORD
------------------------------   --------
CONNECT                          NO
RESOURCE                         NO
DBA                              NO
SELECT_CATALOG_ROLE              NO
EXECUTE_CATALOG_ROLE             NO
DELETE_CATALOG_ROLE              NO
EXP_FULL_DATABASE                NO
IMP_FULL_DATABASE                NO
RECOVERY_CATALOG_OWNER           NO
AQ_ADMINISTRATOR_ROLE            NO
AQ_USER_ROLE                     NO

ROLE                             PASSWORD
------------------------------   --------
SNMPAGENT                        NO
OEM_MONITOR                      NO
HS_ADMIN_ROLE                    NO
JAVAUSERPRIV                     NO
JAVAIDPRIV                       NO
JAVASYSPRIV                      NO
JAVADEBUGPRIV                    NO
JAVA_ADMIN                       NO
JAVA_DEPLOY                      NO
TIMESERIES_DEVELOPER             NO
TIMESERIES_DBA                   NO

22 rows selected.

SQL> alter role timeseries_dba identified by passwd;

Role altered.
```

This action is an added protection so that if a user gets an administrator role that the user should not have, then they would still need the password to access the functions within it.

The number of shipped roles increases to 30 in 9iR1.

Phase 3 ~ Oracle Access Controls

Action 3.5.4

SEVERITY LEVEL 4
O/S VERSION All
ORACLE VERSIONS All

Examine the level of roles used, since too deep a level of roles becomes difficult to manage and leads to security risks that are based purely on the fact that it is not easy to spot what has been granted.

The DBA view DBA_ROLE_PRIVS shows the relationships between "users and roles" and "roles and roles". The DBA view DBA_SYS_PRIVS shows the system privileges granted to roles. The DBA view DBA_ROLES shows all of the roles in the database. A piece of PL/SQL code can be used to check for the role hierarchies:

```
set serveroutput on size 1000000
declare
        cursor c_role is

        select distinct role,granted_role
        from role_role_privs;
        --
        gv_max_level  number:=0;
        gv_level      number:=0;
        --
        procedure get_child (pv_granted_role in varchar2)
        is
                cursor c_child(cv_granted_role in varchar2) is
                select distinct role,granted_role
                from role_role_privs
                where role=cv_granted_role;
                --
                lv_child c_child%rowtype;
                --
        begin
                open c_child(pv_granted_role);
                fetch c_child into lv_child;
                if c_child%found then
                        close c_child;
                        gv_level:=gv_level+1;
                        get_child(lv_child.granted_role);
                else
                        close c_child;
                end if;
        end get_child;
begin
        for lv_role in c_role loop
                gv_level:=1;
                get_child(lv_role.granted_role);
                if gv_level>gv_max_level then
                        gv_max_level:=gv_level;
                end if;
        end loop;
        dbms_output.put_line('Max Level is '||gv_max_level);
end;
/
```

Running this gives:

```
SQL> @role
Max Level is 3

PL/SQL procedure successfully completed.
SQL>
```

Keep the number of levels to a reasonable level. Number fewer than three if possible. If possible, avoid hierarchies all together.

Action 3.5.5

SEVERITY LEVEL: 5
O/S VERSION: All
ORACLE VERSIONS: All

If possible, use a naming convention to distinguish between administrative roles and user roles. It will then make it easier to distinguish the wrong roles that have been granted to users.

Action 3.5.6

SEVERITY LEVEL: 5
O/S VERSION: All
ORACLE VERSIONS: All

Create a simple role for managing user accounts. This would include the ability to add users and modify users and to grant privileges to them and add password management features (possibly via pre-defined profiles). The following roles could be used as a starting point:

```
SQL> create role user_admin identified by secret_password;
Role created.
SQL> grant create user,
  2    drop user,
  3    alter user,
  4    grant any role,
  5    grant any privilege
  6    to user_admin;
Grant succeeded.
SQL>
```

> **Note:** A list of all of the available system privileges can be obtained by running the following query:
>
> ```
> SQL> select *
>   2  from system_privilege_map;
> ```

The above example loses out by having the system privilege GRANT ANY ROLE since this would allow this particular role to be used to alter any other user.

Phase 3 ~ Oracle Access Controls

Step 3.6 — Reviewing Initialization Parameters

PROBLEM: *Oracle uses an initialization file in an operating system file usually stored in $ORACLE_BASE/ admin/< SID>/pfile or $ORACLE_HOME/dbs as a symbolic link. Some of the parameters in this file can cause security issues if incorrectly set. Some others can cause your database to become corrupt or unrecoverable if not set correctly.*

Action 3.6.1

SEVERITY LEVEL: 3
O/S VERSION: All
ORACLE VERSIONS: All

Check that the database is in archivelog mode. If it is not, then suggest strongly that it should be since a complete point in time recovery is not possible unless it is in archivelog mode.

The syntax for ALTER SYSTEM is much the same in 9i. It just has a new option called SCOPE, which can have three values:

- MEMORY: The parameter change is good only for the life of the instance.
- SPFILE: The change will be made in the spfile, but will not affect the current instance. The change will take effect the next time the instance is started.
- BOTH: Change is made in both the current instance and in the spfile. If you are trying to change a static parameter, you must use the SPFILE option.

Sample syntax is:

```
ALTER SYSTEM SET sessions=100 SCOPE=SPFILE;
```

This decision depends upon the type of database being used. Data warehouse applications do not generally need archive logs.

See the SQL check in *Action 1.13.1* to see if the database is in archive log mode. Also see *Phase 6* for details of backup issues.

Putting the database in ARCHIVELOG MODE is done by placing the database in MOUNT state (i.e. not open) and then issuing the following command:

```
ALTER DATABASE ARCHIVELOG;
```

Note: Oracle 9i provides a binary initialization parameter file called the spfiles that allows some parameters to be made permanent without bouncing the database through the use of the ALTER SYSTEM command. In versions of Oracle prior to 9i, the database has to be shut down and restarted to make a changed parameter valid.

It is not possible to list all of the initialization file parameters in a guide like this and and research why some of them could pose security issues. This section lists the most common ones. A paranoid DBA should list out all parameters from the database that are set, understand each of them, what they do and what implications there are for security.

Note: This set of tests depends upon looking at initialization parameters and then changing them. Looking is easy. Simply select the details from the view V$PARAMETER as follows:

SQL> select *
2 from v$parameter
3 where name='<parameter_name>';

Replace the <parameter_name> (without the brackets) with the parameter you wish to check. Some parameters can be changed at the session level with ALTER SESSION and some can be changed at the system level with ALTER SYSTEM.

In 9i, it is now possible to save settings done at the system level without stopping and starting the database. This is done through the new binary parameter file. The syntax has changed slightly to ALTER SYSTEM <blah> SCOPE=SPFILE

Phase 3 ~ Oracle Access Controls

Action 3.6.2

SEVERITY LEVEL: 4
O/S VERSION: All
ORACLE VERSIONS: All

Check that the initialization parameter user_dump_dest in v$parameter is set to a valid directory owned by Oracle and set with Owner read/write permissions only.

If it is incorrect, set a correct value in the *init.ora* file.

Action 3.6.3

SEVERITY LEVEL: 4
O/S VERSION: All
ORACLE VERSIONS: All

Check that the initialization parameter background_dump_dest in v$parameter is set to a valid directory owned by Oracle and set with Owner read/write permissions only.

If it is incorrect, set a correct value in the *init.ora* file.

Note: On Windows, permission on a NTFS partition can be set both at the directory level and file level to ensure that only Oracle owner has permission to Read/write to these files.

On Windows, avoid changing permission from the top level of a directory since the permissions could be replaced at the lower level subdirectories.

Action 3.6.4

SEVERITY LEVEL: 4
O/S VERSION: All
ORACLE VERSIONS: All

Check that the initialization parameter core_dump_dest in v$parameter is set to a valid directory owned by Oracle, and set with Owner read/write permissions only.

If it is incorrect, set a correct value in the init.ora file.

This parameter was made dynamic in Oracle 8i and higher using the ALTER SYSTEM syntax. Note Doc ID: 39793.1 Init.ora Parameter "CORE_DUMP_DEST" [Port Specific] Reference Note on metalink describes this parameter. Oracle should always try and write a trace file first before dumping core. In some cases the core dump will be written to $ORACLE_HOME/dbs if this parameter has not been read. Metalink note: 1812.1 describes how to get a stack trace from a Unix core dump.

Phase 3 ~ Oracle Access Controls

Action 3.6.5

SEVERITY LEVEL: 3
O/S VERSION: All
ORACLE VERSIONS: All

Check that initialization parameter global_names is set to TRUE.

Setting this parameter ensures that Oracle will check that the name of a database link is the same as that of the remote database.

In complex environments or in environments with a large number of databases, this can be very difficult to implement.

Action 3.6.6

SEVERITY LEVEL: 4
O/S VERSION: All
ORACLE VERSIONS: All

Check that initialization parameter log_archive_start is set to TRUE in the initialization file.

Action 3.6.7

SEVERITY LEVEL: 3
O/S VERSION: All
ORACLE VERSIONS: All

Check that initialization parameter max_enabled_roles is set to 30 in the initialization file.

Note: You might be in trouble with, say max_enabled_roles = 20. In a typical case, SYS gets 20 roles by default, and then when you create a new role and grant it to public, SYS cannot log in.

Phase 3 ~ Oracle Access Controls

Action 3.6.8

SEVERITY LEVEL: 2
O/S VERSION: All
ORACLE VERSIONS: All

Check that initialization parameter os_authent_prefix is set to "" (A null string).

Note: If this variable is set to a NULL string, then the account can be used for external authentication or internal but not both. The only way for the account to be used externally is by specifying IDENTIFIED EXTERNALLY when creating a user.

Action 3.6.9

SEVERITY LEVEL: 4
O/S VERSION: All
ORACLE VERSIONS: All

Check that initialization parameter os_roles is set to FALSE.

Oracle can use internal roles or O/S roles. O/S roles are not very granular compared to Oracle. It is only possible to use one or the other, but not both.

The default value for this parameter is FALSE.

Action 3.6.10

SEVERITY LEVEL: 1
O/S VERSION: All
ORACLE VERSIONS: All

Check that initialization parameter o7_dictionary_accessibility is set to FALSE.

In Oracle 7, 8 and 8i, this parameter is set to TRUE. In 9i, it is now set to FALSE. Setting this parameter to FALSE stops those users or roles granted SELECT ANY TABLE access to the data dictionary. Access to the data dictionary is only possible by the owner SYS (does not need to be SYSDBA) and by users explicitly granted access.

Caution: *Some third-party backup software was found to fail when this parameter was set. Any third party software used should be checked for correct operation, and any issues involving this parameter should be reported to your vendor for correction.*

Action 3.6.11

SEVERITY LEVEL: 3
O/S VERSION: All
ORACLE VERSIONS: All

Check that the initialization parameter REMOTE_OS_AUTHENT is set to FALSE. By setting this parameter to TRUE, a security hole would be created. This parameter allows a user to specify the Oracle user name that it wants to connect as without the need for a password. If the parameter SQLNET.AUTHENTICATION_SERVICES = (NONE) is set on either the client or server, the database will attempt to log in the user using the provided username and password. If REMOTE_OS_AUTHENT is set to FALSE, however, the connection will fail.

This parameter is set to FALSE by default.

See Also Step 5.2 for a details of network configuration.

Action 3.6.12

SEVERITY LEVEL: 1
O/S VERSION: All
ORACLE VERSIONS: All

Check that the initialization parameter remote_os_roles is set to FALSE.

This parameter is very dangerous since setting it can lead to spoof attacks. It is not too difficult for an attacker to spoof an O/S role on a machine and then connect remotely to a database using it.

This parameter will allow any user to connect as any user. This parameter is set to FALSE by default.

Action 3.6.13

SEVERITY LEVEL: 3
O/S VERSION: All
ORACLE VERSIONS: All

Periodically check each instance that the running parameters are the same as the configuration parameters. This can be done easily by running the following SQL as SYS and then storing the results and comparing. Use something simple like MS Excel and compare in there or *diff* under Unix. Here is the SQL

```
Select     x.ksppinm   name,
y.ksppstvl  value,
from   sys.x$ksppi x,
       sys.x$ksppcv y
where      x.inst_id = userenv('Instance')
and    y.inst_id = userenv('Instance')
and    x.indx = y.indx
order by
   translate(x.ksppinm, ' _', ' ')
/
```

Note that the x$ tables change regularly both in terms of table names and column names.

The above query is valid for Oracle8 and higher.

Phase 3 ~ Oracle Access Controls

Action 3.6.14

SEVERITY LEVEL: 3
O/S VERSION: All
ORACLE VERSIONS: 9i

Beware of the IFILE facility of the initialization file. This allows another file to be referenced from the real init.ora, and then allows commands to be included in that file.

Check the *init.ora* file with *grep* or similar for the IFILE parameter. If it is there, check why and remove it if it is not necessary. Using a tool like grep will avoid missing rogue IFILE's hidden by a large amount of white space in an editor.

This parameter is used to simulate the link used in Unix from the $ORACLE_HOME/dbs directory to the real *init.ora* file on Windows.

Check under Unix that the *init.ora* in $ORACLE_HOME/dbs is actually a symbolic link and not a trojaned *init.ora* file.

If the IFILE functionality is still required, then it can remain as long as the permissions and the contents of the file pointed at by the IFILE parameter are checked.

Action 3.6.15

SEVERITY LEVEL: 3
O/S VERSION: All
ORACLE VERSIONS: 9i

Check that the initialization parameter REMOTE_LISTENER is set to "" (NULL string).

This parameter was introduced in Oracle 9i and is described in metalink note:
Doc ID: 153376.1 - Init.ora Parameter "REMOTE_LISTENER" Reference Note

REMOTE_LISTENER is added to the initialization file of the instance and describes a listener or list of listeners that are running on a remote machine separate from the database instance. A network name is specified that resolves to an address or address list. The address is specified in *tnsnames.ora* or in any other address repository used.

Action 3.6.16

SEVERITY LEVEL: 2
O/S VERSION: All
ORACLE VERSIONS: All

Ensure that the *pfile* and the *spfile* are both located in a directory that only the owner of the Oracle software has access to, and that the permissions of these files only allow the owner to read and write to them.

Action 3.6.17

SEVERITY LEVEL: 2
O/S VERSION: All
ORACLE VERSIONS: 9i & higher

In Oracle 9i and higher, it is possible to bypass fine-grained security if the privilege EXEMPT ACCESS POLICY is granted to a user. This can be found as follows:

```
SQL> select grantee,privilege
  2  from dba_sys_privs
  3  where privilege = 'EXEMPT ACCESS POLICY';

GRANTEE                         PRIVILEGE
------------------------------  ------------------------------------------
DBA                             EXEMPT ACCESS POLICY

1 rows selected.

SQL>
```

Any users or roles that have this privilege should be reviewed and the privilege revoked if not necessary. This can be done as follows:

```
SQL> revoke exempt access policy from dba;

Revoke succeeded.

SQL>
```

Action 3.6.18

SEVERITY LEVEL: 2
O/S VERSION: All
ORACLE VERSIONS: All

Check that initialization parameters SERIALIZABLE is set to FALSE and ROW_LOCKING is set to ALWAYS in the initialization file. These parameters should not be changed and relate to the way locking works in a multiuser system. If they are changed, data inconsistencies can occur.

Step 3.7 — Objects in System Tablespace

PROBLEM: *The system tablespace contains the data dictionary. The dictionary controls the operation of the database instance and is managed by the Oracle kernel itself. User objects should not be placed in the SYSTEM tablespace. Doing so can result in a Denial of Service. If the system tablespace cannot be extended, the database will hang.*

Action 3.7.1

SEVERITY LEVEL: 1
O/S VERSION: All
ORACLE VERSIONS: All

Check all objects in the system tablespace and confirm their owners as follows:

```
SQL> col owner for a15
SQL> col segment_name for a30
SQL> col segment_type for a30
SQL> select owner,segment_name,segment_type
  2  from dba_segments
  3  where tablespace_name='SYSTEM'
  4  and owner<>'SYS';
```

```
OWNER            SEGMENT_NAME                    SEGMENT_TYPE
---------------  ------------------------------  ------------------------------
OUTLN            OL$                             TABLE
OUTLN            OL$HINTS                        TABLE
SYSTEM           AQ$_QUEUE_TABLES                TABLE
SYSTEM           AQ$_QUEUES                      TABLE
SYSTEM           AQ$_SCHEDULES                   TABLE
SYSTEM           DEF$_AQCALL                     TABLE
SYSTEM           DEF$_AQERROR                    TABLE
SYSTEM           DEF$_ERROR                      TABLE
SYSTEM           DEF$_DESTINATION                TABLE
SYSTEM           DEF$_CALLDEST                   TABLE
SYSTEM           DEF$_DEFAULTDEST                TABLE
MDSYS            SYS_IL0000021709C00013$$        LOBINDEX
MDSYS            SYS_C001167                     INDEX
ORDSYS           ORDT_TIMESERIES_IDX             INDEX
ORDSYS           ORDT_TIMESERIES_IDX1            INDEX
```

On a default installation, there are objects owned by many users including SYSTEM, OUTLN, MDSYS, ORDSYS, OSE$HTTP$ADMIN and AURORAJISUTILITY

Phase 3 ~ Oracle Access Controls

These were obviously created by Oracle itself. Some of these objects could be removed from the SYSTEM tablespace, but approval from Oracle support should be sought first.

Any objects owned by application or database users should be removed from the SYSTEM tablespace. How and when to do this should be considered carefully with the help of the DBA.

Two Metalink notes that describe moving objects from one tablespace to another are:

Note 1012307.6: "Moving tables between tablespaces using export/import"
Note 147356.1: " How to move tables from one tablespace to another"

In Oracle 8i and higher, the following commands can be issued:

```
ALTER TABLE <tab_name> MOVE TABLESPACE <new_tablespace_name>;
ALTER INDEX <index_name> REBUILD TABLESPACE <new_tablespace_name>;
```

These leave all grants and constraints in place.

It is possible to alter default users default tablespace and temp tablespace before running *catsnmp.sql* etc.

Note: Although not easy, it is possible to move some of these objects prior to building a new database or choose not to install them at all. For instance, objects owned by AURORAJISUTILITY and AURORAORBUNAUTHENTICATED are Java VM items. If you run Oracle Expert (An Enterprise Manager management pack utility) against a new database, it will warn you that you should not have placed non-SYS objects in the SYSTEM tablespace, and list all the objects that should be moved out of it.

Phase 3 ~ Oracle Access Controls

Step 3.8 — Excessive System Privileges

PROBLEM: *All privileges in the database can be granted to roles or directly to users. There are a number of default privileges that may be unnecessary for all users. Users may also have been granted extra privileges during the life of the system either directly or through a role. Users granted too many privileges can perform administration tasks.*

Action 3.8.1

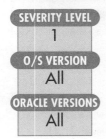

SEVERITY LEVEL: 1
O/S VERSION: All
ORACLE VERSIONS: All

Check for any users who have the privilege DBA as follows:

```
SQL> select    grantee,
  2            default_role,
  3            admin_option
  4  from      dba_role_privs
  5  where     granted_role='DBA';
SQL>

GRANTEE                             DEF  ADM
------------------------------      ---  ---
SYS                                 YES  YES
SYSTEM                              YES  YES
```

Any users who do not need the role DBA should have this role revoked as follows:

```
REVOKE DBA FROM <USER>;
```

Use the *least privilege* principle and grant only the privileges needed to users.

In fact, if possible, do not use the DBA role and create a much less powerful equivalent and grant that to administrators.

Note: An alternative is to revoke excessive privileges from the existing DBA role. Oracle suggests that the pre-defined roles are only supplied for backwards compatibility and will be removed in future releases of Oracle. This will be difficult to achieve as so many customers rely on these roles so either not using them or sanitizing them is really the only option now.

The DBA role can also be granted to database administrators as a non default role. To use the escalated privileges, the administrator needs to use SET ROLE DBA. This will appear in the audit trail if AUDIT ROLE has been enabled.

The DBA role could be dropped from the database but permission should be sought from Oracle support first. The SYS user has the DBA role granted so dropping it would at least need another role to be created with all privileges and then grant it to SYS or grant all privileges directly to SYS.

Note: In addition, roles change from version to version, sometimes they lose system privileges, and sometimes they gain new ones. This can be verified by comparing roles from an Oracle 7.3 database to an 8i database using Change Manager (an Oracle Enterprise Manager Management Pack utility).

Phase 3 ~ Oracle Access Controls

Action 3.8.2

SEVERITY LEVEL: 1
O/S VERSION: All
ORACLE VERSIONS: All

Check for any users or roles that have been granted "all privileges".

There is no direct and easy way to check for all of the privileges. The simplest check would be to count the number of privileges granted to a user or role, and compare this to the count of privileges in the table system_privilege_map.

```
SQL> select count(*) from system_privilege_map;

  COUNT(*)
----------
       126

SQL>
```

Then

```
SQL> select count(*),grantee
  2   from dba_sys_privs
  3   group by grantee;

  COUNT(*) GRANTEE
---------- ------------------------------
         3 AQ_ADMINISTRATOR_ROLE
         1 AURORA$JIS$UTILITY$
         2 AURORA$ORB$UNAUTHENTICATED
         8 CONNECT
       114 DBA
         2 DBSNMP
         5 EXP_FULL_DATABASE
        65 IMP_FULL_DATABASE
       115 MDSYS
         2 OEM_MONITOR
        13 ORDPLUGINS
        13 ORDSYS
         2 OSE$HTTP$ADMIN
         2 OUTLN
         2 PETE
        10 RECOVERY_CATALOG_OWNER
         8 RESOURCE
         1 SNMPAGENT
        10 SYS
         1 SYSTEM
         8 TIMESERIES_DBA
         2 TIMESERIES_DEVELOPER
         2 TRACESVR
         4 USER_ADMIN

24 rows selected.

SQL>
```

The above shows that the role DBA has 114 (124 in 9i and also for WKSYS and CTXSYS and 139 in 9iR2) privileges, but the user MDSYS has 115 privileges. This is because MDSYS has also been granted DBA. Any user with around the same number of privileges as DBA has probably been granted ALL PRIVILEGES.

There is no reason **any** user should have been granted all privileges. Revoke all the privileges from any users who have all privileges and then add back what they really need. If it is a default user, either drop the user if it is not needed, or consult Oracle support.

Note: The above example user MDSYS is created by Oracle in a script provided by them and this user is granted ALL PRIVILEGES. The same applies to the users WKSYS and CTXSYS. This looks like bad practice on the part of the programmer to work out what privileges this user needs and has created a security hole.

Action 3.8.3

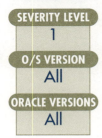

SEVERITY LEVEL 1
O/S VERSION All
ORACLE VERSIONS All

Check for users or roles who have been granted a privilege with the keyword "any" included in it. This can allow access to objects that should not be seen. This can be checked as follows:

```
SQL> select grantee,privilege
  2  from dba_sys_privs
  3  where privilege like '%ANY%';

GRANTEE                        PRIVILEGE
------------------------------ ----------------------------------------
AQ_ADMINISTRATOR_ROLE          DEQUEUE ANY QUEUE
AQ_ADMINISTRATOR_ROLE          ENQUEUE ANY QUEUE
AQ_ADMINISTRATOR_ROLE          MANAGE ANY QUEUE
DBA                            ALTER ANY CLUSTER
DBA                            ALTER ANY DIMENSION
DBA                            ALTER ANY INDEX
….
MDSYS                          UPDATE ANY TABLE
OEM_MONITOR                    ANALYZE ANY
ORDPLUGINS                     CREATE ANY INDEXTYPE
ORDPLUGINS                     CREATE ANY OPERATOR
ORDPLUGINS                     CREATE ANY TABLE
ORDPLUGINS                     CREATE ANY TYPE
ORDPLUGINS                     DROP ANY INDEXTYPE
ORDPLUGINS                     DROP ANY OPERATOR
ORDPLUGINS                     DROP ANY TYPE
ORDSYS                         CREATE ANY INDEXTYPE
ORDSYS                         CREATE ANY OPERATOR

230 rows selected.

SQL>
```

Review each of these privileges and revoke those that are not necessary.

Phase 3 ~ Oracle Access Controls

Action 3.8.4

SEVERITY LEVEL: 2
O/S VERSION: All
ORACLE VERSIONS: All

Check for users or roles that have been granted privileges "with admin" to them. This means that the recipient can grant the same privilege to whomever they wish. "With admin" relates to system privileges.

In SQL*Plus run the following command:

```
SQL> select      grantee,
  2        granted_role pr
  3   from       dba_role_privs
  4   where      admin_option='YES'
  5   union
  6   select     grantee,
  7        privilege pr
  8    from      dba_sys_privs
  9   where      admin_option='YES';
SQL>
GRANTEE                             PR
-----------------------------       ----------------------------------------
AQ_ADMINISTRATOR_ROLE               DEQUEUE ANY QUEUE
AQ_ADMINISTRATOR_ROLE               ENQUEUE ANY QUEUE
AQ_ADMINISTRATOR_ROLE               MANAGE ANY QUEUE
DBA                                 ADMINISTER DATABASE TRIGGER
...
```

Under a default 8.1.7 installation, this gives over 200 records and 339 in 9i.

The results should be reviewed and any privileges granted with admin should in general be revoked.

Action 3.8.5

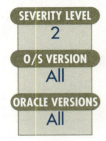

SEVERITY LEVEL: 2
O/S VERSION: All
ORACLE VERSIONS: All

Check for users or roles that have been granted privileges "with grant" to them. This means that the recipient can grant the same privilege to whomever they wish. "With grant" relates to object privileges.

In SQL*Plus run the following command:

```
SQL> select     grantee,
  2      privilege,
  3      table_name
  4  from       dba_col_privs
  5  where      grantable='YES'
  6  union
  7  select     grantee,
  8      privilege,
  9      table_name
 10  from       dba_tab_privs
 11  where      grantable='YES';
SQL>

GRANTEE                     PRIVILEGE                   TABLE_NAME
------------------------    ------------------------    ------------------------
ORDSYS                      SELECT                      DBA_OBJECT_TABLES
ORDSYS                      SELECT                      DBA_TABLES         ...
```

Under a default 8.1.7 installation, this gives 409 records and 781 in 9iR1 and 783 in 9iR2.

The results should be reviewed and any privileges granted with admin should in general be revoked.

Action 3.8.6

SEVERITY LEVEL 1

O/S VERSION All

ORACLE VERSIONS All

Check for users who have been granted system privileges and ascertain why. This can be done with the following SQL:

```
col table_name head "What" for a30
col grantee head "Granted To" for a20
col privilege head "Privilege" for a20

select grantee,'SYSTEM PRIV',privilege
from dba_sys_privs
where grantee not in ('SYSTEM','SYS','PUBLIC')
and not exists (select 'w'
        from dba_roles
           where role=grantee)
union
select grantee,table_name,privilege
from dba_tab_privs
where grantee not in ('SYSTEM','SYS','PUBLIC')
and not exists (select 'w'
        from dba_roles
           where role=grantee)
union
select grantee,table_name,privilege
from dba_col_privs
where grantee not in ('SYSTEM','SYS','PUBLIC')
and not exists (select 'w'
        from dba_roles
           where role=grantee)
/
```

Phase 3 ~ Oracle Access Controls

This gives:

```
SQL> @v

Granted To              What                           Privilege
--------------------    ----------------------------   --------------------
AURORA$JIS$UTILITY$     JIS_EXP                        EXECUTE
AURORA$JIS$UTILITY$     JIS_IMP_AUX                    EXECUTE
AURORA$JIS$UTILITY$     SYSTEM PRIV                    UNLIMITED TABLESPACE
AURORA$ORB$UNAUTHENT    SYSTEM PRIV                    CREATE SESSION
ICATED
...
```

Over 170 records are returned on 8.1.7 default installation and 765 in 9iR1 and 796 in 9iR2. If system privileges granted to PUBLIC are included, then the number of records is over **10,700**. Quite amazing!!

Review the system privileges granted to users and revoke where they are not necessary.

Action 3.8.7

SEVERITY LEVEL 2
O/S VERSION All
ORACLE VERSIONS All

Check for application objects that are owned by privileged users. Start with:

```
SQL> select distinct owner
  2  from dba_objects;

OWNER
------------------------------
AURORA$JIS$UTILITY$
DBSNMP
MDSYS
ORDSYS
OSE$HTTP$ADMIN
OUTLN
PETE
PUBLIC
SYS
SYSTEM

10 rows selected.

SQL>
```

The above list will identify all users; from that list identify which users are privileged. Then check for users with DBA or ALL PRIVILEGES, or users who have been locally defined as an administrator. Check for tablespaces used in the database with the following:

```
SQL> select tablespace_name
  2   from dba_tablespaces;

TABLESPACE_NAME
------------------------------
SYSTEM
TOOLS
RBS
TEMP
USERS
INDX

6 rows selected.

SQL>
```

From this list identify the tablespaces used by applications. Now the application tablespaces can be used in a query against dba_segments as follows to find which users have objects in which tablespaces. Use the list of privileged users found above, and find out why any privileged user has objects in applications tablespaces. Use the following query:

```
select count(*),owner,table_space_name,segment_type
from dba_segments
where tablespace_name in('<TABLE_SPACE_1','TABLE_SPACE_2','..')
group by owner,tablespace_name,segment_type;
```

From the results, move any objects that should be moved to a better tablespace or to a new owner.

Action 3.8.8

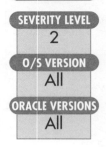

SEVERITY LEVEL: 2
O/S VERSION: All
ORACLE VERSIONS: All

Check for users that have been granted direct privileges on objects and not through roles. This is similar to the test above except that it is just objects/tables. Use the following SQL as an example, and then revoke access to any objects that users should not have access to. Here is the sample:

```
SQL> select grantee,count(*)
  2  from dba_tab_privs
  3  group by grantee;

GRANTEE                          COUNT(*)
------------------------------ ----------
AQ_ADMINISTRATOR_ROLE                  12
AQ_USER_ROLE                            3
CTXAPP                                  4
CTXSYS                                 27
DATA_ALIGNMENT_CHECKER                  2
DBA                                     3
DELETE_CATALOG_ROLE                     1
EXECUTE_CATALOG_ROLE                   28
EXP_FULL_DATABASE                      15
HS_ADMIN_ROLE                          18
IMP_FULL_DATABASE                       7

GRANTEE                          COUNT(*)
------------------------------ ----------
ORDSYS                                 11
OUTLN                                   1
PUBLIC                               9607
SELECT_CATALOG_ROLE                   738
SNMPAGENT                              20
SYS                                    11
SYSTEM                                 29
TRACESVR                                1

19 rows selected.

SQL>
```

Phase 3 ~ Oracle Access Controls

The listing is a count only, since a full listing would be very large. Identify users individually where there could be an issue, and list the objects for that user by using this SQL:

```
select grantee,table_name,privilege
from dba_tab_privs
where grantee='&username';
```

Use the output generated above and revoke access to tables and objects not needed by users.

It is important for a user to own all the code that accesses those users' objects.

Action 3.8.9

SEVERITY LEVEL: 1
O/S VERSION: All
ORACLE VERSIONS: All

Check for users who have been granted "CREATE LIBRARY", "ALTER SYSTEM" or "CREATE PROCEDURE" either directly or through a role.

Check for these privileges with the following query:

```
select grantee,privilege
from dba_sys_privs
where privilege
in ('ALTER SYSTEM','CREATE%PROCEDURE','CREATE%LIBRARY%')
union
select grantee,granted_role
from dba_role_privs
where granted_role
in ('ALTER SYSTEM','CREATE%PROCEDURE','CREATE%LIBRARY%')
```

From the above list, determine if any users have any of these privileges granted directly or if any roles have them. If any role has these privileges, then check for users who have these roles again with the view dba_role_privs. Revoke these privileges from any users or roles in production databases.

A problem exists with KILL SESSION. If an organization wanted to allow developers to kill their own sessions, it would need to allow access to ALTER SYSTEM. ALTER SYSTEM ENABLE RESTRICTED SESSION can be used to lock out all other users. It could also be used to stop archiving of the logs.

CREATE LIBRARY can be used to access O/S files and gain an escalation of privileges on the O/S.

Phase 3 ~ Oracle Access Controls

Action 3.8.10

SEVERITY LEVEL: 3
O/S VERSION: All
ORACLE VERSIONS: All

Create roles to control access to the underlying data through packages, not by directly granting access to tables. Then grant the roles to the relevant business area users.

Action 3.8.11

SEVERITY LEVEL: 2
O/S VERSION: All
ORACLE VERSIONS: All

Check where access other than select has been granted and review if it is necessary. For example, if a table is ever *read only*, then why does every user have insert, update and delete access?

Action 3.8.12

SEVERITY LEVEL: 3
O/S VERSION: All
ORACLE VERSIONS: All

Consider the use of integrity constraints — they can be used not just for data integrity. Having them could make it harder for a malicious person to insert or alter data directly since he would need to understand the application schema. This would not stop a determined attacker, but would prevent casual misuse by someone.

Action 3.8.13

SEVERITY LEVEL: 3
O/S VERSION: All
ORACLE VERSIONS: All

Consider using triggers to insert critical data, thereby removing the need for direct access to critical tables. Lock the schema owner's account, and ensure that the schema owner is the only user who has access to the tables and that no user has SELECT ANY TABLE.

Action 3.8.14

SEVERITY LEVEL: 2
O/S VERSION: All
ORACLE VERSIONS: All

Users should ideally not use more than one role at once and the use of MAX_ENABLED_ROLES and SET ROLE and SET ROLE NONE should be considered in applications, as should the use of password-protected roles. Password protected roles could be considered for use during DML operations. If these roles were not password connected, then users would be able to enable the role and take on additional privileges.

From Oracle8 onwards, when creating an account, if default roles are not defined, then all roles granted will be default enabling more access than intended.

The following example looks for roles that are not password protected:

```
SQL> select *
  2  from dba_roles
  3  where password_required='NO';

ROLE                           PASSWORD
------------------------------ --------
CONNECT                        NO
RESOURCE                       NO
DBA                            NO
SELECT_CATALOG_ROLE            NO
EXECUTE_CATALOG_ROLE           NO
DELETE_CATALOG_ROLE            NO
EXP_FULL_DATABASE              NO
IMP_FULL_DATABASE              NO
RECOVERY_CATALOG_OWNER         NO
AQ_ADMINISTRATOR_ROLE          NO
AQ_USER_ROLE                   NO
```

Phase 3 ~ Oracle Access Controls

```
ROLE                            PASSWORD
------------------------------  --------
SNMPAGENT                       NO
OEM_MONITOR                     NO
HS_ADMIN_ROLE                   NO
JAVAUSERPRIV                    NO
JAVAIDPRIV                      NO
JAVASYSPRIV                     NO
JAVADEBUGPRIV                   NO
JAVA_ADMIN                      NO
TIMESERIES_DEVELOPER            NO
TIMESERIES_DBA                  NO
CTXAPP                          NO

22 rows selected.

SQL>
```

The command to alter a role to use a password is:

```
SQL> alter role ctxapp identified by <password>;
```

Action 3.8.15

SEVERITY LEVEL: 2
O/S VERSION: All
ORACLE VERSIONS: All

The documentation says that the BECOME USER privilege only makes sense for a user of import and export to "become" another user. This privilege does not allow a user to access another's account from, say, SQL*Plus, but this can be abused by a C program making calls to the undocumented upi interface. A check for the BECOME USER privilege is necessary. This can be done as follows:

```
SQL> select grantee,privilege
  2  from dba_sys_privs
  3  where privilege = 'BECOME USER';

GRANTEE                        PRIVILEGE
------------------------------ ----------------------------------------
EXP_FULL_DATABASE              BECOME USER
IMP_FULL_DATABASE              BECOME USER
PETE                           BECOME USER

3 rows selected.

SQL>
```

Any users or roles that have this privilege should be reviewed and the privilege revoked if it is not necessary. This can be done as follows:

```
SQL> revoke become user from pete;

Revoke succeeded.

SQL>
```

Step 3.9 — External Users

PROBLEM: *Oracle allows database users to be defined as external. These users are authenticated by the Operating System. This feature can be useful in some instances but can cause security issues since anyone gaining access to an external O/S account can access the database without further authentication. Finding an external account that has high-level privileges is also a bonus to an attacker.*

This is a problem for external users authenticated by the host-based authentication. Other methods (Kerberos, SSL etc) do not have this problem.

Action 3.9.1

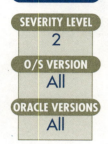

SEVERITY LEVEL: 2
O/S VERSION: All
ORACLE VERSIONS: All

Look for external users in the database by checking dba_users to identify any users who have passwords of external _____. This can be done as follows:

```
SQL> select username
  2  from dba_users
  3  where password='EXTERNAL';
no rows selected

SQL>
```

While this identifies external users, they can only access the database using operating system authentication remotely if REMOTE_OS_AUTHENT=TRUE in the *init.ora* file.

If the parameter os_authent_prefix is set to OPS$, then the external account can also have a database password.

Note that if this parameter is set to FALSE, then "connect /" is only allowed if connecting via a method that can be trusted, such as NTS (Windows only) or bequeath (Unix only) or Oracle Advanced Security.

External users can also be better authenticated using the Advanced Security Option through RADIUS, Kerberos, SSL or Windows (Windows boxes only). SecureID is obsolete in 9iR2 and is replaced by RADIUS.

It is possible at run time to see which authentication method has been used by querying V$SESSION_CONNECT_INFO.

> **Note:** Forbid the usage of external users from other machines. This is especially true when crossing O/S boundaries, e.g. user on Windows database on Unix-flavor.

Phase 3 ~ Oracle Access Controls

Action 3.9.2

SEVERITY LEVEL 1
O/S VERSION All
ORACLE VERSIONS All

Check for users who are external and who are also a DBA as follows:

```
SQL> select     username
  2  from       dba_role_privs,
  3     dba_users
  4  where      username=grantee
  5  and        granted_role='DBA'
  6  and        password='EXTERNAL';

no rows selected

SQL>
```

This check is obvious; any external access gained through one of these users would lead to *any* access of the database.

Action 3.9.3

SEVERITY LEVEL 1
O/S VERSION All
ORACLE VERSIONS All

Check for users who are external and who are also given the "all privileges" privilege. Use the SQL given in *Action 3.9.1* and also check the password of the user to see if it is set to EXTERNAL.

Having "all privileges" is as dangerous as having the privilege DBA; remove the user or revoke the privileges.

Action 3.9.4

SEVERITY LEVEL 2
O/S VERSION All
ORACLE VERSIONS All

In general check that any external users have the weakest roles and privileges possible for the application. It is sometimes not avoidable to use external users, so be prepared to use *least privilege* rigorously.

Phase 3 ~ Oracle Access Controls

Action 3.9.5

SEVERITY LEVEL: 2
O/S VERSION: All
ORACLE VERSIONS: All

Host-based authentication is even more dangerous if allowed remotely, meaning that the authentication takes place at a different server than the one the database resides on (spoofing can easily occur). If you need to improve the security of external authentication, additional tools and procedures (Token cards, Kerberos, SSL, etc.) should be used.

Chapter 9 referenced in the URL in *Action 3.4.1* is a good starting point for this area. External authentication is not available out-of-the-box by Oracle on its own. Oracle teams up with companies such as Baltimore and Verisign to create these solutions. Oracle 9iAS and Oracle 9i can handle certificates, but to manage and implement certificates for a large organization can require specialist software such as Baltimore's UniCERT. See the following URL's for details of these products and companies:

http://www.baltimore.com/unicert/index.asp
http://www.verisign.com

Secure shell (SSH) can also be used.

Action 3.9.6

SEVERITY LEVEL: 1
O/S VERSION: All
ORACLE VERSIONS: All

Ensure that no external users are granted the SYSDBA or SYSOPER roles. This can be checked with the following:

```
SQL> select d.username,d.password,p.sysdba,p.sysoper
  2    from v$pwfile_users p, dba_users d
  3    where d.username=p.username;

USERNAME                       PASSWORD                         SYSDB SYSOP
------------------------------ -------------------------------- ----- -----
SYS                            D4C5016086B2DC6A                 TRUE  TRUE

SQL>
```

If there are external users granted, these roles recreate the password file and revoke these roles.

Phase 3 ~ Oracle Access Controls

Step 3.10 — Public Packages and Privileges

PROBLEM: *Oracle ships a large number of PL/SQL packages that have public privileges. This means that an attacker can use any package available to a user whose account the attacker compromises.*

Action 3.10.1

SEVERITY LEVEL: 1
O/S VERSION: All
ORACLE VERSIONS: 8, 8i, 9i

Revoke the PUBLIC execute privilege on utl_file. This package can be used to access O/S file systems.

```
SQL> revoke all on utl_file from public;
Revoke succeeded.
SQL>
```

See *Action 3.1.1* for details of utl_file_dir.

Note: With UTL_FILE it is only possible to read and write files to the OS if utl_file_dir is set or in 9iR2 a directory object exists.

Action 3.10.2

SEVERITY LEVEL: 1
O/S VERSION: All
ORACLE VERSIONS: 8.1.7 above

Revoke the PUBLIC execute privilege on utl_tcp. This package can be used to write and read sockets.

```
SQL> revoke all on utl_tcp from public;
Revoke succeeded.
SQL>
```

Action 3.10.3

SEVERITY LEVEL: 1
O/S VERSION: All
ORACLE VERSIONS: 8.1.7 above

Revoke the PUBLIC execute privilege on utl_http. This package can write content to a web browser.

```
SQL> revoke all on utl_http from public;
Revoke succeeded.
SQL>
```

Phase 3 ~ Oracle Access Controls

Action 3.10.4

SEVERITY LEVEL: 1
O/S VERSION: All
ORACLE VERSIONS: 8.1.7 above

Revoke the PUBLIC execute privilege on utl_smtp. This package can be used to send mail messages from the database server.

```
SQL> revoke all on utl_smtp from public;
Revoke succeeded.
SQL>
```

Action 3.10.5

SEVERITY LEVEL: 1
O/S VERSION: All
ORACLE VERSIONS: All

Check for all PUBLIC execute privileges on PL/SQL packages owned by sys. It is important for users to have access to what they need, not to everything that is possible in the system. Consider revoking all public access and granting back what's needed.

The SQL used in *Action 3.8.6* above can be modified to just return privileges and objects that can be accessed by PUBLIC. Use this list and review what to delete. This can be a major task since Oracle 8.1.7, for instance, grants over 10,000 PUBLIC privileges.

Again we come back to *least privilege* and the importance of granting what is needed, **not** everything that is available.

Note: Consider writing wrapper functions (e.g. user_lock) owned by SYS that expose subsets of the functionality in the equivalent utl and dbms packages.

Action 3.10.6

SEVERITY LEVEL: 2
O/S VERSION: All
ORACLE VERSIONS: All

Revoke the PUBLIC execute privilege on DBMS_RANDOM. This package is used to generate random numbers and is generally used in security features of applications. Care should be taken in this initialization of this package. Understand the number of bytes used in the initialization of the seed.

If a sufficiently large number of bytes is not used as the seed, the numbers generated are usually not sufficiently random. This package calls the internal number generator within the Oracle kernel.

If better random numbers are needed, the DESGETKEY and DES3GETKEY routines in the DBMS_OBFUSCATION_TOOLKIT package can be used.

Revoke the privilege as follows:

```
SQL> revoke execute on dbms_random from public;
Revoke succeeded.
SQL>
```

Phase 3 ~ Oracle Access Controls

Action 3.10.7

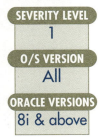

Revoke the PUBLIC execute privilege on DBMS_LOB. This package is used to access LOB's and CLOB's both in the database and in external files. This package in earlier versions can be abused and relative paths can be used to access any file in any directory. This has been fixed in bug 1814582.

After Version 8.1.6.3, a directory object used in the call to DBMS_LOB.OPEN of "/" can be used to access any directory on the server to which the owner of the Oracle software has access.

Some checks/ solutions:
- Check all calls to DBMS_LOB.OPEN()
- Do not allow PUBLIC directory objects. In 8.1.6, for instance, these exist: MEDIA_DIR or WTC_EXP_DIR as PUBLIC directories.
- Do not allow DIRECTORY objects that are set to "/". See metalink Note: 168670.1 How to use BFILE with sub-directories.
- Check all DIRECTORY objects and where they point to.
- Revoke CREATE (ANY) DIRECTORY privileges.

Revoke the privilege as follows:

```
SQL> revoke execute on dbms_lob from public;

Revoke succeeded.

SQL>
```

Action 3.10.8

Revoke any granted PUBLIC execute privileges on DBMS_SQL and DBMS_SYS_SQL. These packages are used to write dynamic SQL. The package DBMS_SYS_SQL can be used to run PL/SQL and SQL as the owner of the procedure, and not the caller. There are no PUBLIC privileges on these packages by default.

dbms_sys_sql is an un-documented package used by Oracle itself in the Oracle Replication Options. There is one interesting function available in this package: parse_as_user, which allows a package using this feature to be run as the invoker rather than the package owner. This particular function is described in the paper at http://downloads.securityfocus.com/library/oracle-security.pdf in the DBMS_SYS_SQL.PARSE_AS_USER section of the document. Hence anyone with execute on DBMS_SYS_SQL has DBA access.

Note: Auditing the usage of some of the critical packages can be useful.

Phase 3 ~ Oracle Access Controls

Action 3.10.9

SEVERITY LEVEL: 1
O/S VERSION: All
ORACLE VERSIONS: All

Any package that is available via a database link that is not part of the application should be revoked. The following example illustrates:

In reviewing a PL/SQL package during an audit, the following was found:

```
v_rc := utl_http.request@mylink ('http://www.some-url.com');
```

To test for this try

```
select utl_http@dblink ('http://www.some-url.com') from dual;
```

The issue here is that the package utl_http was called in another database via a database link. Securing all of these critical packages in the production database is admirable, but if the same packages are then visible via any database links in the database, the effort is futile.

Action 3.10.10

SEVERITY LEVEL: 2
O/S VERSION: All
ORACLE VERSIONS: All

Version 8i and higher of Oracle changed the way PL/SQL packages and procedures work with respect to privileges and implemented *invoker rights*. Before this version, all PL/SQL procedures were run with *definer rights*, that is, the privilege the procedure ran with was that of the *owner* of the procedure. This meant that any object accessed by the procedure could therefore be accessed by anyone running that procedure (provided the owner had granted execute privileges). It is possible for SYS, for instance, to create a procedure to alter a user's password using "execute immediate", and then grant execute on this procedure to all other users. Other users in the database could then also alter SYS's password. This is an extreme example to show the dangers of procedures owned by privileged users. Here it is:

```
SQL> connect sys/<password>
Connected.
SQL> create or replace procedure passwd(passwd in varchar2,
  2   username in varchar2 default user)
  3  is
  4  begin
  5   execute immediate ('ALTER USER '||username||' identified by '||passwd);
  6  end;
  7  /

Procedure created.

SQL> grant execute on passwd to pete;

Grant succeeded.
```

```
SQL> connect pete/<password>
Connected.
SQL> exec sys.passwd('hack0r#','SYS');

PL/SQL procedure successfully completed.

SQL> connect sys/hack0r#
Connected.
SQL>
```

This can be fixed by using *invoker's rights* as follows:

```
SQL> connect sys/<password>
Connected.
SQL> create or replace procedure passwd (passwd in varchar2,
  2   username in varchar2 default user)
  3   authid current_user
  4   as
  5   begin
  6    execute immediate ('ALTER USER '||username||' IDENTIFIED BY '||passwd);
  7   end;
  8  /

Procedure created.

SQL> grant execute on passwd to pete;

Grant succeeded.

SQL> connect pete/<password>
Connected.
SQL> exec sys.passwd('hack0r#','SYS');
BEGIN sys.passwd('hack0r#','SYS'); END;

*
ERROR at line 1:
ORA-01031: insufficient privileges
ORA-06512: at "SYS.PASSWD", line 6
ORA-06512: at line 1


SQL>
```

Adding the line *authid current_users* makes the procedure run as the invoker not the owner.

Just to muddy the waters a bit, *invokers* rights procedures could also be used as a Trojan. A user can create a procedure as current user, and try to get a privileged user to run it. A good article on invoker rights can be found at http://www.oracle.com/oramag/oracle/00-Jan/index.html?1O08i.html

Phase 3 ~ Oracle Access Controls

Action 3.10.11

SEVERITY LEVEL: 2
O/S VERSION: All
ORACLE VERSIONS: All

Check all DIRECTORY objects in the database and note the file names and locations. Check out what files can be accessed and whether they should be accessed. Confirm the permissions of the files and ensure that they can only be accessed by the correct users. The details of directories can be found from the view DBA_DIRECTORIES. Also check out the permissions granted to DIRECTORY objects. This can be done by querying the dba_tab_privs view.

Revoke any PUBLIC privileges on DIRECTORY objects. These can be used to launch attacks. Secure any files accessed. Ensure that DIRECTORY objects can only be accessed by users who need them.

Step 3.11 Direct Privileges

PROBLEM: *If privileges are granted to users directly and not through roles, it makes it much harder to track what those granted privileges are. If no user has any direct privileges, then spotting irregularities becomes easier. Thus the use of roles can simplify privilege assignment.*

Action 3.11.1

SEVERITY LEVEL: 2
O/S VERSION: All
ORACLE VERSIONS: All

Check for any directly granted privileges to users and suggest that they be revoked. The SQL used in *Action 3.8.6* can be used for this purpose.

Because SYS.DBMS_SQL and SYS.DBMS_SYS_SQL are necessary to generate SQL statements dynamically server-side, the trend is to grant system privileges to users directly rather than through roles. SYS packages cannot recognize privileges granted to roles. Roles make administration easier, because a number of system and object privileges can be granted at once. But, of course, it makes it easier for hackers to do the same if they have the ability to grant that role to themselves.

If at all possible, do not use direct grants to objects but use access through roles. This argument doesn't work when package procedures are used, since they need to have access granted directly to underlying objects when those objects are accessed in another schema. The model is still intact since access is through a package.

Phase 3 ~ Oracle Access Controls

Action 3.11.2

SEVERITY LEVEL: 4
O/S VERSION: All
ORACLE VERSIONS: All

Direct access to tables (and similar) should be revoked and access to tables could be granted only through packages or roles. This would make it harder for an attacker to gain access to the data directly.

Implementing this on an existing database / application would be difficult without access to the program code. This recommendation is probably more relevant to a new database and application design.

Step 3.12 — Default Tablespaces

PROBLEM: *Each user in the database is assigned a default tablespace. This is where users' objects are created. If a user's default tablespace is set incorrectly, i.e. to the system tablespace, then that user could eventually cause the database to stop working by consuming all available space. If a user has an application tablespace assigned as default, then problems could occur in the application if objects are created and space is used unnecessarily.*

Action 3.12.1

SEVERITY LEVEL: 1
O/S VERSION: All
ORACLE VERSIONS: All

Set the default tablespace of the system user to something other than system. The SQL for this is covered in Action 2.2.9 in the test for all default users default tablespaces.

Note: If a full import is performed into a database, hoping to recreate the user's objects, and if for some reason the default tablespace for some of the user accounts do not exist, then the user's objects will all end up in SYSTEM.

Note: The system tablespace can be set to autoextend to prevent expansion problems. Then monitor any unusual growth using OEM or homegrown scripts.

Note: It is possible to Dos (Denial of Service: - This essentially means that users are denied access to the server by an attacker ensuring the server runs out of resources) an Oracle instance by filling up the TEMP tablespace with an overly long query.

Phase 3 ~ Oracle Access Controls

Action 3.12.2

SEVERITY LEVEL: 2
O/S VERSION: All
ORACLE VERSIONS: All

Set users default tablespaces and default temporary tablespace to ensure they cannot create objects in tablespaces they should not be able to. Check as follows:

```
SQL> select username,default_tablespace,temporary_tablespace
  2* from dba_users;

USERNAME                DEFAULT_TABLESPACE    TEMPORARY_TABLESPACE
--------------------    --------------------  --------------------
SYS                     SYSTEM                TEMP
SYSTEM                  TOOLS                 TEMP
TRACESVR                SYSTEM                SYSTEM
OUTLN                   SYSTEM                SYSTEM
DBSNMP                  TOOLS                 TEMP
ORDSYS                  SYSTEM                SYSTEM
AURORA$JIS$UTILITY$     SYSTEM                SYSTEM
OSE$HTTP$ADMIN          SYSTEM                SYSTEM
AURORA$ORB$UNAUTHENT    SYSTEM                SYSTEM
ICATED
ORDPLUGINS              SYSTEM                SYSTEM
MDSYS                   SYSTEM                SYSTEM
PETE                    SYSTEM                SYSTEM
PET                     SYSTEM                SYSTEM

13 rows selected.
```

Any users who have SYSTEM defined as either default tablespace or temporary tablespace should be changed to use more suitable tablespaces.

Consider using tablespace quotas, since there is a risk of a denial of service attack if users have UNLIMITED TABLESPACE.

Note: Oracle is not consistent in naming of the default users tablespace. In 7.3 it is called USERS, in 8 it is USER_DATA and in 8i, it is USERS again.

Step 3.13 Standard Roles

PROBLEM: There are a number of standard roles shipped with each version of Oracle, and inevitably some users are assigned these roles as their default basic configuration. Most of these roles, such as RESOURCE or CONNECT, are far too powerful for normal users. This allows the user to create tables or triggers. This should not be necessary for an application user.

Note: Drop the Oracle supplied roles since they are provided for backwards compatibility, and create several new more secure roles such as SYS_ADMIN, SECURITY_ADMIN, and BACKUP_ADMIN

Action 3.13.1

SEVERITY LEVEL: 1
O/S VERSION: All
ORACLE VERSIONS: All

Revoke RESOURCE role from normal application user accounts. This role is too powerful and includes:

```
SQL> select *
  2  from dba_sys_privs
  3  where grantee='RESOURCE';

Grantee              Privilege            ADM
-------------------- -------------------- ---
RESOURCE             CREATE CLUSTER       NO
RESOURCE             CREATE INDEXTYPE     NO
RESOURCE             CREATE OPERATOR      NO
RESOURCE             CREATE PROCEDURE     NO
RESOURCE             CREATE SEQUENCE      NO
RESOURCE             CREATE TABLE         NO
RESOURCE             CREATE TRIGGER       NO
RESOURCE             CREATE TYPE          NO

8 rows selected.

SQL>
```

Drop the RESOURCE role from the database, or if it cannot be dropped, then revoke the key dangerous privileges from it. This would be a good backup to your own new roles if the old ones were used accidentally.

Many sites simply grant this role to all users as a default.

The RESOURCE role also displays a strange behavior. It is not possible to grant space quotas to roles but when the RESOURCE role is granted, it also gives the receiver of this role unlimited tablespace on all tablespaces. This is another reason not to use the RESOURCE role.

Note: Some third-party applications such as Quest's products use the RESOURCE role. In this case, drop the privileges not needed from RESOURCE. Lobby the manufacturer to create its own dedicated role that meets the requirements.

Note: In general, avoid all of the Oracle supplied roles, understand them and understand the privileges they include.

Action 3.13.2

SEVERITY LEVEL: 2
O/S VERSION: All
ORACLE VERSIONS: All

Revoke the CONNECT role from normal application users and replace with a sanitized version, or simply grant CREATE SESSION to new users. This role includes these privileges:

```
SQL> select *
  2  from dba_sys_privs
  3  where grantee='CONNECT';

Grantee                 Privilege                ADM
----------------------  -----------------------  ---
CONNECT                 ALTER SESSION            NO
CONNECT                 CREATE CLUSTER           NO
CONNECT                 CREATE DATABASE LINK     NO
CONNECT                 CREATE SEQUENCE          NO
CONNECT                 CREATE SESSION           NO
CONNECT                 CREATE SYNONYM           NO
CONNECT                 CREATE TABLE             NO
CONNECT                 CREATE VIEW              NO

8 rows selected.

SQL>
```

This role is granted in organizations by default to most users.

Drop the CONNECT role from the database, or if it cannot be dropped, then revoke the key dangerous privileges from it. This would be a good backup to your own new roles if the old ones were used accidentally.

Note: When Creating a new USER, DBA Studio has a hidden default of assigning the CONNECT ROLE, which may well be much more privileged than the user needs. This does not happen when issuing the raw SQL CREATE USER command

Note: Many third-party applications use the default roles, particularly the CONNECT role. Therefore in some cases, it is not easy to remove this role without affecting support arrangements of these applications. In this case, remove the unnecessary privileges from the CONNECT role i.e. CREATE VIEW.

Action 3.13.3

SEVERITY LEVEL: 3
O/S VERSION: All
ORACLE VERSIONS: All

Consider adding passwords to any critical roles and administration roles used in the application.

Action 3.13.4

SEVERITY LEVEL 3
O/S VERSION All
ORACLE VERSIONS All

Revoke all non-essential roles and rights from the PUBLIC group.

Use the following SQL to find all PUBLIC rights granted:

```
select 'SYSTEM','SYSTEM',privilege
from  dba_sys_privs
where grantee='PUBLIC'
union
select  'OBJECT',table_name,privilege
from dba_tab_privs
where grantee='PUBLIC'
union
select 'COLUMN',table_name,privilege
from dba_col_privs
where grantee='PUBLIC'
union
select 'ROLE','ROLE',granted_role
from dba_role_privs
where grantee='PUBLIC';
```

Review this massive list and revoked all unnecessary privileges.

Phase 3 ~ Oracle Access Controls

Step 3.14 — The Use of Profiles to Help Prevent Attacks

PROBLEM: *Oracle provides the concept of profiles, which can be used to control access and some resource items. There is a default profile assigned to users. This is not always restrictive enough. For instance, the number of failed login attempts is unlimited in some cases, and this would allow a brute force attack against any user with that role.*

Action 3.14.1

SEVERITY LEVEL: 3
O/S VERSION: All
ORACLE VERSIONS: 8 & above

In default profile, set the parameter PASSWORD_LIFE_TIME to 60.

See *Action 2.1.3* for details on how to modify the default profile.

Note: One problem with default installations is that the password management features are not set and most default profile settings are set to UNLIMITED.

Action 3.14.2

SEVERITY LEVEL: 3
O/S VERSION: All
ORACLE VERSIONS: 8 & above

In the default profile set the parameter PASSWORD_GRACE_TIME to 3.

See *Action 2.1.3* for details on how to modify the default profile.

Action 3.14.3

SEVERITY LEVEL: 2
O/S VERSION: All
ORACLE VERSIONS: 8 & above

In default profile set the parameter PASSWORD_REUSE_MAX to 20.

See *Action 2.1.3* for details on how to modify the default profile.

Phase 3 ~ Oracle Access Controls

Action 3.14.4

SEVERITY LEVEL: 3
O/S VERSION: All
ORACLE VERSIONS: 8 & above

In default profile set the parameter FAILED_LOGIN_ATTEMPTS to 5.

See *Action 2.1.3* for details on how to modify the default profile.

Setting this parameter will prevent someone from brute forcing a database account, but could also allow a Denial of service attack to take place.

Action 3.14.5

SEVERITY LEVEL: 3
O/S VERSION: All
ORACLE VERSIONS: All

Investigate the use of profiles in general in the database, and assign users profiles for their business role or administration tasks, rather than every user having the default profile.

Profiles and their settings can be seen in the view DBA_PROFILES, and the profiles assigned to users can be viewed in the view DBA_USERS.

Action 3.14.6

SEVERITY LEVEL: 2
O/S VERSION: All
ORACLE VERSIONS: All

Ensure that the users profile settings include the following parameters:
- CPU_PER_SESSION
- PRIVATE_SGA
- LOGICAL_READS_PER_SESSION
- SESSIONS_PER_USER
- CONNECT_TIME
- IDLE_TIME

Check that these parameters have appropriate values consistent with the applications and database. These settings will help prevent uncontrolled applications and queries that could cause a denial of service to occur. They will also help prevent multiple logins on the same user account, and on accounts that do not need to remain connected.

The following SQL can be run to check these:

```
SQL> col profile for a12
SQL> col resource_name for a30
SQL> col limit for a30
SQL> l
  1  select profile,resource_name,limit
  2  from dba_profiles
  3  where resource_name in ('CPU_PER_SESSION',
  4      'PRIVATE_SGA',
  5      'LOGICAL_READS_PER_SESSION',
  6      'SESSIONS_PER_USER',
  7      'CONNECT_TIME',
  8      'IDLE_TIME')
  9  order by profile
SQL> /

PROFILE      RESOURCE_NAME                  LIMIT
------------ ------------------------------ ------------------------------
DEFAULT      SESSIONS_PER_USER              1
DEFAULT      CPU_PER_SESSION                UNLIMITED
DEFAULT      IDLE_TIME                      UNLIMITED
DEFAULT      PRIVATE_SGA                    UNLIMITED
DEFAULT      CONNECT_TIME                   UNLIMITED
DEFAULT      LOGICAL_READS_PER_SESSION      UNLIMITED
LIMIT_USERS  SESSIONS_PER_USER              1
LIMIT_USERS  CPU_PER_SESSION                DEFAULT
LIMIT_USERS  IDLE_TIME                      DEFAULT
LIMIT_USERS  PRIVATE_SGA                    DEFAULT
LIMIT_USERS  CONNECT_TIME                   DEFAULT
LIMIT_USERS  LOGICAL_READS_PER_SESSION      DEFAULT

12 rows selected.

SQL>
```

Step 3.15 — Hidden Initialization Parameters

PROBLEM: *There are a lot of initialization parameters that can be set for an Oracle instance. These are added to a configuration file, and some can be altered on line for the current session. In Oracle 9i, some of these alterations can be made permanent. There are also a lot of undocumented parameters supplied for internal use by Oracle, some of which can cause damage to the database or cause it to give up information it would not normally do.*

Action 3.15.1

SEVERITY LEVEL: 3
O/S VERSION: All
ORACLE VERSIONS: All

Ensure that the hidden parameter _trace_files_public is set to false. This parameter, if set to TRUE, allows users access to read trace files. This parameter is set in the *init.ora* file.

See the SQL in *Action 3.15.2* to read the value of this parameter.

Action 3.15.2

SEVERITY LEVEL: 3
O/S VERSION: All
ORACLE VERSIONS: All

Review all hidden parameters in the database and ensure that none of them change. Regularly looking at the parameters and checking them against a known set of defaults can do this. The following SQL can be used:

```
select   pin.ksppinm called,
         pcv.ksppstvl itsvalue
from     sys.x$ksppi pin,
         sys.x$ksppcv pcv
where    pin.inst_id=userenv('Instance')
and      pcv.inst_id=userenv('Instance')
and      pin.indx=pcv.indx
and      translate(pin.ksppinm,'_','^') like '^%';
```

Some key parameters can be used to open a corrupted database. It is important that these are not enabled.

Step 3.16 — Object Owners

PROBLEM: *If an application uses a certain set of tablespaces, and user objects are created within the space so that data is added, problems could ensue. At a minimum, it would cause space calculations to be incorrect resulting in fragmentation. It could also cause application failures if space is exceeded by unauthorized objects.*

Note: If tablespace data files are set to autoextend, and the tablespace happens to be on the same volume as the archived logs destination directory, theoretically someone could cause the tablespace to extend to the point where no archived logs can be written. When that happens, the database halts.

Action 3.16.1

SEVERITY LEVEL: 3
O/S VERSION: All
ORACLE VERSIONS: All

For all application tablespaces, check who owns the objects in them. Objects not owned by the application schema owners should be moved or dropped. The following SQL will show which users own objects in which tablespace:

```
select count(*),owner,tablespace_name,segment_type
from dba_segments
where tablespace_name<>'SYSTEM'
group by owner,tablespace_name,segment_type;
```

This process should be used regularly to look for rogue objects. A check for tables with autoextend set on can be done as follows:

```
SQL> select tablespace_name,status,extent_management
  2  from dba_tablespaces;

TABLESPACE_NAME                STATUS     EXTENT_MAN
------------------------------ ---------- ----------
SYSTEM                         ONLINE     DICTIONARY
TOOLS                          ONLINE     DICTIONARY
RBS                            ONLINE     DICTIONARY
TEMP                           ONLINE     DICTIONARY
USERS                          ONLINE     DICTIONARY
INDX                           ONLINE     DICTIONARY
DRSYS                          ONLINE     DICTIONARY
DATACHECK_TABLE                ONLINE     DICTIONARY
DATACHECK_INDEX                ONLINE     DICTIONARY
9 rows selected.

SQL>
```

Phase 3 ~ Oracle Access Controls

Step 3.17) Users Quotas

PROBLEM: *Users can be assigned a quota in Oracle. Having a quota allows a user to create objects in the database. This is a risk to integrity, performance and security.*

Action 3.17.1

SEVERITY LEVEL
3

O/S VERSION
All

ORACLE VERSIONS
All

Check the quota assigned to users. Having a quota allows objects to be created. Moreover, a user needs to be granted explicit permission to create objects. Having a quota set allows controls to be placed on the amount of space a user can use. If quotas are not limited, then it is possible to mount a denial of service attack against a database. The following SQL can be used to view quotas assigned:

```
SQL> select *
  2   from dba_ts_quotas;
no rows selected

SQL>
```

If a user has a quota in another user's tablespace, and the relevant grants have been performed, then a user can create objects in another user's tablespace.

Establishing quotas can be difficult to achieve in production and almost impossible in development.

Granting the RESOURCE role to a user (we do not recommend this) also gives UNLIMITED TABLESPACE to the same user. This is a problem with the RESOURCE role. UNLIMITED TABLESPACE cannot be granted to a role so this is either a bug or one of the privileges included in the RESOURCE role brings UNLIMITED TABLESPACE to the user. Either way **do not use** this role.

Note: The RESOURCE role entirely bypasses tablespace quota restrictions.

Note: Beware that if enough space quotas on tablespaces are not granted then large imports can fail.

Action 3.17.2

SEVERITY LEVEL
3

O/S VERSION
All

ORACLE VERSIONS
All

Establish separate users for the schema management and data management in each application.

Assign unique tablespaces for each application.

Note: If objects were created in a schema previously, when the account had more privileges, then the user will have all the DML privileges for those objects. The user will NOT have DDL privileges over those objects.

Phase 3 ~ Oracle Access Controls

Step 3.18 ~ Naming Conventions

PROBLEM: *Having all users use their surnames or initials or combinations of surnames and forenames is a security risk. If an attacker learns or guesses the convention, then his work is greatly reduced. At a minimum, the convention for usernames should differ from that used for company e-mail accounts. Ideally, there should be no convention for usernames.*

Action 3.18.1

SEVERITY LEVEL: 3
O/S VERSION: All
ORACLE VERSIONS: All

Consider using naming conventions for schema owners, DBA's and normal users to make identification of users' types easier. Also consider a naming convention that is **not** based on user's names or email accounts or any other easy way to identify who they are. This could help stop an attacker building an attack profile.

Having complex naming conventions does, however, cause problems with user's memories and usernames, and passwords then tend to be written down.

Note: Naming conventions tend to cause a religious debate. This step is included here just to remind the reader that they could be used, but they do not have to be, hence the low rating of this action. This could also be described as security through obscurity – see the URL in Step 1.1.

Step 3.19 ~ Triggers Owned by Users

PROBLEM: *It is possible with the correct permissions for a user to create a database trigger and steal data that he has absolutely no permissions to read or write. See http://downloads.securityfocus.com/library/oracle-security.pdf for an example.*

Action 3.19.1

SEVERITY LEVEL: 2
O/S VERSION: All
ORACLE VERSIONS: All

Check for users who have database triggers where they are not the schema owners and should not have triggers. These triggers can be used to steal data. See http://downloads.securityfocus.com/library/oracle-security.pdf

To check for users who own triggers and on what, run the following SQL. (Note: the user of this SQL should include in the "not in" clause any schema owners used in the database).

```
SQL> select trigger_name,owner,table_name,table_owner
  2  from dba_triggers
  3  where owner not in('SYS','SYSTEM');
TRIGGER_NAME                   OWNER        Object                        TABLE_OWNE
------------------------       ----------   -------------------------     ----------
SDO_GEOM_TRIG_DEL1             MDSYS        USER_SDO_GEOM_METADATA        MDSYS
SDO_GEOM_TRIG_INS1             MDSYS        USER_SDO_GEOM_METADATA        MDSYS
SDO_GEOM_TRIG_UPD1             MDSYS        USER_SDO_GEOM_METADATA        MDSYS
SDO_DROP_USER                  MDSYS                                      SYS

4 rows selected.
```

The same type of trick of stealing data can be applied to any user who has the privilege SELECT ANY TABLE.

Check which users own triggers, and revoke those triggers owned by non-application users.

Check for users who have the privilege CREATE (ANY) TRIGGER with the following SQL:

```
SQL> select grantee,privilege
  2    from dba_sys_privs
  3    where privilege in ('CREATE TRIGGER','CREATE ANY TRIGGER');

GRANTEE                        PRIVILEGE
------------------------       ------------------------------------
DBA                            CREATE ANY TRIGGER
DBA                            CREATE TRIGGER
IMP_FULL_DATABASE              CREATE ANY TRIGGER
MDSYS                          CREATE ANY TRIGGER
MDSYS                          CREATE TRIGGER
RECOVERY_CATALOG_OWNER         CREATE TRIGGER
RESOURCE                       CREATE TRIGGER
TIMESERIES_DBA                 CREATE ANY TRIGGER

8 rows selected.

SQL>
```

Step 3.20 Access to Critical Views

PROBLEM: *If an unauthorized user has access to any of the SYS owned tables or views that allow information about users, passwords or password hashes to be revealed, then they can potentially build an attack profile against any database or any particular user.*

Action 3.20.1

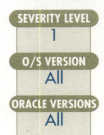

Check that no users have access to dba_users, sys.link$, sys.user$ or sys.user_history$. These tables and views all have either a password in clear text, or password hashes stored in them. This can be done with the following SQL:

```
SQL> select grantee,table_name,privilege
  2  from dba_tab_privs
  3  where table_name in('USER$','DBA_USERS','LINK$','USER_HISTORY$');

Grantee                 Object                    Privilege
--------------------    ------------------------  --------------------
SELECT_CATALOG_ROLE     DBA_USERS                 SELECT

SQL>
```

If any users have access, then revoke that access.

Third-party applications quite often implement their own authentication mechanisms and store the data in the database.

Note: In 9iR2, a user XDB has access granted in a default installation to sys.user$.

Phase 3 ~ Oracle Access Controls

Action 3.20.2

SEVERITY LEVEL: 1
O/S VERSION: All
ORACLE VERSIONS: All

Check that no user has access to dba_% views, v_$ views, v$ synonyms, x$ tables or any dictionary objects. The check needed for all the above is complicated but can be reduced to access on SYS owned tables and views in the first instance.

The following SQL will show this:

```
SQL> select grantee,table_name,privilege
  2  from dba_tab_privs p
  3  where owner='SYS'
  4  and grantee<>'PUBLIC'
  5  and (exists (select 'x'
  6  from dba_tables t
  7  where t.table_name=p.table_name)
  8  or exists (select 'x'
  9  from dba_views v
 10  where v.view_name=p.table_name))
SQL> /

Grantee               Object                      Privilege
--------------------  --------------------------  --------------------
AQ_ADMINISTRATOR_ROL  AQ$_PROPAGATION_STATUS      SELECT
E

DELETE_CATALOG_ROLE   AUD$                        DELETE
SELECT_CATALOG_ROLE   CODE_PIECES                 SELECT
SELECT_CATALOG_ROLE   CODE_SIZE                   SELECT
....
```

This select goes on to produce 835 records on a default 8.1.7 installation, and 1008 in 9iR1 and 1415 in 9iR2, so the issue is getting worse! Furthermore, this SQL does not include privileges granted to PUBLIC. These are dealt with in the section above on PUBLIC privileges. See *Step 3.11*.

The task on reducing these privileges is a large one, BUT it should be recommended again that *least privilege* be observed. All privileges granted on the SYS schema to other database users should be revoked and only granted back to those users who actually need them.

Phase 3 ~ Oracle Access Controls

Consensus has revealed that the following V$ and DBA views can be accessed in non-production databases by developers, but not by normal users. Access should not be granted to these views in production databases for non-administrators. Access can be granted to these SYS owned views (Note for v$ views the grant needs to be done on the underlying v_$ view) as follows:

```
grant select on sys.v_$log to {username};
grant select on sys.v_$rollstat to {username};
grant select on sys.v_$rollname to {username};
grant select on sys.v_$parameter  to {username};
grant select on sys.v_$latch to {username};
grant select on sys.v_$sqlarea to {username};
grant select on sys.v_$sqltext to {username};
grant select on sys.v_$sysstat to {username};
grant select on sys.v_$dispatcher to {username};
grant select on sys.v_$lock to {username};
grant select on sys.v_$locked_object to {username};
grant select on sys.v_$session to {username};
grant select on sys.v_$session_longops to {username};
grant select on sys.v_$process to {username};
grant select on sys.v_$sqltext to {username};
grant select on sys.dba_data_files to {username};
grant select on sys.dba_segments to {username};
grant select on sys.dba_tablespaces to {username};
-- optional
-- grant select on sys.v_$sgastat to {username};
-- grant select on sys.v_$sql to {username};
-- grant select on sys.v_$sqltext_with_newlines to {username};
-- grant select on sys.v_$sql_bind_data to {username};
-- grant select on sys.v_$sql_bind_metadata to {username};
-- grant select on sys.v_$sql_cursor to {username};
-- grant select on sys.v_$sql_shared_cursor to {username};
-- grant select on sys.v_$sql_shared_memory to {username};
```

Action 3.20.3

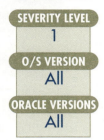

SEVERITY LEVEL: 1
O/S VERSION: All
ORACLE VERSIONS: All

Check which users have the privilege SELECT ANY TABLE and revoke this privilege from all users who do not need it. The following SQL can be used:

```
SQL> select grantee,privilege
  2  from dba_sys_privs
  3  where privilege in ('SELECT ANY TABLE');

GRANTEE                         PRIVILEGE
------------------------------  ----------------------------------------
DBA                             SELECT ANY TABLE
EXP_FULL_DATABASE               SELECT ANY TABLE
IMP_FULL_DATABASE               SELECT ANY TABLE
MDSYS                           SELECT ANY TABLE
SYS                             SELECT ANY TABLE
TRACESVR                        SELECT ANY TABLE

6 rows selected.

SQL>
```

Revoke the privilege as follows:

```
SQL> revoke select any table from tracesvr;

Revoke succeeded.

SQL>
```

Phase 3 ~ Oracle Access Controls

Step 3.21 ~ Object Creation and Access

PROBLEM: *If any user except a DBA or application schema owner can create objects, then potentially they can cause damage, denials of service or find ways to steal data.*

Action 3.21.1

SEVERITY LEVEL: 2
O/S VERSION: All
ORACLE VERSIONS: All

Revoke object creation privileges from all users except DBA and application schema owners. Revoking object creation privileges will make it harder for anyone to create any objects in the database that could be used maliciously.

Action 3.21.2

SEVERITY LEVEL: 2
O/S VERSION: All
ORACLE VERSIONS: All

Object access -- This one is hard to define. The aim is to ensure that users can only see objects that they should see. This will make it harder for an attacker to gain any account and steal any data.

This depends on the style of the application design used, whether users access tables directly or through views or through packages. This is a manual investigation that should start by understanding the business requirements and the different groups of users that use the application. Establish the interfaces, and then the objects that should be accessed, then review which other objects users in each group can see, and which views and packages allow them access to other objects.

A good starting point is to pick a representative user from each business group of users and then use the SQL below and supply the username:

```
select 'SYSTEM','SYSTEM',privilege
from  dba_sys_privs
where grantee='&&username'
union
select  'OBJECT',table_name,privilege
from dba_tab_privs
where grantee='&&username'
union
select 'COLUMN',table_name,privilege
from dba_col_privs
where grantee='&&username'
union
select 'ROLE','ROLE',granted_role
from dba_role_privs
where grantee='username';
```

> **Note:** Even people who submit queries can launch a DoS attack against a database, by submitting a query with an infinite loop. If profiles are not implemented, that query can cause a database to crash within minutes. The more powerful the server, the faster they can crash.

Step 3.22 Access to Views

PROBLEM: *In some versions of Oracle it is possible to create views that allow the underlying data accessed through the view to be modified. This is one way for a malicious user to alter data without access to the underlying tables.*

Action 3.22.1

SEVERITY LEVEL
2

O/S VERSION
All

ORACLE VERSIONS
All

Check the access privileges allowed on views and ensure that only select access is available.

The *with check option on views* allows constraints to be met while accessing data and changing it through views.

The following little demonstration will show that a user with no privileges whatsoever on the underlying table can, with access granted to a view, be able to change data. **This is good** if it is intentional. It also can cause an access point to change data to existing tables if it is not monitored.

Know what views can be used to alter data in tables.

Here is the demo, run this code and see that a table can be modified through a view:

```
spool lis.lis

connect sys/<password> as sysdba

drop user pete cascade;
drop user fred cascade;

create user pete identified by <password>
default tablespace users
temporary tablespace temp;

grant connect,resource to pete;

grant unlimited tablespace to pete;

create user fred identified by <password>;

grant connect,resource to fred;

connect pete/<password>

create table pete_01
(
col_01 number
);
```

Phase 3 ~ Oracle Access Controls

```
insert into pete_01(col_01)values(1);

create view pete_view as
select *
from pete_01;

grant update on pete_view to fred;

connect fred/<password>

update pete.pete_01
set col_01=3;

update pete.pete_view
set col_01=4;

spool off
```

Check which views have access granted other than select access. This can be done with the following SQL:

```
SQL> col grantee for a20
SQL> col privilege for a10
SQL> col table_name for a30
SQL> select grantee,table_name,privilege
  2  from dba_tab_privs
  3  where exists (select 'x'
  4                from dba_views
  5                where view_name=table_name)
  6  and privilege<>'SELECT'
  7  union
  8  select grantee,table_name,privilege
  9  from dba_col_privs
 10  where exists (select 'x'
 11                from dba_views
 12                where view_name=table_name)
 13  and privilege<>'SELECT'
SQL> /
```

Phase 3 ~ Oracle Access Controls

```
GRANTEE                    TABLE_NAME                      PRIVILEGE
-----------------------    -----------------------------   ----------
PUBLIC                     ALL_SDO_GEOM_METADATA           DELETE
PUBLIC                     ALL_SDO_GEOM_METADATA           INSERT
PUBLIC                     ALL_SDO_GEOM_METADATA           UPDATE
PUBLIC                     USER_SDO_GEOM_METADATA          DELETE
PUBLIC                     USER_SDO_GEOM_METADATA          INSERT
PUBLIC                     USER_SDO_GEOM_METADATA          UPDATE

6 rows selected.

SQL>
```

Any access found should be removed if it is not controlled and necessary.

Access to the base tables ideally should be through package procedures and not through views or directly on the base tables.

Step 3.23) Control Brute Force Password Attack

PROBLEM: *If a hacker attempts to brute force accounts, then he will succeed if precautions are not taken to stop him.*

Action 3.23.1

SEVERITY LEVEL: 2
O/S VERSION: All
ORACLE VERSIONS: All

Gaining access to an account is a significant step up for a hacker. Use database facilities to stop brute force attacks on accounts. Use the profiles facilities and the login attempts parameter to avoid this.

If special database administrator accounts have been created, and the SYSTEM account has been locked by brute force attempts, this should not pose much of an issue. The new database administrator accounts should not be named in a way that would easily identify them.

See *Phase 4* and add audit details to monitor for brute force attacks.

Note: It is important to be careful with this action; otherwise a denial of service attack could ensue. It would not be wise for DBA and operator accounts to be locked out after three bad attempts.

Phase 3 ~ Oracle Access Controls

Step 3.24 — DBA's / Operators Reading System Tables

PROBLEM: *If a database contains highly secret data, it can be necessary to stop the DBA reading the SYS tables.*

Action 3.24.1

SEVERITY LEVEL: 2
O/S VERSION: All
ORACLE VERSIONS: All

Where there are a number of administrators, it is not necessary for them all to read the SYS tables directly. Dictionary access should be controlled with the O7_DICTIONARY_ACCESSIBILITY parameter in the initialization file. See *Action 3.6.10*. This stops SELECT ANY TABLE privilege having direct access to SYS objects. This parameter is covered elsewhere; as is encryption of data in *Action 7.18.1* to prevent even DBA's seeing critical data.

Audit can be used to monitor the use of the SYS user. See *Phase 4* for details of this.

Step 3.25 — Preventing DBA's from Reading Application Data

PROBLEM: *If a database contains highly secret data it is necessary to stop the DBA reading data from the applications tables directly.*

Action 3.25.1

SEVERITY LEVEL: 4
O/S VERSION: All
ORACLE VERSIONS: All

DBA's typically have SELECT ANY TABLE privilege, which allows access to application data — HR records etc.

Revoke this privilege if it is not absolutely necessary and use encryption on critical data. See *Step 7.18* for more information.

This step should only be performed in highly secure environments and where the management wishes to restrict access to data from all employees including Database Administrators.

Note: This step assumes that a] the DBA does not have access to the "canned" DBA role supplied by Oracle and b] the DBA has in fact the privileges needed to work. This step is easily bypassed since a DBA that has been granted the DBA role could change the SYS password and then log in or use the password file to log in and then read any data.

Phase 3 ~ Oracle Access Controls

Step 3.26 — Integration and Server to Server Authentication

PROBLEM: *It is possible to inject transactions into a database though message-oriented middleware.*

Action 3.26.1

SEVERITY LEVEL: 2
O/S VERSION: All
ORACLE VERSIONS: All

Controls are needed to authenticate the source of messages. For example, pump your data in as an HTTP post to a known port on an integration server.

Some simple database based solutions could be to:
- use *sqlnet.ora* to limit server access
- Use stored procedures to prevent SQL injection attacks against the server.
- Use stored procedures so large amounts of data cannot be "grabbed" in one go.

Better solutions would be written into the application to confirm the source of the message before processing it. Problems arise in application-based solutions due to the fact that the protocol can be worked out and spoofed in most cases.

Step 3.27 — Internet Access from the Oracle Database

PROBLEM: *Oracle 9iR2 enables two new ports by default within the database server. An attacker can use these ports to guess account names and lock those accounts. Unsuccessful attempts to do this are not logged.*

Action 3.27.1

SEVERITY LEVEL: 2
O/S VERSION: All
ORACLE VERSIONS: 9iR2 & higher

In Oracle 9i Rel. 2, the default installation comes with two new ports (ftp: 2100 and http: 8080) from the now integrated OSE-stack in the database.

Anyone with a network connection to the database can use a web browser in order to attempt to break into the database. You can see these ports in *lsnrctl* (status command) or with the Enterprise Manager 9i2. By default, (unsuccessful) attempts are not logged. It is possible to change the log-level in Enterprise Manager.

The easiest way to disable these two ports is to change the *init.ora* and remove line:

```
dispatcher=(PROTOCOL=TCP) (SERVICE=orat92XDB)
```

Shutdown and restart the database.

Step 3.28 — Performance Pack Allows Access to SQL

PROBLEM: *The stats pack functionality, which was added to allow a user to get much better statistics over a period of time than the old bstat and estat utilities, gives public permissions to access SQL executed in the database.*

Action 3.28.1

SEVERITY LEVEL
2

O/S VERSION
All

ORACLE VERSIONS
8i & higher

One of the scripts used to install stats pack, *spctab.sql*, grants select to public on the tables stats$sqltext and stats$sql_summary. Check if these permissions are present in the database and if so, revoke the public grants on stats pack objects (identified as STATS$.) and grant back the permissions to those who need them.

PHASE 4
Auditing

Step 4.1 — Configure the Storage for Auditing

PROBLEM: If audit is turned on, and is being written to the database, then the records are written to a table in the system tablespace called sys.aud$. If an attacker can guess which auditing rules are enabled, then it could be possible to mount a Denial of service (Dos) attack against the database.

Action 4.1.1

SEVERITY LEVEL
2

O/S VERSION
All

ORACLE VERSIONS
All

If auditing is turned on, and set to write audit records to the database, then the parameter audit_trail will be set to DB. This parameter can also be set to TRUE or FALSE in Oracle 8 and higher. The parameter can also be set to OS.

```
SQL> SELECT NAME,VALUE FROM V$PARAMETER WHERE NAME='audit_trail';
```

Oracle note 1020945.6 "How to set-up auditing", available on Metalink is a good source for configuring audit.

If the parameter is set to OS, then the parameter audit_file_dest will show the directory that audit files will be written to. If audit is written to the database, then the audit records are written to a database table called sys.aud$. The tablespace used for this by default is system. The table should be moved to another tablespace, since not doing so could allow a denial of service attack to be mounted (See the note below for cautions on doing this).

Windows does not use the parameter audit_file_dest but instead writes operating system audit records to the Windows Event Viewer. Note 99137.1 "Setting up, Interpreting Auditing Using Windows Event viewer" describes this. The parameter audit_file_dest exists since Version 7.3.4 on other platforms Doc ID: 39796.1 Init.ora Parameter "AUDIT_FILE_DEST" Reference Note describes its use.

Note: Consider using the O/S for audit records since it is easier to secure the trail and also it is more difficult to mount a Denial of service attack on the database when this has been done.

Note: If SYS.AUD$ is filled, and is still in the SYSTEM tablespace, then the database will halt. This can be due to bad maintenance or due to a Denial of service attack.

If the sys.aud$ table fills up and you are auditing create session, you may not be able to connect to Oracle. You must login to sqlplus as sysdba, then set noaudit connect before purging the sys.aud$ table.

Moving the SYS.AUD$ table is an option, but it is uncertain whether Oracle will support you if you do. They previously sanctioned moving it but not after one recorded case where the database could not be recovered because of this.

Oracle also does not recommend moving SYS.AUD$ since it can break the patch and upgrade process.

Phase 4 ~ Auditing

Step 4.2 Audit DML Failures

PROBLEM: *If someone were to try to alter critical data, would you know? Auditing DML actions against critical tables and objects can help.*

Action 4.2.1

SEVERITY LEVEL
2

O/S VERSION
All

ORACLE VERSIONS
All

Audit INSERT failures attempted into critical data objects. Identify the tables that are critical to your database and enable auditing on insert failures on those tables. Issue the following command as an example:

```
SQL> audit insert,update,delete on mdsys.user_cs_srs by access whenever not successful;
Audit succeeded.
SQL>    audit select on mdsys.user_cs_srs by access whenever not successful;
Audit succeeded.
SQL>
```

Note: If you have followed the actions in Phase 3, then no users other than those intended should be able to access your tables so auditing DML should not be necessary!

Auditing DML will show when anyone either makes a mistake or could potentially catch SQL Injection, which quite often relies on multiple tries at accessing an object to read the error messages and find out the structure.

Potentially this requires a massive overhead, but by keeping the tables audited to a select minimum, it is possible to have a good overview on what people are doing and what access is attempted. Remember if your application is written correctly, there should be no failures.

Note: It is possible to use the Oracle log miner tool as a device to allow forensic investigation and find out what has happened in the database. Remember the logs show inserts, updates and deletes in 8i, and from 9i selects are stored as well. A good document that describes the basic functionality of Oracle log miner is Note: 62508.1 "The Oracle8i Log Miner Utility" on Metalink. The log Miner package became available in Oracle 8.

Phase 4 ~ Auditing

Action 4.2.2

SEVERITY LEVEL: 2
O/S VERSION: All
ORACLE VERSIONS: All

Triggers can be used to capture audit trail information. The new system-triggers can capture logon as well as logoff as well as database start and stop information. Using these triggers is fraught with error, if the objective is to capture accurate IP addresses, application names etc. All of these can easily be spoofed.

Write triggers against tables and system events that you would like to capture, and write the results to a database table or using UTL_FILE (PL/SQL) or Println (Java) write to an operating system file.

Autonomous transactions can be used within a trigger to capture audit information as well as using or not using the audit trail.

Note: Always have auditing checked for its output. Auditing should not be misused as an Intrusion Detection System. Use it when needed, and turn it off afterwards. Fine-grain auditing is great. Having everything audited creates an amount of data no normal human will read or analyse.

Step 4.3 — Set-up Basic Auditing

PROBLEM: Many people could be attacking your live production database every day and attempting to brute force users' accounts. Other users could be attempting actions that they should not do. Unless some sort of auditing is used, no one will ever know.

Action 4.3.1

SEVERITY LEVEL: 2
O/S VERSION: All
ORACLE VERSIONS: All

Audit CREATE SESSION for either successful or unsuccessful operations to monitor when people are logging on and off, and from where and with what. Combine this with a look at what processes are running in the database on a regular basis. Issue the following command to do this:

```
SQL> audit session;
Audit succeeded.
SQL>
```

This will audit access by all users whether successful or not. Access to the database via a database link will add the source TNS information in the comment field. This has been tested in 9iR2.

Note: All auditing is turned off by default in an Oracle installation.

Note: In 9iR2 it is possible to audit the actions of the SYS user.

Action 4.3.2

SEVERITY LEVEL 2
O/S VERSION All
ORACLE VERSIONS All

Audit the use of all GRANT statements on "Application schema owner" accounts. Run the following SQL to generate the statements needed and then run those statements:

```
SQL> set feed off
SQL> set head off
SQL> set pages 0
SQL> set verify off
SQL> select 'audit '||name||' by pete;'
  2   from system_privilege_map
  3   where name like '%GRANT%';
audit GRANT ANY ROLE by pete;
audit GRANT ANY PRIVILEGE by pete;
SQL>
```

The example assumes that the user PETE is the owner of the data.

Phase 4 ~ Auditing

Action 4.3.3

SEVERITY LEVEL: 3
O/S VERSION: All
ORACLE VERSIONS: All

Audit the use of all DROP statements on "Application schema owner" accounts. Run the following SQL to generate the statements needed and then run those statements:

```
SQL> select 'audit '||name||' by pete;'
  2   from system_privilege_map
  3   where name like '%DROP%';
'AUDIT'||NAME||'BYPETE;'
--------------------------------------------------------
audit DROP TABLESPACE by pete;
audit DROP USER by pete;
audit DROP ROLLBACK SEGMENT by pete;
audit DROP ANY TABLE by pete;
audit DROP ANY CLUSTER by pete;
audit DROP ANY INDEX by pete;
audit DROP ANY SYNONYM by pete;
audit DROP PUBLIC SYNONYM by pete;
audit DROP ANY VIEW by pete;
audit DROP ANY SEQUENCE by pete;
audit DROP PUBLIC DATABASE LINK by pete;
audit DROP ANY ROLE by pete;
audit DROP ANY PROCEDURE by pete;
audit DROP ANY TRIGGER by pete;
audit DROP PROFILE by pete;
audit DROP ANY SNAPSHOT by pete;
audit DROP ANY DIRECTORY by pete;
audit DROP ANY TYPE by pete;
audit DROP ANY LIBRARY by pete;
audit DROP ANY OPERATOR by pete;
audit DROP ANY INDEXTYPE by pete;
audit DROP ANY DIMENSION by pete;
audit DROP ANY CONTEXT by pete;
audit DROP ANY OUTLINE by pete;

24 rows selected.

SQL>
```

Action 4.3.4

SEVERITY LEVEL: 2

O/S VERSION: All

ORACLE VERSIONS: All

Audit the use of all ALTER statements on "Application schema owner" accounts. Run the following SQL to generate the statements needed and then run those statements:

```
SQL> set head off
SQL> set feed off
SQL> set pages 0
SQL> set verify off
SQL> select 'audit '||name||' by pete;'
  2   from system_privilege_map
  3   where name like '%ALTER%';
audit ALTER SYSTEM by pete;
audit ALTER SESSION by pete;
audit ALTER TABLESPACE by pete;
audit ALTER USER by pete;
audit ALTER ROLLBACK SEGMENT by pete;
audit ALTER ANY TABLE by pete;
audit ALTER ANY CLUSTER by pete;
audit ALTER ANY INDEX by pete;
audit ALTER ANY SEQUENCE by pete;
audit ALTER ANY ROLE by pete;
audit ALTER DATABASE by pete;
audit ALTER ANY PROCEDURE by pete;
audit ALTER ANY TRIGGER by pete;
audit ALTER PROFILE by pete;
audit ALTER RESOURCE COST by pete;
audit ALTER ANY SNAPSHOT by pete;
audit ALTER ANY TYPE by pete;
audit ALTER ANY LIBRARY by pete;
audit ALTER OPERATOR by pete;
audit ALTER ANY INDEXTYPE by pete;
audit ALTER ANY DIMENSION by pete;
audit ALTER ANY OUTLINE by pete;
SQL>
```

Phase 4 ~ Auditing

Action 4.3.5

SEVERITY LEVEL: 3
O/S VERSION: All
ORACLE VERSIONS: All

Audit the use of the CREATE USER statement on "Application schema owner" accounts. Example:

```
SQL> audit create user;
Audit succeeded.
SQL>
```

Action 4.3.6

SEVERITY LEVEL: 3
O/S VERSION: All
ORACLE VERSIONS: All

Audit the use of the CREATE ROLE statement on "Application schema owner" accounts. Example:

```
SQL> audit create role;
Audit succeeded.
SQL>
```

Action 4.3.7

SEVERITY LEVEL: 3
O/S VERSION: All
ORACLE VERSIONS: All

Audit the use of CREATE statement on "Application schema owner" accounts. Run the following SQL to generate the audit commends needed:

```
SQL> select 'audit '||name||' by pete;'
  2  from system_privilege_map
  3  where name like '%CREATE%'
SQL> /
```

```
'AUDIT'||NAME||'BYPETE;'
--------------------------------------------------------
audit CREATE SESSION by pete;
audit CREATE TABLESPACE by pete;
audit CREATE USER by pete;
audit CREATE ROLLBACK SEGMENT by pete;
audit CREATE TABLE by pete;
audit CREATE ANY TABLE by pete;
audit CREATE CLUSTER by pete;
audit CREATE ANY CLUSTER by pete;
audit CREATE ANY INDEX by pete;
audit CREATE SYNONYM by pete;
audit CREATE ANY SYNONYM by pete;
audit CREATE PUBLIC SYNONYM by pete;
audit CREATE VIEW by pete;
audit CREATE ANY VIEW by pete;
audit CREATE SEQUENCE by pete;
audit CREATE ANY SEQUENCE by pete;
audit CREATE DATABASE LINK by pete;
audit CREATE PUBLIC DATABASE LINK by pete;
audit CREATE ROLE by pete;
audit CREATE PROCEDURE by pete;
audit CREATE ANY PROCEDURE by pete;
audit CREATE TRIGGER by pete;
audit CREATE ANY TRIGGER by pete;
audit CREATE PROFILE by pete;
audit CREATE SNAPSHOT by pete;
audit CREATE ANY SNAPSHOT by pete;
audit CREATE ANY DIRECTORY by pete;
audit CREATE TYPE by pete;
audit CREATE ANY TYPE by pete;
audit CREATE LIBRARY by pete;
audit CREATE ANY LIBRARY by pete;
audit CREATE OPERATOR by pete;
audit CREATE ANY OPERATOR by pete;
audit CREATE INDEXTYPE by pete;
audit CREATE ANY INDEXTYPE by pete;
audit CREATE DIMENSION by pete;
audit CREATE ANY DIMENSION by pete;
audit CREATE ANY CONTEXT by pete;
audit CREATE ANY OUTLINE by pete;

39 rows selected.

SQL>
```

Save the SQL to a file and then run it to create the audit.

Action 4.3.8

SEVERITY LEVEL: 3
O/S VERSION: All
ORACLE VERSIONS: All

Establish business procedures to review the basic audit records collected in the above steps and also purge the audit trail regularly. See *Actions 4.4.4* and *4.4.5*.

Reviewing audit trails can be a real drain on resources, and usually the effort put into it decreases after the initial excitement of seeing audit records and being able to see what people are doing. To reduce this major issue, it is important that the audit collected is what is needed, **not** what is available, and also that the reports and tools created (SQL scripts) are basic and return what is needed and no more. Simple reporting is better and more likely to continue to be used.

Review of the audit trail reports should be done by a non database administrator or non system administrator. This will provide better security because this person will not be linked to the data he is reviewing.

Action 4.3.9

SEVERITY LEVEL: 4
O/S VERSION: All
ORACLE VERSIONS: All

It is possible for the Log Miner tool to perform some database auditing. This tool provides the following advantages and disadvantages:

Advantages
- It is not necessary to modify the database.
- It is possible to audit everything (not just successful / unsuccessful events)
- No performance degradation

Disadvantages
- Use of Log Miner requires programming skill if used from the command line.
- Selects are not recorded in the redo logs prior to 9i.
- The real SQL cannot easily be reconstructed, i.e. if you "audit" update on xxxx by user, Log miner would not recognize the update as easily as the audit functionality. The work to find access by users would be up to the user of Log Miner, rather than it being done by the audit functionality. (i.e. the real SQL is not known, only what Log Miner suggests it could have been)
- Because Log Miner uses PGA memory, it cannot be used in an MTS environment.
- Log Miner doesn't fully support objects.
- Log Miner doesn't support chained or migrated rows. This issue is fixed in 9i.
- Log miner doesn't support analysis of IOT's or clustered tables or indexes.

This tool can be used but the above issues need to be taken into account.

Phase 4 ~ Auditing

Step 4.4 — Basic Auditing Steps

PROBLEM: *Basic auditing can ensure that unauthorized actions are being caught. A privileged user can alter auditing easily or destroy or remove the audit trail completely without being caught themselves by audit records, so again, it is important to regulate user privileges sensibly.*

Action 4.4.1

SEVERITY LEVEL: 2
O/S VERSION: All
ORACLE VERSIONS: All

Initialization parameter AUDIT_TRAIL set to DB or OS. Basic audit will allow access by privileged users to be logged.

Note: The audit trail should be copied regularly somewhere else, in case the sys.aud$ table is flushed / truncated. There should be a trigger that fires BEFORE the sys.aud$ table is deleted, to leave a record somewhere that the sys.aud$ table was deleted. It is possible to set up audit on audit, and it writes to the alert log. I would suggest that O/S auditing is used so that privileged access is captured. One other option is to replicate the audit trail to another database and write the records immediately to write-once media.

Action 4.4.2

SEVERITY LEVEL: 2
O/S VERSION: All
ORACLE VERSIONS: All

Review which users have audit roles and consider limiting to one or two users to make it harder to revoke audit commands.

This can be done with the following commands:

```
SQL> select grantee,privilege
  2  from dba_sys_privs
  3  where privilege like '%AUDIT%';

GRANTEE                         PRIVILEGE
------------------------------  ------------------------------------

DBA                             AUDIT ANY
DBA                             AUDIT SYSTEM
IMP_FULL_DATABASE               AUDIT ANY
MDSYS                           AUDIT ANY
MDSYS                           AUDIT SYSTEM

SQL>
```

Note: Oracle can also use the O/S audit trail on some platforms. This can reduce the number of users that can modify the audit trail.

Phase 4 ~ Auditing

Action 4.4.3

SEVERITY LEVEL: 2
O/S VERSION: All
ORACLE VERSIONS: All

Protect the audit trail with AUDIT ALL ON SYS.AUD$ BY ACCESS. This will alert administrators to attempts to alter the audit trail.

Auditing of *truncate* is not captured. O/S auditing is better on systems that support it.

Action 4.4.4

SEVERITY LEVEL: 3
O/S VERSION: All
ORACLE VERSIONS: All

Review the backup procedures used to protect the audit trail. Ensure that the audit records are backed up regularly to ensure that no one deletes the contents of the audit trail.

Action 4.4.5

SEVERITY LEVEL: 4
O/S VERSION: All
ORACLE VERSIONS: All

Review the purging procedures used for the audit trail. Ensure that the audit trail is purged regularly.

Step 4.5 Date / Time Stamps of Objects

PROBLEM: *In a default installation with default users, it is quite easy to find a user who can alter objects within the database, whether it is by adding new ones, amending source code of existing packages or simply re-compiling objects. Changing objects in a production database can go undetected and should not be allowed.*

Action 4.5.1

SEVERITY LEVEL: 3
O/S VERSION: All
ORACLE VERSIONS: All

Check date time stamps for creation, reload and compilation of database objects. Store the results somewhere in the database or to an operating system file, and check if anyone is changing or adding objects.

The following SQL will highlight any objects that have been altered or added during the last 30 days:

```
SQL> select owner,object_name,object_type,last_ddl_time,created
  2    from dba_objects
  3   where last_ddl_time>sysdate-30;

OWNER            OBJECT_NAME                     OBJECT_TYPE                       LAST_DDL_ CREATED
---------------  ------------------------------  --------------------------------  --------- ---------
SYS              AUD_LOGIN                       TABLE                             08-SEP-02 08-SEP-02
SYS              CHECK_LOGIN                     TRIGGER                           08-SEP-02 08-SEP-02
SYS              TEST                            PROCEDURE                         18-SEP-02 31-AUG-02

OWNER            OBJECT_NAME                     OBJECT_TYPE                       LAST_DDL_ CREATED
---------------  ------------------------------  --------------------------------  --------- ---------
PUBLIC           PRODUCT_PROFILE                 SYNONYM                           08-SEP-02 08-SEP-02
PUBLIC           PRODUCT_USER_PROFILE            SYNONYM                           08-SEP-02 08-SEP-02
SYSTEM           PRODUCT_PRIVS                   VIEW                              08-SEP-02 08-SEP-02

OWNER            OBJECT_NAME                     OBJECT_TYPE                       LAST_DDL_ CREATED
---------------  ------------------------------  --------------------------------  --------- ---------
SYSTEM           PRODUCT_USER_PROFILE            SYNONYM                           08-SEP-02 08-SEP-02

7 rows selected.

SQL>
```

If objects are being amended, then investigate the culprit's permissions and revoke them. This report could be run regularly and the results could be stored in a simple database table for comparison with previous results.

Phase 4 ~ Auditing

Step 4.6 — Procedures for Reviewing Audit Logs

PROBLEM: *Having audit set up and in use will help you spot unauthorized attempts to access the database and authorized users poking about in areas where they do not belong. However, merely having all the audit information is **no** guarantee that an attacker or a malicious employee will be detected unless the audit logs are reviewed and acted upon regularly.*

Action 4.6.1

SEVERITY LEVEL: 3
O/S VERSION: All
ORACLE VERSIONS: All

Ensure adequate reports are in place to review the gene-rated audit records for potential intrusions and wrongdoings by employees. Also review the procedures for reading the reports and taking action based on any findings. Just generating audit records is not enough: knowing what to look for and taking action is necessary. This can be made easy with realistic reports.

Setting up of alerts is easily within the capabilities of most DBA's or Administrators. Simple SMS or email messages should suffice. For auditing to be effective, as much work as possible should be done automatically.

Step 4.7 — Row-Level Auditing

PROBLEM: *The standard audit facilities up to Oracle 8i are at a high level. It is not possible to capture amendments to individual rows of critical tables. If a malicious employee manages to find his salary stored in a table and change just this one record, would anyone notice? Row level auditing can be done in Oracle easily.*

Action 4.7.1

SEVERITY LEVEL: 3
O/S VERSION: All
ORACLE VERSIONS: All

Consider row level auditing using triggers (the newer features for fine-grained audit are not included in this item). The only disadvantage is that on error row level, audit will be rolled back.

This problem can be overcome with the use of autonomous transactions in the newer versions of Oracle.

Action 4.7.2

SEVERITY LEVEL: 3
O/S VERSION: All
ORACLE VERSIONS: 8 & above

Use Virtual Private Database (VPD), Fine-Grained Auditing and Oracle Label Security to protect the data.

Fine-grained auditing provides another level of auditing and will most likely find use in critical and top-secret databases.

Fine-grained auditing (FGA) facilities are accessed using the database package DBMS_FGA. Fine-grained auditing allows audit records to be generated when defined records are selected from a table. A list of the FGA policies can be found by querying the view DBA_AUDIT_POLICIES. The audit records generated are stored in DBA_FGA_AUDIT_TRAIL.

A good high-level description of fine-grained auditing can be found at

http://otn.oracle.com/deploy/security/oracle9iR2/pdf/9ir2secwp.PDF

Oracle 8i introduced the concept of a virtual private database (VPD). VPD allows separation of data using fine-grained access control functionality. Using this mechanism, it is possible to ensure that users only have access to the data that they need to see. It would be possible to store multiple companies' data in the same database without them being able to access each others' data.

Configuration for VPD is done using the package DBMS_RLS (Row Level Security). To view the existing VPD configurations, do the following:

```
SQL> select *
  2   from sys.v$vpd_policy;
```

Oracle label security (formally trusted Oracle) uses the Virtual Private Database (VPD) functionality of Oracle 8i and greater to implement row level security. Access to individual rows is controlled based on the user's security tag or label. Oracle label security is configured and controlled using the Policy Manager. This is a GUI based part of the Enterprise Manager.

A good article on this subject can be found at the following URL:

http://www.interealm.com/roby/technotes/8i-rls.html

Phase 4 ~ Auditing

Step 4.8 Failure to Be Alerted of Suspicious Activity

PROBLEM: *If suspicious activity takes place, knowing how to easily solve it and stop it from happening is not enough. Knowing it has happened is the key.*

Action 4.8.1

SEVERITY LEVEL: 2
O/S VERSION: All
ORACLE VERSIONS: All

Unless there is some process to monitor, and preferably alert, on high priority incidents, the attacker could be long gone before it is noticed, if at all. It is important that the level of auditing be adequate and simple enough to not overwhelm users and also to not impact performance.

Step 4.9 Failure to Audit the Security Profile

PROBLEM: *If a DBA is adding users or altering privileges or an attacker has done it, would you know?*

Action 4.9.1

SEVERITY LEVEL: 2
O/S VERSION: All
ORACLE VERSIONS: All

The audit facilities are rich enough to audit the use of privileges, in particular creating new users, and the use of grants. With an audit on the security profile, DBA's will leave a trail, or create a mess trying to clean up their actions. (The smoking gun principle).

Phase 4 ~ Auditing

Step 4.10 — Failure to Audit the Log Files

PROBLEM: *Even without audit turned on, Oracle writes to many log files during its operations. Failure to review these logs could mean that a critical system error is not found in time or that malicious activity is not noticed.*

Action 4.10.1

SEVERITY LEVEL: 2
O/S VERSION: All
ORACLE VERSIONS: All

The change from client server to n-tier-systems also plays a role in checking log-files. In client server environments, it was only necessary to check the *listener.log* for SQL-connection data. In an n-tier-environment, this data is distributed in different places.

This could lead to administrative problems, if different persons are responsible for application servers and databases.

Example:

If iSQL*Plus (default installation in 9i Rel 2) is used, and a user connects to an application server, and this application server tries to connect to the database with this users' credentials, you find in the *listener.ora* only the entries from the application server. Which IP-address tried to login to SQL*Plus is logged on the middle tier (*access_log*).

There is a similar problem with http-based access of XML-DB.

It is important for an Administrator to know **what** it logged **where**, and **how** to recognize suspicious activities. Some of the more common logs are listed below. A useful free tool from Oracle to manage logs is mentioned in *Action 1.9.2*.

Type	File / System	What
Operating System	Eventviewer (Windows)	
Operating System	Syslog (Unix)	
Oracle	Listener.log (location defined by environment)	Connection attempts are logged.
Oracle	access_log (location defined in httpd.conf)	Every access
Oracle	error_log (location defined in httpd.conf)	Errors
Oracle	Sqlnet.log (many locations, users home directories)	Especially logs connection failures in Net8 and Net9.
Oracle	Apache.log (located in $ORACLE_HOME/Apache/Apache/logs. Use in 9iAS and Oracle database from 8.1.7)	Shows access violations.

PHASE 5
Networking

Step 5.1 — Listener Configuration

PROBLEM: *A default installation of Oracle and its clients leaves connections to the database open to remote O/S authentication, accepts connections from any source and raises many other security issues.*

Action 5.1.1

SEVERITY LEVEL: 1
O/S VERSION: All
ORACLE VERSIONS: All

In $ORACLE_HOME/network/admin/listener.ora, ensure the parameter ADMIN_RESTRICTIONS_{LISTENER_NAME}=ON is added.

This parameter prevents the listener from accepting SET commands while it is running. This parameter was added to prevent reading and writing of O/S files when the listener password has not been set.

Note: It is possible to install and run an 8.1.7 or later listener for an earlier version of the database to resolve some of the security issues.

Action 5.1.2

SEVERITY LEVEL: 4
O/S VERSION: All
ORACLE VERSIONS: All

In $ORACLE_HOME/network/admin/listener.ora, ensure that the parameter REMOTE_DBA_OPS_DENIED is added. This parameter is only relevant if running SQL*Net V1. This parameter and REMOTE_DBA_OPS_ALLOWED are both irrelevant from SQL*Net V2.

Note: Oracle uses a structured method to network configuration files. It looks in the home directory and also at wherever the environment variable TNS_ADMIN is pointing. Then it looks in $ORACLE_HOME/network/admin. A lesser known fact is that a .tnsnames (yes "dot" tnsnames.ora) will be looked at first in the user's home directory. Ensure that no one has set one up on the machine to avoid the use of the correct files.

Phase 5 ~ Networking

Action 5.1.3

SEVERITY LEVEL: 5
O/S VERSION: All
ORACLE VERSIONS: All

Regularly check client machines for *listener.ora* files and ensure that the *listener.ora* on the server is the only one.

This can be very impractical in large environments, which explains the low severity level of this action.

Action 5.1.4

SEVERITY LEVEL: 3
O/S VERSION: Windows
ORACLE VERSIONS: All

In $ORACLE_HOME/network/admin/listener.ora, ensure that the parameter USE_SHARED_SOCKET is added.

This should only be done when there is a need to pipe through a firewall, since this would otherwise hurt performance.

> **Note:** This parameter is only available on Windows Operating systems.

Action 5.1.5

SEVERITY LEVEL: 4
O/S VERSION: All
ORACLE VERSIONS: All

Force the MTS dispatcher to use specific ports. One reason to do this is to get around non-Oracle-aware firewall issues. When dispatcher ports are automatically assigned, they are assigned randomly, and the random port will be blocked by the firewall.

When the port number is assigned manually, then that port can be opened on the firewall to allow outside access to the database. If ports are configured manually, then all dispatchers have to be configured separately. Here is an example configuration added to the instance initialization file *init.ora*.

```
MTS_DISPATCHERS="(ADDRESS=(PARTIAL=TRUE)(PROTOCOL=TCP) \
(HOST=pete.finnigan.com)(PORT=1220)) \
(DISPATCHERS=4)(CONNECTIONS=100)"
```

Phase 5 ~ Networking

Action 5.1.6

SEVERITY LEVEL: 2
O/S VERSION: All
ORACLE VERSIONS: All

Avoid running the listener on the normal ports of 1521 or 1526, and the other regular services on their standard ports. Choose port numbers in completely different ranges so that it is harder for an attacker to easily find an Oracle listener.

Avoid calling the listener by the default names. Set a distinct listener name.

Some very good tools are available from Patrik Karlsson's web site http://www.cqure.net for discovering Oracle SID's and also for auditing an Oracle instance.

Note: Doing this will probably not deter a determined or experienced hacker since nmap / nessus will find the ports easily. Using different ports, however, **will** stop attackers who are just looking for machines with ports 1521/1526 active for Oracle.

Note: Regularly review the listener log file for failed attempts to connect to the listener. The default location is $ORACLE_HOME/network/admin.

Action 5.1.7

SEVERITY LEVEL: 2
O/S VERSION: All
ORACLE VERSIONS: All

Do not use the default database service name or SID name or ORCL. If the database is named ORCL, then unfortunately renaming it is not easy, although it is possible. For a well written document that describes this on Metalink, see:

DocID 15390.1 How to Determine and Change DB_NAME or ORACLE_SID (without recreating).

Action 5.1.8

SEVERITY LEVEL: 2
O/S VERSION: All
ORACLE VERSIONS: All

In smaller environments, do not use hostnames in the *listener.ora*; this places an unnecessary dependency on a DNS server. In a larger organization, a DNS server is needed to make administration practical.

Phase 5 ~ Networking

Action 5.1.9

SEVERITY LEVEL: 2
O/S VERSION: All
ORACLE VERSIONS: All

Use a personal firewall on all database administration computers.

Action 5.1.10

SEVERITY LEVEL: 2
O/S VERSION: All
ORACLE VERSIONS: All

Set appropriate file permissions on the listener configuration file *listener.ora*. This can be done as follows:

```
Unix - $ chmod 600 $ORACLE_HOME/network/admin/listener.ora
Windows - File properties -> Security -> Permissions
```

Phase 5 ~ Networking

Step 5.2 — IP Access Restrictions

PROBLEM: *A standard installation of Oracle accepts connections from any IP address that can reach the machine hosting the database. It is possible for an application to be deployed to a certain department, but access to the database could still be available in all departments using any tool that can access the database. Restricting IP addresses is one way of preventing access.*

Action 5.2.1

SEVERITY LEVEL: 3
O/S VERSION: All
ORACLE VERSIONS: All

In $ORACLE_HOME/network/admin/protocol.ora, ensure that the following parameters are set:

```
tcp.validnode_checking = YES
tcp.invited_nodes= (xxx.xxx.xxx.xxx, xxx.xxx.x.x)
tcp.excluded_nodes= (xxx.xxx.xxx.xxx, xxx.xx.x.xx, xxx.xx.x.xx)
```

Setting these parameters will allow connections only from specific nodes and deny any others.

Note that these parameters need to be set in the sqlnet.ora file in 9i and later.

Note: Never use hostnames in the protocol.ora file since these are easily spoofed.

This method can either allow IP address or deny IP addresses but not both. In addition, wild cards like 128.193. or xxx.xxx or 128.193.0.0 are not allowed. So for large subnets, it is impossible to limit IP ranges easily.

A simple example of a database procedure that could check for IP ranges when accessing a role is shown below. Beware that it is reasonably easy to spoof IP addresses, and also that this function could instead be used in conjunction with the logon trigger shown in *Action 5.7.3*.

```
create role some_role
identified using sys.confirm;

create or replace procedure confirm
authid current_user is
      lv_ip varchar2(30)
begin
      select sys_context('userenv','ip_address')
      into lv_ip
      from dual;
      --
      if substr(lv_ip,1,4) != '172.' then
            return;
      end if;
      dbms_session.set_role('some_role');
end;
/
```

Note: This is not really a protection, since a skilled hacker could change its IP address, but is still worth doing in our opinion.

Assuming you can have more than a few databases, it would be a big task to add lots of IP addresses. Restricting access to a specific IP address in a lot of databases is not workable in large sites.

Phase 5 ~ Networking

Action 5.2.2

SEVERITY LEVEL
2

O/S VERSION
All

ORACLE VERSIONS
All

The problem here is **controlling the source of connection requests**. IP is generally considered a weak approach to authentication. IP filtering at the listener can be part of a belt and braces approach (firewall, router filtering etc); however, static IP's are less common these days, so unless there is a very clear segregation of business function to network address, restricting interactive users by IP is problematic. Restricting access to application servers and a DBA local area network segment can be useful.

Where IP filtering is required, it would be better to see some kind of screening router. For a small organization, this can be beneficial.

Connection manager can restrict on origin, destination and sid. Uses *cman.ora* in the CMAN_RULES section: four sections to each rule.

- SRC
- DST
- SVR
- ACT

It is possible to supply hostname or IP address of the database server and use wildcards such as 110.x.x.x. Rules can be any combination of src, dest, sid. Each rule is separate in a RULES_LIST. The default action is to accept the request. It is possible to define multiple rules. If there is a conflict, the earlier rule is taken.

To use connection manager (CMAN), add an entry to the *sqlnet.ora* file on the client.

USE_CMAN=TRUE.

If not set or false, the connection route will be random. It should be noted that this parameter needs to be first or last in the .ora file, otherwise it does not work.

Information: *Oracle names provides a method to centralize resolution and configuration of connection strings. The file names.ora is used for configuration. Connection requests first are directed to the names server, which then returns the address information to the client, who in turn then makes the connection request to the database server.*

Connection Manager (CMAN) provides access control and allows connections to be concentrated. CMAN also allows connections to be made between different network protocols. When connection concentration is used, MTS is required and connection pooling cannot be used. The rules are stored in the cman.ora file and allow source, destination, sid and action to be specified. This allows source and destinations to be specified including wild cards.

Note: Oracle names is being phased out in favor of Oracle Internet Directory (OID).

Phase 5 ~ Networking

Step 5.3 Listener Password

PROBLEM: *The Oracle listener is a standalone process that manages connections to the database. Users ask the listener to make a connection and a Transparent Network Substrate (TNS) session is granted and opened. There are several well-known exploits that can be performed against the listener. It is possible to log onto it and perform various administration tasks against it. This is easy for an attacker if the listener password has not been set.*

Action 5.3.1

SEVERITY LEVEL
1

O/S VERSION
All

ORACLE VERSIONS
All

Ensure that the listener password has been set. The listener can have a clear text password, multiple passwords or an encrypted password. The following shows how:

Setting an unencrypted password: In the listener.ora file, add the following line for a listener called PETES_LISTENER:

PASSWORDS_PETES_LISTENER=(passwd,another)

Any number of passwords can be added like this. If only one password is set, then the syntax is:

PASSWORDS_PETES_LISTENER=passwd

Note: The above example of setting a clear text password is only shown here to highlight the fact that a clear text password can be set. The reader should be aware of this and not use it. **Please do not use clear text passwords.**

Setting an encrypted password: See below:

```
$ lsnrctl

LSNRCTL for Solaris: Version 8.1.7.0.0 - Production on 27-JUN-2002 18:55:32

(c) Copyright 1998 Oracle Corporation.  All rights reserved.

Welcome to LSNRCTL, type "help" for information.

LSNRCTL> change_password
Old password:
New password:
Reenter new password:
Connecting to (DESCRIPTION=(ADDRESS=(PROTOCOL=IPC)(KEY=EXTPROC)))
Password changed for LISTENER
The command completed successfully
LSNRCTL>
```

Scripts to shut down/start up listener have a big disadvantage: It is necessary to store an unencrypted password in the file system somewhere for use in these scripts.

Phase 5 ~ Networking

It is possible to start up/shut down password-protected listener with jobs in Enterprise Manager. With this solution, it is not necessary to store unencrypted passwords and works with every script.

The following script can be used to stop a listener that is password protected:

```
#!/bin/ksh
export ORACLE_HOME=...
export PATH=$ORACLE_HOME/bin
my_password=`cat .passwd`
lsnrctl <<EOF
set password $my_password
stop
quit
EOF
```

Note: The default listener password on some platforms is listener or Oracle.

Step 5.4 — Listener Banner Information

PROBLEM: *By default the listener gives out a lot of information when making a connection to the database. Also, querying the listener can give out information about the services running, database SID and other information. Ensure that the listener displays the minimum banner information.*

Action 5.4.1

SEVERITY LEVEL: 3
O/S VERSION: All
ORACLE VERSIONS: All

Ensure that the listener gives out the minimum banner information when status commands are run, or other commands that give out details of the server or database.

There is no easy way to do this and the most effective is to set the password. Restricting access to the *lsnrctl* command to only the owner and group is also effective. A simple C program could be written that opens a read-only pipe to the real listener could be used, and simple messages such as "listener is up" or "listener is down" could be returned.

Note: Changing banner information with a hex editor most likely would not be supported by Oracle and could cause issues with support contracts. Therefore, lobby Oracle to allow customers to edit banner strings on its products. Oracle currently has configurable banner info for IFS and is working towards a configurable banner in the Transparent Network Substrate (TNS) listener.

Phase 5 ~ Networking

Step 5.5 — Oracle Firewall

PROBLEM: *Organizations protect their outer perimeters with firewalls and a DMZ, but then may leave all of their valuable machines and data completely open to all within the protected network. Often a company's most valuable possessions are in a database and open for all to attempt to access.*

Action 5.5.1

SEVERITY LEVEL: 2
O/S VERSION: All
ORACLE VERSIONS: All

Adding a firewall or packet filtering to the server that hosts the Oracle database is advantageous. The organization will be provided with firewalls, De-Militarised Zone (DMZ) and internal firewall, but the database server will be open to all intranet and internal network traffic. Placing a firewall and the server on its own subnet would add an extra level of security to the database. This way an external attacker would need to pass through three firewalls to get to the database and an internal attacker would need to pass just one.

See also *Step 7.18* for details on encrypting critical data within the database.

Information: *Oracle generally uses fixed port numbers by default, although these can easily be changed. 1521 and 1526 are generally used by the database.*

Keep database communications on a separate secure link: have the public web server communicate with the Database through a firewall that only allows the web server through (prevent internal access around the firewall). In addition, keep the backup network secure for the database. (Backup servers usually have broad access to network and aren't secured).

Not only should the database be protected from direct access with a firewall inside the protected network, but make sure all application servers or backup servers connected to that same database server are also protected from direct access.

Phase 5 ~ Networking

Step 5.6 — Security of Client Configuration Files

PROBLEM: *Each client machine that accesses an Oracle database or application uses an Oracle client and TNS. If the configuration for TNS is stored locally, quite often the files are written to cover all databases within an organization, and they are often insecure. An attacker gaining access to a machine with the Oracle client configuration installed is then able to enumerate available databases and details for connecting to them.*

Action 5.6.1

SEVERITY LEVEL: 4
O/S VERSION: All
ORACLE VERSIONS: All

Check the file permissions of the configuration files on the client. These files are generally difficult to secure. But efforts should be made to secure the client TNS files.

Note: Use the version of tnsping from Oracle 9i. This version shows which parameter files are used, and is a very useful feature for any DBA.

Note: A lot of companies have a tnsnames.ora on a Windows drive that is mapped to all clients. This is a bad idea for various reasons. Another solution in this case is to use Oracle Names or Oracle Internet Directory for database name resolution.

Action 5.6.2

SEVERITY LEVEL: 5
O/S VERSION: All
ORACLE VERSIONS: All

Check the contents of client configuration files. General files shipped out to all desktops with details of all databases might be easy to ship, but allow an attacker to know about **all** the databases in an organization.

Phase 5 ~ Networking

Action 5.6.3

SEVERITY LEVEL: 2
O/S VERSION: All
ORACLE VERSIONS: All

Look for stray *sqlnet.log* files on the server and also on clients. If an attacker manages to read them, information could be gleaned from connect strings to allow an attack. If, for example, someone enters the password where the username is expected, then it is displayed in the log file. Searching for *sqlnet.log* files in a large organization and removing them can be a major task.

A simple solution could be to redirect sqlnet log files to /dev/null on Linux / Unix systems. This would obviously default the use of these files for finding errors, but would reduce the chance of passwords being logged.

Attempt to secure the trace files and log files generated from either the server or clients.

Secure the wallet directory.

A regular port scan of the servers looking for Oracle would allow the DBA and security administrator to know if databases and Oracle applications are secure. If Oracle Enterprise Manager (OEM) can be captured then all databases can be.

The following URL's can be checked for information about port scans: http://packetstorm.decepticons.org, http://www.insecure.org. Nmap is a utility for network exploration or security auditing that can also be used.

There is a free port scanner available from nessus at http://www.nessus.org that includes various plug-ins for Oracle. These cover most of the known vulnerabilities. New plug-ins are added regularly. A list of those covered at the time of writing is here.

Nessus ID	Description	Risk
10594	Oracle XSQL Stylesheet Vulnerability	High
10613	Oracle XSQL Sample Application Vulnerability	Low
10658	Oracle tnslsnr version query	High
10840	Oracle 9iAS mod_plsql Buffer Overflow	High
10848	Oracle 9iAS Dynamic Monitoring Services	High
10849	Oracle 9iAS DAD Admin interface	High
10850	Oracle 9iAS Globals.jsa access	Medium/High
10851	Oracle 9iAS Java Process Manager	High
10852	Oracle 9iAS Jsp Source File Reading	Medium/High
10853	Oracle 9iAS mod_plsql cross site scripting	High
10854	Oracle 9iAS mod_plsql directory traversal	High
10855	Oracle XSQLServlet XSQLConfig.xml File	High

Phase 5 ~ Networking

CRITICAL ISSUE. At one site that did a kind of text string search on their Windows servers, looking for files that might contain an administrator password, they located the password in the clear in the SQLNET.LOG files in locations where SQL files had been executed. That file logs errors in SQL connections. The passwords were in the clear because people had made simple typing errors when trying to connect to a database, and the error was written to the log file (e.g. CONNECT MYPASSWORD/MYID@MYDABATASE instead of CONNECT MYID/MYPASSWORD@MYDATABASE). Technically, Oracle didn't write the password in the clear here, it just wrote a bad text string. Either way, it compromised the security of the password.

To disable writing to *sqlnet.log* — You can change to another directory with some environment variables (TNS_ADMIN). There is no known way to disable writing to log files. If the 'LOG_DIRECTORY_CLIENT' or 'LOG_DIRECTORY_SERVER' syntax is not stated in the *sqlnet.ora* file, it will default to the current working directory: $ORACLE_HOME/BIN.

If the 'LOG_DIRECTORY_CLIENT' or 'LOG_DIRECTORY_CLIENT' syntax is stated in the *sqlnet.ora* file, it should give you the directory:

LOG_DIRECTORY_CLIENT=c:\NET\ADMIN
LOG_DIRECTORY_SERVER=/tmp/trace

It is possible to disable logging to *listener.log* or *sqlnet.log*.

listener.log: LOGGING_listener = OFF   or   lsnrctl set log_status off

(See http://metalink.oracle.com/metalink/plsql/ml2_documents.showDocument?p_database_id=FOR&p_id=98740.996). Another good document on Metalink is "Note: 39357.1"

Use a name service such as Oracle Names or Oracle Internet Directory if possible to remove need for *tnsnames.ora* file. If using *tnsnames.ora* file, consider storing the file on a network drive rather than the local PC. When stored on the network drive, it is possible to have separate, unique Transparent Network Substrate (TNS) configuration files for different user groups based on drive mappings.

Note: On the Unix operating system, logging can be disabled by pointing the parameters to /dev/null.

Step 5.7 — Database Links

PROBLEM: *Database links can provide an easy way into an otherwise secure database. By getting into a less secure database such as a development or test database, you can often find links to other databases. The worst-case scenario is when these links use the schema owner or privileged users.*

Action 5.7.1

SEVERITY LEVEL 1
O/S VERSION All
ORACLE VERSIONS All

Check database links used where there is a clear text password in the hard coded link. Use the following SQL to check this:

```
select  name,
        host,
        password,
        authusr,
        authpwd,
        userid
from    sys.link$
where   password is not null;
```

If the applications and database must have public database links, then restrict access to sys.link$, otherwise always try to use private database links.

There are three types of database links: PUBLIC, PRIVATE and GLOBAL. PUBLIC links can be used by any user in the database. PRIVATE can be used only by the owner, and GLOBAL links are stored on a names server when Oracle Names is used, and apply to all databases on the network.

There are three ways of establishing a connection to the remote database while using a database link:

- Fixed user: This always uses an embedded username and password.
- Connected user and current user do not store connection credentials. A connected user is the user you have connected to the database such as SCOTT in SQL*Plus. A current user is where the user SCOTT is connected to SQL*Plus, but is executing a procedure owned by the user FRED, and is running in that user's context. A connected user link executes code in the remote database as the local connected user. A current user link executes code in the remote database as the current user on the local database. To create a connected user link, simply omit the "CONNECT TO" clause when creating it. To create a current user link, add the syntax "CONNECT TO CURRENT USER".

Current user database links are more secure since they do not require storing a database password in SYS.LINK$.

See the note in *Action 1.12.1* about exports and database link passwords.

> **Note:** Database links can be used to "escalate" privileges, e.g. a user with little privileges on one database connects to another database using an account with more privileges. Sometimes this is done through applications. There is no easy way to match privileges across various databases and compare by database links.
>
> Never have database links in a production database that connect to any non-production databases or from any non-production databases to a production database.

Phase 5 ~ Networking

Action 5.7.2

SEVERITY LEVEL: 2
O/S VERSION: All
ORACLE VERSIONS: All

Check which objects a link user can see in the database being accessed. Use some of the previous actions above, but over the database link using the username and password you have found above. Then revoke the privileges granted to that user where not needed.

Action 5.7.3

SEVERITY LEVEL: 1
O/S VERSION: All
ORACLE VERSIONS: All

Develop a policy for managing database links. Include procedures for changing link passwords, as well as for checking which databases can be accessed from the production system, and which databases can access the production system.

The following code example shows how to write a simple *after logon* trigger to capture the details of the database session logging in. While some of the details captured can be spoofed easily, it is still worth implementing such a trigger in parallel with audit facilities described in Phase 4. Most users would not know how to spoof these details.

```
drop table aud_login
/
create table aud_login
(
        username        varchar2(30) not null,
        login_date      date not null,
        osuser          varchar2(30),
        machine         varchar2(64),
        program         varchar2(64)
) tablespace tools
/
```

Phase 5 ~ Networking

```
create or replace trigger check_login
after logon on database
declare
        --
        pragma autonomous_transaction;
        lv_username   aud_login.username%type;
        lv_osuser     aud_login.osuser%type;
        lv_machine    aud_login.machine%type;
        lv_program    aud_login.program%type;
        lv_stmnt      varchar2(2000);
        --
begin
        lv_username:=upper(sys_context('userenv','session_user'));
        lv_stmnt:='insert into aud_login(username,login_date,osuser,machine,program)';
        lv_stmnt:=lv_stmnt||' values(:1,:2,:3,:4,:5)';
        begin
                select  s.osuser,
                        s.machine,
                        s.program
                into    lv_osuser,
                        lv_machine,
                        lv_program
                from    v$session s
                where   sys_context('userenv','SESSIONID')=s.audsid;
                execute immediate lv_stmnt using lv_username,sysdate,lv_osuser,
                        lv_machine,lv_program;
                commit;
        exception
                when others then
                        null;
        end;
end;
/
```

Phase 5 ~ Networking

Testing this gives:

```
SQL> @login

Table dropped.

Table created.

Trigger created.

SQL> connect dbsnmp/dbsnmp
Connected.
SQL> connect sys/change_on_install
Connected.
SQL> select *
  2  from aud_login;

USERNAME        LOGIN_DAT  OSUSER     MACHINE    PROGRAM
--------------- ---------- ---------- ---------- ------------------------------

DBSNMP          08-SEP-02  oracle     sputnik    sqlplus@sputnik (TNS V1-V3)
SYS             08-SEP-02  oracle     sputnik    sqlplus@sputnik (TNS V1-V3)

SQL>
```

Phase 5 ~ Networking

Action 5.7.4

SEVERITY LEVEL: 1
O/S VERSION: All
ORACLE VERSIONS: All

Check if the user connected to in any database links is a DBA. This is a potential access point to a database (if it is a DBA, then it is easy to masquerade as any other user) and easy if combined with a public link.

Apply all of the checks and tests listed in this guide to the database that can be reached over the database link.

Action 5.7.5

SEVERITY LEVEL: 1
O/S VERSION: All
ORACLE VERSIONS: All

Investigate the database links that are enabled both in the database being checked as well as in the database accessed by the link. Check for access both to and from other data-bases. The use and types of database links should be kept to a minimum.

Use an Oracle account, **not** an O/S account. (i.e., do not use an Oracle account that is enabled for external access to the database) and limit the account to using only a procedure and no table access.

Set DBLINK_ENCRYPT_LOGIN in the *init.ora* file. This parameter is defaulted to false. Database link accesses are sniffable by default on the second attempt. Of course, an argument can be made that storing a password in the database is bad anyway. But this makes it worse and can be fixed easily.

An alternative to public database links is *current user* database links. These types of links do not require the password to be stored in sys.link$.

See also Actions *1.6.3* and *1.6.4* for more details on these parameters.

Phase 5 ~ Networking

Step 5.8 — Network File Permissions

PROBLEM: *All users connect to Oracle using Oracle networking, which in turn uses configuration files in $ORACLE_HOME/network/admin to control the listener. These files can be altered in many ways to make access easier or to get Oracle to run programs it shouldn't.*

Action 5.8.1

SEVERITY LEVEL: 2
O/S VERSION: All
ORACLE VERSIONS: All

Check the file permissions of all the configuration files in the $ORACLE_HOME/network/admin directory. Consider making them the minimum permissions for Oracle to operate and only temporarily alter the permissions to edit them.

See the Oracle documentation referenced in *Action 1.2.1* for details of Oracle's recommended file permissions. In this case, if possible make the permissions tighter but seek advice from Oracle support first.

Action 5.8.2

SEVERITY LEVEL: 2
O/S VERSION: All
ORACLE VERSIONS: All

The ideal client installation would only include a *tnsnames.ora* file (if needed) or better, a *sqlnet.ora* file containing just the name of the Oracle Names Server.

Phase 5 ~ Networking

Step 5.9 — Listener Exploits

PROBLEM: *There are now a number of well-publicized exploits against the Oracle listener. One example is reading details from the listener memory left by previous connections.*

Action 5.9.1

SEVERITY LEVEL: 2
O/S VERSION: All
ORACLE VERSIONS: All

Keep up to date with Oracle security vulnerabilities on Oracles security alert page on their web site (*See Step 0.1*) and apply patches as soon as they become available. The listener is a good target for attackers.

Step 5.10 — Remote Access

PROBLEM: *Remote access to the database is the end goal for any intruder. Therefore, by allowing the listener ports to be visible to the Internet, or providing any direct access to the database or a shell prompt is like leaving your front door open at home.*

Action 5.10.1

SEVERITY LEVEL: 1
O/S VERSION: All
ORACLE VERSIONS: All

It should not be possible for any remote client to obtain access to a shell. For remote DBA, there really aren't many good alternatives. Oracle authentication and security parameters need to be secure in this case. Use *ssh* or any other Virtual Private Network (VPN) solution.

For proper security of an Oracle installation, never open a listener port to the Internet.

Phase 5 ~ Networking

Action 5.10.2

SEVERITY LEVEL: 2
O/S VERSION: All
ORACLE VERSIONS: All

All remote access should be through an application gateway firewall that supports Oracle network firewall proxy. Virtual Private Network (VPN) can be used to the network that the database is available on.

Step 5.11 — tnsnames.ora

PROBLEM: *The tnsnames.ora file contains the connection details for each service that a client can connect to. This includes database instances and the external procedure service. Because of the order Oracle uses to look for configuration files, it is possible to create a local one for Oracle to use.*

Action 5.11.1

SEVERITY LEVEL: 2
O/S VERSION: All
ORACLE VERSIONS: All

In the $ORACLE_HOME/network/admin/tnsnames.ora file, set SERVER=DEDICATED.

Normally, if a client is running in multi-threaded server, and it is necessary to force a connection to be dedicated, this parameter would be used for example:

```
<service name> =
  (DESCRIPTION =
    (ADDRESS_LIST =
      (ADDRESS =
        (COMMUNITY = <community>)
        (PROTOCOL = <protocol>)
        (Host = <server>)
        (Port = 1526)
      )
    )
    (CONNECT_DATA =
     (SID = <sid>)
        (SERVER=DEDICATED)            <---
     )
```

Do not use the default ports of 1521 and 1526 as discussed in the listener section above.

A *.tnsnames.ora* file can be set up by an attacker to bypass the real tnsnames.ora file.

See also *Action 5.1.2*.

Solutions include using Oracle Names or Oracle Internet Directory (OID). Note: 1036577.6: "How to Make Dedicated Connections from a Client When Using Oracle Names" available from Metalink describes this.

Phase 5 ~ Networking

Action 5.11.2

SEVERITY LEVEL
3

O/S VERSION
All

ORACLE VERSIONS
All

There are a number of default ports used by Oracle for the database, applications and tools. These are listed here:

Ports	Oracle products
1521,1526	Oracle RDBMS – All versions
8888,80,2649(udp)	Oracle web application server ver 3.0.2
80,443(SSL)	Oracle application server ver 4.0.x
7777,80,443(SSL)	Oracle iAS Apache listener
9000	Oracle forms server
2002	Oracle webdb listener
10021-10029,15000	Oracle TFC server
1526	Oracle report view agent
9010,9020	Oracle metric server and client

Be aware of the default ports used and check using a port scanner for active ports. If the facilities are not required, then stop the listeners and services. If the facilities are required, start the listeners on non-default ports.

Step 5.12 — Intelligent Agent

PROBLEM: *The intelligent agent provides a mechanism for monitoring and administrating multiple databases. This can be abused through many avenues to gain access to not one but many databases in a company. The intelligent agent must be screwed down tight.*

Action 5.12.1

SEVERITY LEVEL: 2
O/S VERSION: All
ORACLE VERSIONS: All

Connects by default using "dbsnmp/dbsnmp". If the account exists, chances are someone can install the OEM on their PC and try to connect to the database that way. They need to "Discover" it using the OEM Console. They can enter a hundred host names in the list and wait for the OEM to discover an Oracle database on one of them. This will work if the Oracle Intelligent Agent is left running on the machine. A connection is then made. To use Schema Manager, Security Manager, etc., the user does need an account name and password. Oracle makes the OEM available for free from their web site.

When 8.1.7 and 9i have been installed, a default http server is installed and started. This should be stopped and removed if it is not necessary. If installing using a *custom.rsp* file, you can eliminate the starting of the http server. It is one of the parameters to the installer.

Intelligent Agent logons/password combinations (preferred credentials for both O/S and database) are stored inside the OEM repository. This allows an end user with an OEM console super administrator logon to have complete access to all databases and to discover additional databases. This also includes the ability to "change roles".

In 8i, OEM administrator logons can discover any nodes and administer any of the databases; in 9i, only super administrators can discover nodes and have to grant access to any discovered node to an administrator. The password algorithm is weak since patterns are seen for sequential usernames for OEM. At the very least, the file containing the passwords should be protected.

User defined events can run any script in any programming language against a node or database.

Administrators that run events or jobs need advanced O/S rights such as "logon as a batch job" and read/write to the ORACLE_HOME/network/admin on Windows, as well as a valid DBA account for Unix. Any files with a .q extension contain the jobs that OEM runs. These files need to be secured. Otherwise alerts, scripts, backups etc. can be corrupted.

Any Oracle Management Server that has not been restricted at the network/O/S level of reaching your database will be able to discover your organization's database nodes.

SNMP functionality is integrated with OIA and can be configured inappropriately allowing traps to be intercepted.

To stop SNMP, issue the following command.

```
LSNRCTL DBSNMP_STOP
```

Phase 5 ~ Networking

In 9i, use *agenttcl* start and *agenttcl* stop to stop and start the agent.

Scripts run by the IA can damage everything. Good directory permissions are essential with regular checks. Use Enterprise Manager to check the jobs on all machines that run the Intelligent Agent.

SANS lists SNMP vulnerabilities as one of the top 20 methods; see http://www.sans.org/top20.html, item U7. Follow the guidelines in this document to secure SNMP devices.

Protect the file $ORACLE_HOME/rdbms/admin/catsnmp.sql since this file contains the password for the user *dbsnmp*. The script *catproc.sql* executes *catsnmp.sql*. If OEM is not used, execute $ORACLE_HOME/rdbms/admin/catnsnmp.sql to remove all of the objects and also remove $ORACLE_HOME/bin/dbsnmp, which is SUID root by default.

Note: OEM uses encrypted RPC to communicate with the intelligent agent. SNMP is not used because of the insecurities. The Oracle intelligent agent (dbsnmp process) is SNMP compatible, so that it can function as an SNMP agent with existing SNMP tools, but OEM doesn't use SNMP.

Action 5.12.2

SEVERITY LEVEL: 2
O/S VERSION: All
ORACLE VERSIONS: All

In the *snmp_rw.ora* file, the following lines exist after the dbsnmp has been started.

```
SNMP.CONNECT.<service name>.NAME=<new name>
SNMP.CONNECT.<service name>.PASSWORD=<password>
```

The files *snmp_ro.ora*, *snmp_rw.ora* and *sqlnet.ora* need to be protected. If the password is changed, then the password is visible along with lots of other information: they are read/write for the owner of the Oracle software and the group used for ORAINVENTORY.

Do not use the intelligent agent if the server is on the Internet.

Note: The listener-password in 9i will become encrypted after the first start of IA. The parameter listed above will change and the password will be encrypted.

Phase 5 ~ Networking

Step 5.13 — Transmissions between Oracle Clients and Servers

PROBLEM: *The communication between all Oracle clients and the database is in clear text (not just SQL*Plus) except for Oracle client passwords, which are encrypted. So, critical information may be disclosed from a sniffer attack.*

Action 5.13.1

SEVERITY LEVEL: 3
O/S VERSION: All
ORACLE VERSIONS: All

To encrypt the connection, use Oracle Advanced Security, which supports SSL, DES, Triple DES and RC4. An alternative option is to use IPSec.

Action 5.13.2

SEVERITY LEVEL: 3
O/S VERSION: All
ORACLE VERSIONS: All

To "Enable Secure Socket Layer (SSL) Authentication", one of the tasks is to "Configure SSL on the Client". One of the steps within this task is to optionally set "SSL as an authentication service". Do not set the SQLNET.AUTHENTICATION_SERVICES parameter in the *sqlnet.ora* file so that the SSL authentication service is not set. You must set this parameter only if the following two conditions **both** apply:

You want to use SSL authentication in conjunction with another Authentication method supported by Oracle Advanced Security. For example, you want the server to authenticate itself to the client by using SSL and the client to authenticate itself to the server by using Kerberos or SecurID.

You are not using Net8 Assistant to configure the client or the Server. If both of the above conditions apply, add TCP with SSL (TCPS) to this parameter in the *sqlnet.ora* file by using a text editor. For example:
SQLNET.AUTHENTICATION_SERVICES = (BEQ, TCPS, identix, securid)

If either or both of the above conditions do not apply, you do not need to set this parameter. See "Note: 132852.1 - Enabling SSL Authentication" on Metalink.

To use SSL authentication, a wallet needs to be created.

An excellent introduction to Oracle Advanced Security and encryption can be found in the Oracle on-line documentation in the "Oracle Advanced Security Administrators Guide" book. This can be found at:

http://download-west.oracle.com/otndoc/oracle9i/901_doc/network.901/a90150/toc.htm

Oracle Advanced Security will provide real end-to-end security since encryption via SSL is often used via the Internet, but the internal network from 9iAS to the database (using Net8/Net9) is unencrypted.

Note: By default the client has SSL enabled in versions greater than 8.1.7.

Phase 6 — Availability / Backup / Recovery

PHASE 6
Availability / Backup / Recovery

This phase, which covers the basics of backup, is not intended to be a treatise on backup methods. It should serve as a reminder that a complete security solution for an Oracle database must include backup and recovery procedures.

Step 6.1 Backup and Recovery

PROBLEM: If a failure takes place with the database or an intruder destroys part or the entire database, then it is crucial to have correct backup and recovery procedures in place. Consider the idea of backup tapes stored off site: think about how easy it would be for an attacker to telephone the tape storage facility, tell the attendant that there has been a major problem, and that backups for last week should be sent immediately to reception for collection. The attacker walks in off the street, walks to the receptionist and says, "I have come to pick up some tapes for Mr....". Then off he goes and rebuilds your database at his leisure.

Action 6.1.1

SEVERITY LEVEL: 3
O/S VERSION: All
ORACLE VERSIONS: All

Review the backup and restore procedures, and ensure that the process is fully documented. Regularly test complete restores and partial restores to a point in time to ensure that the backup process in place is adequate.

Phase 6 ~ Availability / Backup / Recovery

Action 6.1.2

SEVERITY LEVEL: 3
O/S VERSION: All
ORACLE VERSIONS: All

Review recovery procedures. Write them down, and test them regularly.

Note: When objects are created, NOLOGGING an immediate backup is needed for tablespaces / indexes. Delays are possible, but backups are needed at some stage soon.

Action 6.1.3

SEVERITY LEVEL: 3
O/S VERSION: All
ORACLE VERSIONS: All

Adequate backups need to be done and tapes (or whatever media is used) should be stored and recorded off site.

Note: Any standby database (in manual or managed recovery mode) is in the same state of vulnerability as a normal read/write database, but with restricted database access. This provides an additional copy of production data with an additional copy of archive logs to protect at the O/S level.

There are typically on-line database backups of database files and exports stored on the hard drive of the server itself, providing opportunity at the file system level for compromise.

Action 6.1.4

SEVERITY LEVEL: 3
O/S VERSION: All
ORACLE VERSIONS: All

In addition to hot backups or exports, cold backups should be scheduled and done as regularly as possible. A cold backup is also necessary to backup the rest of the Oracle installation in order to allow a complete rebuild from one point in time to take place.

Phase 6 ~ Availability / Backup / Recovery

Action 6.1.5

SEVERITY LEVEL: 3
O/S VERSION: All
ORACLE VERSIONS: All

Backup media integrity should be checked regularly.

Action 6.1.6

SEVERITY LEVEL: 2
O/S VERSION: All
ORACLE VERSIONS: All

Ideally backups should not be available on-line but off site (obviously a lot of organizations keep very recent backups available on-line for ease of recovery). This would make it harder for an attacker to easily steal the database from recent backups.

Action 6.1.7

SEVERITY LEVEL: 2
O/S VERSION: All
ORACLE VERSIONS: All

Procedures should be in place for backup tape retrieval from off site to prevent social engineering taking place to steal the tapes. Document the process, ensure that the person collecting the tapes and receiving them is the person authorized to do so. Use identification methods for the individuals involved.

Phase 6 ~ Availability / Backup / Recovery

Step 6.2 — Mirroring of Redo and Control Files

PROBLEM: *If the online redo logs are on a disk or accessed through a controller that failed and they are not mirrored, then the database will very likely need recovery.*

Action 6.2.1

SEVERITY LEVEL: 2
O/S VERSION: All
ORACLE VERSIONS: All

Ensure that the on-line redo logs are mirrored, and that more than one group exists. Use the following SQL to check their locations:

```
select lo.group# group,
       fi.member filename,
       lo.bytes/1024 log_size
from   v$log lo,
       v$logfile fi
where  lo.group# = fi.group#;
```

Note: If the redo logs are lost, it is still possible to start up the database if it was running in archivelog mode. There is an undocumented init.ora parameter that can let a database open even if the redo log files are corrupt. This is **not** recommended, however, since this means some data corruption is likely. Get permission from Oracle support before doing this.

The parameter _allow_resetlogs_corruption is the parameter mentioned above. The parameter _allow_read_only_corruption can also be used. Both of these parameters will damage the database, and should be used **only** to get it open to retrieve what you can after a corruption. Oracle will not support you if you use them (unless, of course, they recommend that you do so).

Step 6.3 — Archive Logs

PROBLEM: *If a database is not in Archivelog Mode, and it is hacked or damaged in any way, then a point in time recovery is not possible and data will be lost. It's as simple as that.*

Action 6.3.1

SEVERITY LEVEL: 2
O/S VERSION: All
ORACLE VERSIONS: All

Ensure the database is in archivelog mode. Use the following SQL:

```
select log_mode
from   v$database;
```

It is important that the permissions are set correctly on the directories used to store archive logs. See also *Action 1.13.1*.

Action 6.3.2

SEVERITY LEVEL: 2
O/S VERSION: All
ORACLE VERSIONS: All

Ensure that the archivelog directories exist and are writable by the Oracle user. Use the following SQL to find then:

```
SQL> select name,value
  2   from v$parameter
  3   where name like '%arch%';
SQL> /

NAME                             VALUE
-------------------------------- ----------------------------------------
log_archive_start                FALSE
log_archive_dest
log_archive_duplex_dest
log_archive_dest_1
log_archive_dest_2
log_archive_dest_3
log_archive_dest_4
log_archive_dest_5
log_archive_dest_state_1         enable
log_archive_dest_state_2         enable
log_archive_dest_state_3         enable
log_archive_dest_state_4         enable
log_archive_dest_state_5         enable
log_archive_max_processes        1
log_archive_min_succeed_dest     1
standby_archive_dest             ?/dbs/arch
log_archive_trace                0
log_archive_format               %t_%s.dbf

18 rows selected.

SQL>
```

Check the directories listed via the O/S.

Phase 6 ~ Availability / Backup / Recovery

Action 6.3.3

SEVERITY LEVEL: 3
O/S VERSION: All
ORACLE VERSIONS: All

Ensure that the Archive log files are saved to tape or to a separate disk. A point in time recovery is not possible unless the archive log files are available. If the directory containing the files is not cleared, there could be a potential Denial of Service if a hacker issued a large amount of bogus updates.

Step 6.4 — File Locations and Directory Structure

PROBLEM: *If a single disk or single controller has a problem, and the data and Oracle are on that disk or controller, then the database can be lost either temporarily or until a restore is done. This is a single point of failure action.*

Action 6.4.1

SEVERITY LEVEL: 3
O/S VERSION: All
ORACLE VERSIONS: All

Split the location of the Oracle software distribution; redo logs and data files to separate disks and controllers for resilience. This can be done at design time before implementation or to an existing database without changing the applications.

> **Note:** In the event of failure it depends what files are associated with a specific controller. If the SYSTEM tablespace is affected, there is a need to restore the SYSTEM tablespace somewhere else. Manipulate the control files and try to bring up the database gradually. If a tablespace data file disappears due to disk corruption, that tablespace can be placed off-line and the rest of the database will remain accessible, provided it is not SYSTEM. Other tablespaces have to be available such as rollback. Temp is needed if any DML requires a sort.

Action 6.4.2

SEVERITY LEVEL: 3
O/S VERSION: All
ORACLE VERSIONS: All

Only put database files on disks or volumes used by Oracle, thereby reducing the need for other users to access those disks.

ORACLE SECURITY Step-by-Step

Phase 6 ~ Availability / Backup / Recovery

Action 6.4.3

SEVERITY LEVEL: 5
O/S VERSION: All
ORACLE VERSIONS: All

Use the Oracle Flexible Architecture (OFA) naming conventions. This makes it easier for a new DBA or anyone involved with the application and database to find and understand the layout. OFA in Oracle 8i places the archive logs on the same volume as the Oracle binaries. Oracle also places trace files in OFA in the same volume as the binaries. Trace and archive logs can both fill the executable volume.

Note: Using the OFA conventions also has a downside: not only is it easy for a new DBA to understand the layout used, it is just as easy for a hacker to do likewise.

Action 6.4.4

SEVERITY LEVEL: 4
O/S VERSION: All
ORACLE VERSIONS: All

Ideally the file systems holding the data should be mirrored and / or striped / RAID for resilience.

Phase 6 ~ Availability / Backup / Recovery

Step 6.5 — Disk Failures

PROBLEM: *If a disk used to store database files should fail and is replaced, do **not** leave it lying around the computer center or toss it in a trashcan. Remember, this disk recently had critical business data on it. It is not inconceivable that an observant attacker could take the disk from the trashcan and retrieve some of the business data. It's not easy, but it **is** possible.*

Action 6.5.1

SEVERITY LEVEL: 2
O/S VERSION: All
ORACLE VERSIONS: All

Consider having old disks, no longer used disks and failed disks wiped magnetically to ensure that database data cannot be stolen later. Oracle provides a tool called Data Recovery UnLoader (DUL) and another database block editor called BBED that allows data to be accessed on disk from a database without a database running. The DUL tool is owned by a Dutch consultant and is *rented* back to Oracle for use in recovering databases. It is not inconceivable that someone could get and use this tool to steal data.

It is also not inconceivable that someone will write a *free* version of this tool for use by anyone.

BBED is available from Oracle 8.1.5 on Windows as a binary file and on Unix as a library that can be built into a binary file.

Step 6.6 — Disaster Recovery

PROBLEM: *In the event of a machine failure or some natural disaster or an attacker destroying a database completely, some form of backup process needs to be in place. For critical applications a disaster recovery system should be in place to allow the database and associated applications to continue running or at least to be restored promptly.*

Action 6.6.1

SEVERITY LEVEL: 4
O/S VERSION: All
ORACLE VERSIONS: All

Disaster recovery procedures need to be reviewed and tested. Write them down, and test them regularly.

> **Note:** One very important fact needs to be stated here; that is the disaster recovery site and its systems need to be **as secure** as the production environment. The full contents of this guide need to be applied to the disaster recover site.

Phase 6 ~ Availability / Backup / Recovery

Action 6.6.2

SEVERITY LEVEL: 4
O/S VERSION: All
ORACLE VERSIONS: All

Users should be formally included in recovery procedures. Document recovery procedures, and ensure that key users are involved in the planning stage and are also involved in testing. This is an important step to ascertain that business requirements and functionality work correctly after recovery.

PHASE 7
Application Development

Step 7.1 — Issues with PL/SQL and Java

PROBLEM: *More and more applications are taking advantage of Oracle's built-in features to create business logic within the database itself, using PL/SQL or Java. This code, if not secured, can give away a lot of details about your applications schema and function and allow an enterprising attacker to assemble a picture of how things work. For example, PL/SQL code that can execute dynamic SQL is open to SQL Injection attempts.*

Note: Secure programming is a highly underestimated area. Every organization should have someone with a lot of experience in this field to evaluate the development team / area and their actions and code.

Action 7.1.1

SEVERITY LEVEL: 2
O/S VERSION: All
ORACLE VERSIONS: All

Identify all application PL/SQL code by querying the dba_objects view, and use the wrap program provided by Oracle to wrap the source code. The wrap program can be used to *encode* the PL/SQL source code and make it unreadable. It should be noted that this utility encodes and does not *encrypt*.

The *wrap* process converts the PL/SQL to microprocessor independent P-Code. This means that this process could be reverse-engineered. I am not aware of anyone who has done this yet. The process is still safer than leaving all of the applications source code in clear text for all to view. Use the tool as follows:

Note: A good website for these web based coding problems is www.owasp.org.

```
wrap iname=input_file [oname=output_file]
```

The code stored in the database per user can be found as follows:

```
SQL> select count(*),owner
  2  from (select owner,name
  3   from dba_source
  4   where line=1
  5   group by owner,name)
  6   group by owner;
```

```
  COUNT(*) OWNER
---------- ------------------------------
        41 CTXSYS
        53 MDSYS
        13 ORDPLUGINS
        55 ORDSYS
       259 SYS
         2 SYSTEM

6 rows selected.

SQL>
```

The wrapped code can be found as follows:

```
SQL> select owner,count(*)
  2  from (select owner,name,max(line) max_line
  3  from dba_source
  4  where (text like '% wrapped%'
  5  and line=1)
  6  group by owner,name)
  7  group by owner
SQL> /

OWNER                            COUNT(*)
------------------------------ ----------
CTXSYS                                 32
MDSYS                                  35
ORDPLUGINS                             13
ORDSYS                                 25
SYS                                   181
SYSTEM                                  1

6 rows selected.

SQL>
```

Phase 7 ~ Application Development

It should also be noted that code that is wrapped with Oracle's utility only wraps the program structure, not variables and constants. See the following example:

```
$ cat test.sql
create or replace procedure wrap
is
begin
   dbms_output.put('test string');
end;
/

$ wrap iname=test.sql

PL/SQL Wrapper: Release 9.0.1.0.0- Production on Thu May 30 18:26:14 2002

Copyright (c) Oracle Corporation 1993, 2001.  All Rights Reserved.

Processing test.sql to test.plb
$ grep "test string" test.plb
1test string:
```

This issue can be resolved by obfuscating the strings first. This means the program logic needs to be able to rebuild strings on the fly. Another option is to build strings from concatenated parts.

Note: It may make sense at this stage to offer differing advice for production and development, but the risk is just as high if someone gains access to a development database. So the advice is to ensure that **all** databases are as secure as each other.

Note: The new 9i facility to compile PL/SQL to native binaries can be used also via the plsql_native interface to convert a wrapped PL/SQL package to binary. This is done via generated C Source code. The C source code generated after an experiment does not reveal any usable information, but the use of plsql_native process should still be guarded against.

Action 7.1.2

SEVERITY LEVEL 3
O/S VERSION All
ORACLE VERSIONS All

Checksum the PL/SQL source code, Java classes stored in the database and Java jar files and store the results for checking later to see if any database source code has been altered. It is not inconceivable for someone to plant a Trojan, and to manipulate the date / time stamps in the data dictionary.

Configuration management and release management should also control all source code.

Do not grant access to the views DBA_SOURCE, ALL_SOURCE and the SYS owned table SOURCE$ to any users. These views and tables allow database stored source code to be viewed or changed.

Note: A related or sub issue is with readable, executable code (code that has been interpreted from the source at runtime). In addition, deployment techniques where code is compiled / converted to executable formats (e.g. Java classes) on the production system should be guarded against.

Phase 7 ~ Application Development

Action 7.1.3

SEVERITY LEVEL: 3
O/S VERSION: All
ORACLE VERSIONS: All

Check PL/SQL code for hard coded usernames, passwords and other critical data.

> **Note:** Some simple advice on reviewing an Oracle installation: The main focus in security assessment is understanding the architecture of applications and systems that are using databases. Focus primarily on how the application connects. Based on this, the security assessment can go in a number of directions. Most of them have been covered in the document:
>
> • Check on how development and production instances are separated.
>
> • Check how development and production schemas are separated, if in same instance.
>
> • Check developer privileges in production schemas / instances.
>
> • Check hard-coding of Oracle connection (username / password) in scripts / source code / executable (check how each of these are protected).
>
> • Check copy-down procedures for use of production data in test and development.
>
> • Check developer membership in privilege groups at O/S level.

Action 7.1.4

SEVERITY LEVEL: 2
O/S VERSION: All
ORACLE VERSIONS: All

Audit the PL/SQL code for SQL Injection and PL/SQL Injection possibilities. Some simple guidelines when writing PL/SQL follow:

- Always try to use bind variables instead of concatenation if possible. Using bind variables will almost eliminate the possibility of SQL or PL/SQL injection.
- Perform a security review of newly developed code. If possible, this should be performed by someone who is **not** in the development team.
- Create PL/SQL programs as AUTHID CURRENT_USER if possible.
- Do not use dynamic PL/SQL if the same function can be achieved with dynamic SQL.
- If dynamic PL/SQL is used, try to use numbers and not strings in the variable part and validate the numbers before use.
- Filter dynamic input and do not allow certain characters such as a semi-colon and "<" and ">" when some of the htp package procedures are used.

The above ideas were gleaned from an excellent book on PL/SQL *Learning Oracle PL/SQL* from O'Reilly.

Phase 7 ~ Application Development

Action 7.1.5

SEVERITY LEVEL: 3
O/S VERSION: All
ORACLE VERSIONS: All

Ensure that as little information as possible about a schema structure is available through reading the PL/SQL from the database.

This can sometimes be a nuisance when planning and investigating. But in line with "no one should log in as the application schema owner", there is nothing wrong with "no one logs in as the procedure owner".

Action 7.1.6

SEVERITY LEVEL: 3
O/S VERSION: All
ORACLE VERSIONS: All

Java source code needs to be compiled to classes in the database itself and loaded. This can be a risk to security in exposing the source code to the database.

Java source code can also be read from the data dictionary if the Java is available as a JAVA SOURCE in the sys.obj$ table. The source can be read using DBMS_LOB.

This source needs to be secured, and permissions to view objects in DBA_OBJECTS, ALL_OBJECTS and SYS.OBJ$ should be revoked as should the use of DBMS_LOB.

Java classes can be loaded compiled into the database using the loadjava utility. Obfuscated classes can also be loaded preventing classes from being decompiled.

Step 7.2 — Applications that Access the Database

PROBLEM: *An organization may have an application to access their data in an Oracle database and believe that this is the only way of accessing the data. They may design the roles and hierarchy based around this model. Now imagine a user in the accounts department who decides to use MS Excel and ODBC to access the database one day, to try to download some figures into a spreadsheet. He realizes that he can now see data he couldn't see through the application, and soon a few more people are using this method. Worse still, a user connecting to the database using an Admin tool like TOAD would find it even easier to alter the database schema.*

Action 7.2.1

SEVERITY LEVEL: 2
O/S VERSION: All
ORACLE VERSIONS: All

Review what applications access the database. This can be done using audit or by querying v$session. Look for non-standard applications such as MS Excel, Toad, and MS Access etc.

Unfortunately, it is too easy for a determined attacker to spoof where he is, what he is using and any other information that is available in the v$ view.

The security issues with ODBC vary with the version and the driver used. Later drivers allow the connected user to see all of the objects granted to that user and all PUBLIC objects. This behavior is to be expected. The only real solutions to the uncontrolled use of ODBC are for all users' privileges to be locked down as discussed in this guide. Then any user connected through ODBC should only be able to see the objects that the user was designed to see.

Note: This can happen anywhere where the security is managed within application code, and it is not the only route users take into the database. A poorly configured ad-hoc reporting system — discoverer, business objects, brio etc. can all produce the same problems.

Action 7.2.2

SEVERITY LEVEL: 2
O/S VERSION: All
ORACLE VERSIONS: All

Implement processes to control what applications access your database, such as MS Access or MS Excel. One method is to use the DBMS_APPLICATION_INFO package and have all of your genuine applications use this package to make themselves known to the database. Standard applications, even if renamed to spoof the database, would find it more difficult to spoof the use of this package.

Oracle 9i brings application roles that will make it easier to control **what** and **who** accesses the database.

Note: Really no problem? Portable software is usually not developed for optimal security. The database is often used as a simple storage medium. Special security features (like VPD, dbms_obfuscation_toolkit ...) are often not used, because they are not portable between the different non-Oracle database platforms. Therefore the smallest common denominator is used.

Note: Apart from a specific bug on Window, the output of the DBMS_OBFUSCATION_TOOLKIT is portable between different Oracle platforms and O/S platforms. VPD uses PL/SQL to do its work so it, too, is portable between different platforms.

Phase 7 ~ Application Development

Action 7.2.3

SEVERITY LEVEL: 3
O/S VERSION: All
ORACLE VERSIONS: All

The same as 7.2.2 above, but this time restricts more destructive applications such as TOAD, HORA, and PL/SQL Developer, etc. from normal users.

As stated above in 9i, application roles can be used to restrict the access of more advanced applications such as TOAD from normal database users.

Step 7.3 — Decommissioning Products / Applications

PROBLEM: *Old applications, even parts that still exist in an environment, leave holes in an organization's armament. If the previous legacy application binaries are still there along side the new, and they are not controlled, then access can be gained to the database through an alternate route.*

Action 7.3.1

SEVERITY LEVEL: 4
O/S VERSION: All
ORACLE VERSIONS: All

When applications are decommissioned, ensure that all of the binaries, users, batch processes, and access rights are removed. Leaving parts of old legacy applications in place leave openings that are uncontrolled. They can leave additional, less secure access points to the new database.

Phase 7 ~ Application Development

Step 7.4 — Adding a New Application

PROBLEM: *New applications inevitably have slack permissions and access. One reason for this is that issues may need to be resolved quickly and the highest privileges are granted to resolve them, and this leaves an opening. Furthermore, new applications are less understood and therefore may not be configured securely.*

Action 7.4.1

SEVERITY LEVEL: 4
O/S VERSION: All
ORACLE VERSIONS: All

Review the procedures for adding new applications that access your database, and for adding users and access rights to that database. Quite often when a new application is added, the highest access rights are given to far too many users, since it is easier than deciding who should have these rights.

Note: The pressure to put systems online is enormous. Therefore new applications tend to be placed into production before a comprehensive security audit has been done. Security is quite often an afterthought, and not incorporated into the initial application and database design.

Step 7.5 — Movers, Leavers and Joiners

PROBLEM: *Having dormant accounts in a database can provide accounts for an attacker to use that may not be monitored. Usually, dormant accounts exist because of staff movements within an organization or due to attrition.*

Action 7.5.1

SEVERITY LEVEL: 2
O/S VERSION: All
ORACLE VERSIONS: All

Review procedures for movers, leavers and joiners. Most sites do not have any formal procedures and leave large numbers of dormant accounts in place.

Consider using audit to review user's accounts for activity. If an account has not been used after a set number of days, lock it and after a further set number of days, remove it.

The SQL used in *Action 2.3.3* and the audit options discussed in *Phase 4* will help here.

One way around this issue is to use "an account for the job". This is a bad way of solving this issue, since the previous person will know the password and details of the account. So this is **not** an ideal way of solving this issue.

Old accounts should be removed and new accounts created for the new person. In some applications, removing users can cause issues with timestamps and application audit trails.

Note: Just looking for accounts in the database that are dormant for a set period of days is a good first step. Actually finding them should start two processes, the first to remove the accounts, and the second to review the procedures that allowed these accounts to still exist and lie dormant.

Phase 7 ~ Application Development

Step 7.6 — Application File Permissions

PROBLEM: *Controlling the permissions of application files and binaries is just as important as controlling the file permissions of Oracle itself. World-readable configuration files for an application can reveal important details of how the application works or communicates with the database server. SUID permissions on application binaries can provide opportunities for buffer overflows and escalation of privileges. World-executable permissions of application binaries allow anyone to attempt to run the applications.*

Action 7.6.1

SEVERITY LEVEL: 3
O/S VERSION: All
ORACLE VERSIONS: All

Check that all application files — server-based, client-based and batch processes — are owned by the correct owner and have the correct permissions for the application and for correct access to the database as the correct user.

Note: Interface between O/S and DBMS, such as passing in parameters via files, use of O/S commands and processes, OCI compiled into programs with C, C++, etc. There are LOTS of opportunities for data type inconsistencies, different string terminators, dependence on internal, O/S-dependent representation, buffer overflows.

Step 7.7 — Development on Production Databases

PROBLEM: *Allowing developers to alter any of the schema or change PL/SQL or Java code in the database can cause security issues. Access to objects can be granted beyond what is needed, and source code can be changed in the database itself causing the latest code to exist only in the database and nowhere else.*

Action 7.7.1

SEVERITY LEVEL: 3
O/S VERSION: All
ORACLE VERSIONS: All

Check for evidence of development taking place on production databases, i.e., altering of objects or creation of new objects — audit could be used to check for this.

There should be a clear separation of duties between developers and production staff.

The column last_ddl_time on sys.obj$ can be used to check for objects that have changed.

Developers should not have read or write access to production databases. Sometimes it is necessary for developers to track down bugs on production databases. This should be done through read only access that is created for the purpose and revoked immediately after.

Note: Is the process for moving files from development to production secure? Can it be subverted, or convinced to publish a file that shouldn't be published? Is there version control? What protections are there against corruption? Are there code reviews and walk-through sessions? Are there any opportunities for Trojans or back doors being installed?

Phase 7 ~ Application Development

Step 7.8 Ad-Hoc Queries

PROBLEM: *Allowing ad-hoc access to a live production database to query any data is a risky business. The schema, users and roles may be well designed and access controlled through a good application, but ad-hoc query tools allow simple browsing of all the accessible data. Simply put, anyone using a client-based copy of Crystal Reports or MS Access can see much more than they should. Performance and availability of the database should also be considered, since running ad-hoc queries can impair the performance of the rest of the application.*

Action 7.8.1

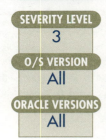

SEVERITY LEVEL: 3
O/S VERSION: All
ORACLE VERSIONS: All

Ad-hoc queries should be disallowed against the production database. Access should be restricted to correct applications, approved reporting tools and DBA access.

Most of the steps above should help accomplish this. But the process needs to be monitored.

Ad-hoc query access allows developers and support staff to potentially read data they could be restricted from seeing through the application, and could also cause a Denial of service if an overly long query is executed.

Phase 7 ~ Application Development

Step 7.9 — Development and Test Databases

PROBLEM: *Development and test databases offer a large area of opportunity for an attacker to gain access to data they would like to steal. Often, developers or testers are given far higher privileges than they need. These sometimes lead to incorrect privileges and developer accounts being created in a production database. Database links created between a development system and a production system to help development or testing can provide an easy way into a production database.*

The production database may be very well protected and properly audited, but a thief may be able to find the data they wish to steal in a development system, where it has not been well protected.

Action 7.9.1

SEVERITY LEVEL: 2
O/S VERSION: All
ORACLE VERSIONS: All

Review test and development databases for users with extra permissions not granted in production. Use the techniques described in *Phase 3*, and then compare between the two databases.

Revoke any extra permission granted in production. Review the level of permissions a developer has in production. It should not be taken for granted that a developer gets the same permission in production as he does in development. In fact, he should get less.

Note: It is common practice to have development and production schemas on same instance or to have development and production instances on same host operating system environment. This causes many risks related to operating system security, Oracle system privileges and production schema object privileges

Note: Comparing databases: You can use Enterprise Manager (Change Manager) to compare schemas and automatically create alter scripts.

Action 7.9.2

SEVERITY LEVEL: 2
O/S VERSION: All
ORACLE VERSIONS: All

Check for database links with access to production databases. Use the following SQL:

```
SELECT *
FROM DBA_DB_LINKS;
```

Phase 7 ~ Application Development

Action 7.9.3

SEVERITY LEVEL: 2
O/S VERSION: All
ORACLE VERSIONS: All

Check that data held in development and test databases are sufficiently obfuscated or mangled. If it is real data, the data in a test system or development system might be a much easier target for an attacker or malicious employee.

The level of data held in development and test should be very low. There are a number of examples where this is probably not the case, i.e., stress testing, testing data migration software.

Action 7.9.4

SEVERITY LEVEL: 2
O/S VERSION: All
ORACLE VERSIONS: All

Ideally test and development databases should not be located on the same server as the production system.

Ideally there should be no test instances on production servers, different instances should be on different servers, and production should have a restricted subnet.

If the database backs a web site, then the web server should not be on the same server as the production database.

One common problem from development to production is the developer who acquires extra privileges. In that case, the code works on development, but it doesn't work on production. A common solution is to 'fix' production rather than backing out and fixing the code strategy.

Action 7.9.5

SEVERITY LEVEL: 2
O/S VERSION: All
ORACLE VERSIONS: All

Ideally there should not be access from the test or development databases to the production database.

Phase 7 ~ Application Development

Action 7.9.6

SEVERITY LEVEL: 1
O/S VERSION: All
ORACLE VERSIONS: All

Ideally there should not be direct developer access to the production database.

See also *Step 7.20* on change control.

Action 7.9.7

SEVERITY LEVEL: 2
O/S VERSION: All
ORACLE VERSIONS: All

Check that developer accounts do not exist in production.

Action 7.9.8

SEVERITY LEVEL: 2
O/S VERSION: All
ORACLE VERSIONS: All

There is an issue of using backups (or exports) to create test databases — especially with the resulting password cloning and database link existence.

Ensure that when test and development databases are recreated, passwords are changed before giving access to developers and testers.

Also ensure that data used in test and development is sufficiently altered so that users who should not have access to critical data do **not** have the ability to see it.

Phase 7 ~ Application Development

Action 7.9.9

SEVERITY LEVEL: 2
O/S VERSION: All
ORACLE VERSIONS: All

If possible, place production databases on a different network segment from test and development databases.

Step 7.10 — Application Objects

PROBLEM: *When application objects are placed in the system tablespace, there is a remote chance that a Denial of Service could occur. If extending an application's objects prevented the system tablespace from extending as well, then this would hang the database, causing a Denial of Service.*

If application objects are not confined to one user and exist among many, then accessing those objects and the data contained within becomes very easy for an attacker.

Action 7.10.1

SEVERITY LEVEL: 2
O/S VERSION: All
ORACLE VERSIONS: All

Identify all tablespaces used by the application / applications, and then select all of the objects and owners from those tablespaces. Any objects sharing the storage owned by the application and not owned by the application owner should be moved to a more appropriate tablespace.

The same SQL used in *Action 3.7.1* can be modified and used. First select all of the tablespace names from DBA_TABLESPACES, and then replace the SYSTEM tablespace name in the query above, and remove the lines that check for the owner being SYS.

Any objects not owned by the owner of the tablespace should be moved or dropped.

Phase 7 ~ Application Development

Action 7.10.2

SEVERITY LEVEL: 2
O/S VERSION: All
ORACLE VERSIONS: All

Identify the owner or owners of all of the objects / tables that make up the application. Ensure that one owner owns all objects, and if any objects are not owned, move them to the application "schema" owner. As part of this test, note whether any objects are owned by any privileged users. If they are, as a minimum move these objects to a non privileged user.

Note: This is not just about the system tablespace. Any tablespace could cause a Dos attack. If you have 'autoextend' files, then you could force the file size beyond Oracle's inherent limit on many platforms and crash the system. If you do not, then any application may stop because space has been robbed quite deliberately. You need a strategy for prediction and detection, which includes a pre-emptive block on runaway space usage: e.g. tablespace quotas, maxextents, autoextend with strict limits.

Step 7.11 Resource Limits

PROBLEM: *While not strictly a security issue, resources in the database, if incorrectly allocated or used, can cause problems.*

Action 7.11.1

SEVERITY LEVEL: 2
O/S VERSION: All
ORACLE VERSIONS: All

Check the values shown in the view v_$resource_limit and ensure that the database is not approaching the limits for the applications being used.

Increase any resources as necessary, or investigate which users are causing resources to be used to the limit. This is a potential indicator of Dos activity.

If a database cannot be temporarily stopped, or if there is a need to alter resource limits or they must be altered temporarily, it is possible to turn on or off the enforcement of resource limitation using the SQL command ALTER SYSTEM. After an instance is started, an ALTER SYSTEM command overrides the value set by the RESOURCE_LIMIT parameter. To enable resource limits for a database issue the following SQL:

```
ALTER SYSTEM
    SET RESOURCE_LIMIT = TRUE;
```

If a database can be shut down, resource limits can be turned on or off by the RESOURCE_LIMIT parameter in the init.ora file. Valid values for the parameter are TRUE (enables enforcement) and FALSE; by default, this parameter's value is set to FALSE.

Note: If resource limits are not in place, an ad hoc query with a cross-product or PL/SQL with an infinite loop can cause the database to hang.

Phase 7 ~ Application Development

Step 7.12 — Application Authentication

PROBLEM: *Spending time writing authentication code for applications is sometimes a futile exercise. As often as not, the application authentication is weak and easy to bypass.*

Action 7.12.1

SEVERITY LEVEL: 1
O/S VERSION: All
ORACLE VERSIONS: All

It is important when writing applications not to duplicate the Oracle authentication, and then effectively ignore Oracle's authentication. If you do so, this usually means it is possible to bypass your authentication easily by using another account and to steal what you need.

See also *Action 2.1.5* describing proxy authentication.

New audit commands have been added to allow *proxy* connections to be audited. The new commands have the syntax:

```
AUDIT <OPERATION> BY <PROXY>,<PROXY> .. ON BEHALF OF <CLIENT>,<CLIENT>..;
```

Or

```
AUDIT <OPERATION> BY <PROXY>, <PROXY> ON BEHALF OF ANY;
```

If connections by one user on behalf of another user are audited, then only the proxy connections are audited. If each of the users connects in their own right, then this would not show in the audit trail. These connects can be audited of course as well. If the *proxy* authentication is used, it is possible in n-tier environments to now audit the "real" users.

> **Note:** A certain well-known third-party application that uses Oracle as its database allows users to login with a known external user, then the more privileged database account name and password are read from the application's own user table. These are then used to login. The password is encrypted in this case but with a reversible text compression tool! This leaves a glaring hole that can be used to circumvent this third-party applications security.

Action 7.12.2

SEVERITY LEVEL: 2
O/S VERSION: All
ORACLE VERSIONS: All

In applications that use one login, i.e., application authentication, it is not uncommon for people to write their own authentication functions. These basically look something like this.

```
SELECT *
FROM app_users
WHERE username='foo' AND password='bar'.
```

If the SQL statement above returns a row, then the user has performed a successful login. This means that the application must already be connected to the database to validate the login of users. This in turn means that all users use the same Oracle login, which is discussed earlier in this guide, and is always a bad solution.

Phase 7 ~ Application Development

Step 7.13 — Application Access

PROBLEM: *Experience has shown that in many organizations, access to a database is achieved using the schema owner. This is obviously very dangerous since all application schema objects are then visible. Data can be accessed easily, or worse, altered. Making an application schema owner also a DBA provides potential for damage or an attack.*

Action 7.13.1

SEVERITY LEVEL: 2
O/S VERSION: All
ORACLE VERSIONS: All

Audit the users used to administer the database, and if the schema owner is being used for admin tasks, stop administrators from using it. Either lock the account and only allow access to it when product releases are done, or in earlier versions of Oracle, use the undocumented values command in alter user to set the password to an unusable one.

Note: If the users know the username and password of the application schema owner, what is to stop them from connecting to that schema via sqlplus, or ODBC? Not to mention the OEM console.

Action 7.13.2

SEVERITY LEVEL: 2
O/S VERSION: All
ORACLE VERSIONS: All

Select the dictionary view dba_role_privs to see if the application schema owner has the privilege DBA. See example below

```
SQL> sho user
USER is "SYS"
SQL> select grantee
  2  from dba_role_privs
  3  where granted_role='DBA';

GRANTEE
------------------------------
CTXSYS
PETE
SYS
SYSTEM

SQL>
```

This example shows that the schema owner pete is a DBA. If the schema owner is a DBA, then revoke this privilege.

Phase 7 ~ Application Development

Action 7.13.3

SEVERITY LEVEL: 2
O/S VERSION: All
ORACLE VERSIONS: All

Identify the schema owner and check if the account is locked. This can be done as follows in Oracle 8 and above:

```
SQL> alter user pete account lock;
User altered.
SQL> select username,account_status
  2    from dba_users
  3    where username='PETE';

USERNAME                       ACCOUNT_STATUS
------------------------------ ------------------------------
PETE                           LOCKED

SQL>
```

Setting an impossible password can also lock an account.

Step 7.14 Public Synonyms

PROBLEM: *While not a major security issue, public synonyms provide easy access to objects owned by other users. Public synonyms allow an attacker to access objects by name without fully qualifying the name.*

Action 7.14.1

SEVERITY LEVEL: 5
O/S VERSION: All
ORACLE VERSIONS: All

Consider ensuring only public synonyms that exist only for objects that need them and no more.

An export of a schema will not include public synonyms since they are not in a schema and have to be exported with a full export. There is no easy way to export them.

The existence of a PUBLIC SYNONYM, by itself, doesn't allow access, unless the prospective accessor has been GRANTED a privilege.

Phase 7 ~ Application Development

Step 7.15 Application Security

PROBLEM: *Applications can cause many security issues just by being there. Passwords and user-names hard-coded in an application's source code can be seen easily with string utilities. The language used to write an application should be carefully considered. Some of the more modern languages can more easily be de-compiled allowing secrets of the application's function to be revealed.*

Applications that alter the structure of the database schema are potentially dangerous since an attacker could cause elements of the database to be destroyed or altered to their advantage.

Action 7.15.1

SEVERITY LEVEL: 2
O/S VERSION: All
ORACLE VERSIONS: All

Do not hard code usernames and passwords in application source code. Develop a common best practice for developers that forbids this type of action. This should include DBA shell and SQL scripts as well as 3GL and 4GL application source code.

One solution is to get a senior developer or project manager to sign a document that states that no hard coded passwords exist in the applications code. Failure to sign the document would stop the application code being taken into production.

Action 7.15.2

SEVERITY LEVEL: 2
O/S VERSION: All
ORACLE VERSIONS: 8 & Above

Consider not using Java in applications, since it is easier to de-compile or reverse engineer than say 'C'. This is actually debatable since decompilers are available for both languages, but better ones are available for Java.

Using IDA*Pro, for instance, a password is just as visible in C or Java.

If obfuscation is available, then it should be used to protect the Java code.

Phase 7 ~ Application Development

Action 7.15.3

SEVERITY LEVEL: 2
O/S VERSION: All
ORACLE VERSIONS: All

If applications are altering the database schema Data Definition Language (DDL), then consider not allowing them to do so.

There are dangers with sloppy precedence assumptions such as

A = 'xxx' OR B < max_num AND B > min_num.

There are dangers with user-supplied DML, if a user supplies DML not just content. For example, "anyanswer' OR 1=1 '" (See BUGTRAQ at the following URL for lots more examples: http://www.securityfocus.com/bugtraq).

It is common practice for people writing web based applications to store passwords and usernames for the databases in clear text in files on the server. This practice should be avoided, and if not the file should be locked down tight.

One possibility would be to supply a list of demands to a third party software supplier that includes the following:
- Improve security of these applications with VPD, private synonyms
- Demand some things from your software-maker:
  - security
  - rights
  - user management
  - application audits
  - ...

In this context there is also a problem with the single-instance-concept. Unsecured software can threaten the whole single instance (server). An attacker will choose the weakest application to break into the system, e.g., via SQL Injection, too many rights, brute force attack.

Possible Solution:
Instead of a single (unsecured) instance, split this instance into three different security instances and zones (low, medium, high).

High: support LDAP-server for authentication, data encryption ...

Medium: secure user management (brute-force attack, account-lock, complex passwords)

Low: own user management, no special security, grant to public...

Phase 7 ~ Application Development

Step 7.16 — Batch Processes

PROBLEM: *Batch processes are necessary with a lot of applications. Quite often the user assigned to run batch processes is not defined or is a single, very powerful user, since the code developers may have assumed higher privileges than necessary for the application to run. Even worse is the fact that this user may not be too strictly maintained, so the password could be well known or it could be hard-coded in scripts or documents.*

Action 7.16.1

SEVERITY LEVEL: 1
O/S VERSION: All
ORACLE VERSIONS: All

Batch processes should ideally access the database through one account designed specifically for that purpose.

> **Note:** There are tools available to encrypt passwords for the use in scripts/batch-files.

Action 7.16.2

SEVERITY LEVEL: 1
O/S VERSION: All
ORACLE VERSIONS: All

Do not use external accounts for batch processes. On the surface, they seem like a good choice, but allow a simple way to access your database.

Action 7.16.3

SEVERITY LEVEL: 1
O/S VERSION: All
ORACLE VERSIONS: All

If a scheduler is used, the getting and use of a password should be secure. Passwords should ideally **not** be a command line parameter, and **not** an environment parameter.

Phase 7 ~ Application Development

Action 7.16.4

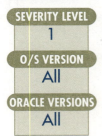

Use a time based approach to enabling the account that can access batch processes, and conversely disable all other accounts while batch processes run. Having only one account available during the night makes it harder for an attacker to gain access, and also makes attempts to access the database easier to spot.

Step 7.17 — Restrict Access to SQL*Plus

PROBLEM: *The standard interface tool provided with an Oracle database is SQL* Plus. Up to Version 8.1.7, Server Manager is also provided. In Oracle 9i, SQL* Plus provides all of the facilities of the desupported Server Manager. SQL* Plus is a very powerful tool that allows a user to pass any SQL to the database they wish, according to their level of permission. Some enterprising individual in an organization might also load this tool on a client.*

Action 7.17.1

Use the product_user_profile table to restrict access to SQL*Plus and its facilities. This is controlled by inserting records into the table PRODUCT_USER_PROFILE to control users access to SQL*Plus, whether or not they are able to load the software, and it can also be used to restrict access to DDL and other commands within SQL*Plus.

VPD can be used more effectively to stop access to data itself in the database.

For a good document on how to restrict tools used, see:
DocID 19042517.6 *How to Set Oracle Privileges Based on Tool Used*.

It should be noted that ODBC does not use product_user_profile. It is possible, however, to restrict SQL*Plus, SQL and some PL/SQL commands using this functionality. A sample entry into this table is shown next to demonstrate how to restrict the HOST command from SQL*plus users:

```
SQL> connect system/manager
Connected.
SQL> @?/sqlplus/admin/pupbld.sql

....
```

Phase 7 ~ Application Development

```
SQL> insert into product_user_profile (product,userid,attribute,scope,
  2  numeric_value,char_value,date_value,long_value)
  3  values ('SQL*Plus','PETE','HOST',NULL,NULL,'DISABLED',NULL,NULL);

1 row created.

SQL> commit;

Commit complete.

SQL> connect pete/pete
Connected.
SQL> !ls
SP2-0544: invalid command: ! (HOST)
SQL> host ls
SP2-0544: invalid command: host
SQL>
```

SQL*Plus uses the Unix environment variable $SHELL to decide what to run when *!* or *host* is used to access the shell. Set this variable to *cat* or *echo* for extra safety.

Action 7.17.2

SEVERITY LEVEL 3
O/S VERSION All
ORACLE VERSIONS All

Check the permissions of the binaries for *svrmgrl* and *SQL*Plus* on the server, and ensure that their use is restricted to the owner of the Oracle software. Check as follows:

```
$ ls -al $ORACLE_HOME/bin/sqlplus*
-rwxr-x--x    1 oracle    oinstall    466799 Jun 10 20:18 /db001/app/oracle/product/bin/sqlplus
-rwxr-xr-x    1 oracle    oinstall    466843 Mar 21  2000 /db001/app/oracle/product/bin/sqlplusO
$ ls -al $ORACLE_HOME/bin/svrmgrl*
-rwxr-x--x    1 oracle    oinstall    896110 Jun 10 20:19 /db001/app/oracle/product/bin/svrmgrl
-rwxr-xr-x    1 oracle    oinstall    896158 Mar 30  2000 /db001/app/oracle/product/bin/svrmgrlO
```

If host based access to the database with these tools is not required, then set the permissions of these binaries to "000" with the *chmod* command as follows:

```
$ chmod 000 $ORACLE_HOME/bin/sqlplus*
$ chmod 000 $ORACLE_HOME/bin/svrmgrl*
```

Note that from Oracle 9i, Server Manager is no longer available.

Phase 7 ~ Application Development

Step 7.18 — Encryption of Critical Data

PROBLEM: *Even if the database and all the applications are secure, and all of the roles and users are correctly designed, all or most of an organization's data is still readable by DBA's. It is very difficult to design roles, applications and users that will not have to change over time to protect critical data. You may also not wish certain data to be seen by your administration staff. Encryption could be the solution.*

Action 7.18.1

SEVERITY LEVEL: 2
O/S VERSION: All
ORACLE VERSIONS: All

Identify critical application data and encrypt it. This can be done using the Oracle supplied package DBMS_OBFUSCATION_TOOLKIT. This package has problems with not having a good spread of encryption options and doesn't support public key encryption (Note: PKI would not be used to encrypt large amounts of data since it suffers from being slow, but for extra security of small amounts of critical data, it could be considered).

It also cannot support multiple encryptions of the same data due to U.S. law restrictions; a header is prepended to the data to prevent this. There is always the main problem of hiding the key effectively from the DBA and users and developers. The key can be embedded in applications or stored encrypted in the database somewhere, but this should be avoided since it leads to the "spiral of death", where the key to encrypt the key needs to be stored and so on.

This key can be a password or even a private key stored on the client. When a user connects to the database, he passes his credentials, which unlock (decrypt) a private key. This is then used to decrypt symmetrical keys used to decrypt the actual data in the tables. It is important not to lose the key.

For a very good white paper on this, see:

http://www.appsecinc.com/presentations/Encryption_of_Data_at_Rest.pdf

Encryption is the only way to prevent a DBA from reading your data. Such prevention is necessary in highly secure applications. Two examples are military secrets and medical records.

The key is to only encrypt critical data. Attempting to encrypt all data could cause performance and maintenance issues.

Another option would be to audit the key tables thoroughly and track what happens to them. This would not prevent the DBA from viewing the data, but you would know he had viewed it.

Third-party solutions exist to encrypt data. Look at http://www.appsecinc.com for their product DbEncrypt. Protegrity also offer products to do this at http://www.protegrity.com/The_Secure.Data_Suite.html.

> **Note:** Encryption is important, but there are also ways to get around this. Even encrypted data will be sorted very often. To sort data, the data must be unencrypted. If you now set the sort_area_size=0 (no problem for a DBA), the unencrypted data will be swapped to disk. Now, you could take the tablespace offline and use a block editor to view the unencrypted data.
>
> This obviously depends on the implementation of encryption. Preventing this level of abuse would require more detailed investigation.

ORACLE SECURITY Step-by-Step

Phase 7 ~ Application Development

Step 7.19 — Generated Applications

PROBLEM: *Applications generated with tools can introduce serious security weaknesses. Quite often, users can share the same account to access the database or the application. Usernames and passwords are also often stored in plain text. Generated applications often generate template code that, if susceptible to any weakness reported in security forums, means that you are seriously susceptible and need to take immediate action.*

Action 7.19.1

SEVERITY LEVEL: 2
O/S VERSION: All
ORACLE VERSIONS: All

Investigate any applications that have been generated with tools — these generally introduce serious security weaknesses. For example, users may share an account. The password and usernames could be stored in plain text in the applications or in text files. Certain sections of code or actions can be predicted from knowledge of the tool. Tools could easily add a security issue to many places within an application rather than in one place from a hand coded application. A known security issue with the generator tool immediately puts your whole business in danger.

Beware of the security limits that generated code puts on an organization and understand the issues. Monitor security forums regularly for security violations with "your" tool.

Action 7.19.2

SEVERITY LEVEL: 2
O/S VERSION: All
ORACLE VERSIONS: All

Programs are using public libraries: Many software developers (even Microsoft) use public libraries (e.g. zlib-library) for their programs. If there is a bug in such a library, you must replace the DLL/LIB, re-link the programs or get a patched version of the program.

Check security forums for violations / issues with any public libraries "your" application uses.

Phase 7 ~ Application Development

Step 7.20 — Change Control Management

PROBLEM: *If code management techniques are not used, then incorrect code can be introduced to production, and Trojan horses could be buried somewhere into the source.*

Action 7.20.1

SEVERITY LEVEL: 2
O/S VERSION: All
ORACLE VERSIONS: All

Implement and record change control procedures for development and release to production.

Step 7.21 — Advanced Queues

PROBLEM: *If advanced Queue processes are used, it is seen as a benefit that the queuing process does not know the reader of the queue and vice versa. This potentially leaves the database open to processing anything an attacker manages to place in a queue.*

Action 7.21.1

SEVERITY LEVEL: 2
O/S VERSION: All
ORACLE VERSIONS: All

If Advanced Queues are used, it is often seen as a benefit that the enqueue processes do not need to know the dequeue processes. On the other hand, we need to ensure that the enqueue processes are dealing with data from trusted sources. The same argument applies to the dequeue processes.

Protect the queues by not granting access to any users on Advanced Queues. Also revoke unnecessary privileges from the Advanced Queue packages from PUBLIC.

Some files with the extension .q can be seen in the $ORACLE_HOME directories in the *dbsnmp* area. These files should be protected from anyone attempting to alter them and subvert the queue process.

Phase 7 ~ Application Development

Step 7.22 — Tools

PROBLEM: *Many developers use third-party and Oracle tools to manage the database. A lot of these tools store passwords locally for ease of use, but inevitably they use weak encryption themselves, leaving the databases open to attack.*

Action 7.22.1

SEVERITY LEVEL: 2
O/S VERSION: All
ORACLE VERSIONS: All

It is often easier to crack a developer's computer shares and read the unencrypted passwords from there, instead of hacking a well-secured DB-Server.

Every Oracle-Developer/DBA/Security-Officer must ask questions about tools before using them. Where and how are passwords stored? Are they encrypted and how? Is it possible to copy the encrypted password and use these encrypted to connect to a database (Roaming-Feature)

Check for weak encryption: Create user passwords like 'AAAAAAAAAAAAAAAAAAAA'. Are there any or identical strings? If yes, then it is weak encryption.

Oracle provides a tool called BBED, the block editor. This tool has a very weak protection system. This tool can be used to alter database files without the database being opened.

Delete the file bbed.exe from Windows distributions. This file is only distributed on Windows and 8.1.5 and above.

Step 7.23 — Reporting Facilities Have a Different Access Model to Interactive Interfaces

PROBLEM: *When an application implements a reporting tool that has a different interface and authentication than the main application, potentially there is an easier way into an application for an attacker.*

Action 7.23.1

SEVERITY LEVEL: 2
O/S VERSION: All
ORACLE VERSIONS: All

Review the authentication mechanisms used by differing interfaces to an application and ensure that no tool offers an easy access to the database.

Phase 7 ~ Application Development

Step 7.24 — Introduction of Backdoors, Viruses, and Malignant Code by Developers

PROBLEM: *In organizations where there are weak controls, developers can introduce extra code. This could remain dormant for a period before the payload is executed.*

Action 7.24.1

SEVERITY LEVEL: 2
O/S VERSION: All
ORACLE VERSIONS: All

A number of solutions spring to mind: source control, change management, release control. Checksumming of the source code using an algorithm such as MD5 could be done since algorithms such as CRC are less secure. Public domain programs exist to modify files and adjust the CRC checksum. An alternative is to use SHA-1 instead. This is algorithm is thought to be more secure — in fact, the US government does not allow its use so maybe it is. Tools such as *Tripwire* can be used.

In Oracle 8.1.6, the dbms_obfuscation_toolkit package was added to provide database encryption. In Oracle 8.1.7, this was enhanced to include MD5 hashing. This functionality can be used to MD5 checksum the PL/SQL and Java code stored in clear text in the database or even the hashed PL/SQL that has been wrapped. In Tom Kyte's book, *Expert One-on-One Oracle*, he gives a good example of using the package dbms_obfuscation_toolkit to write some functions to MD5 checksum strings. The PL/SQL or Java code can be read from sys.source$ and checksummed with these routines.

> **Note:** A cyclic redundancy check can be described simply as a check sum of the source code. Each source code module is summed and the number generated is stored. This can then be used for comparison purposes later. A CRC is actually not a simple summing of the code, but the application of a CRC algorithm to the code.

Step 7.25 — iSQL*Plus

PROBLEM: *If the Oracle HTTP Server is started by a user who is a member of the OSDBA or OSOPER groups on Unix, or who is a member of the ORA_DBA, ORA_OPER, ORA_SID_DBA, or ORA_SID_OPER groups on Windows, the iSQL*Plus DBA URL is automatically authenticated for Oracle9i by the operating system.*

Information
Since 9i (or beta 8.1.7), there has been a web version of *SQL*Plus* called iSQL*Plus. Using a web browser, a user can connect to an Oracle database and write queries or administer the database using SQL.

Action 7.25.1

SEVERITY LEVEL: 1
O/S VERSION: All
ORACLE VERSIONS: 9i & higher

To avoid the DBA URL being automatically authenticated, start the Oracle HTTP Server (OHS) as an operating system user who is not a member of the OSDBA or OSOPER groups on Unix, or who is not a member of ORA_DBA, ORA_<sid>_DBA, ORA_OPER or ORA_<sid>_OPER on Windows.

Starting the Oracle HTTP Server as a user who is not in these groups will stop operating system authentication that allows privileged connections "as sysdba" and "as sysoper". Using the privileges field in the login screen to access as SYSDBA or SYSOPER will still work using the OHS authentication file.

> **Note:** Unless iSQL*Plus is configured correctly, all users who use it will automatically be authenticated.

Phase 7 ~ Application Development

Action 7.25.2

SEVERITY LEVEL: 3
O/S VERSION: All
ORACLE VERSIONS: 9i & higher

Two considerations for security and authentication need to be made when using iSQL*Plus:
- The HTTP protocol connection between the Oracle HTTP Server and the browser.
- The Oracle networking connection between the iSQL*Plus module in the Oracle HTTP Server and the Oracle 9i database.

Security between the OHS and the browser is provided by HTTPS. Secure listener connections are provided using an encryption mechanism via the Secure Sockets layer (SSL). Installing the *mod_ssl* module when installing the OHS will provide this functionality. See *The Oracle Advanced Security Administrators Guide* for details.

Securing the listener is accomplished by using the same techniques as described in *Phase 5*. For further information on Oracle Net connection security, see *The Oracle Net Services Administrator's Guide* and *The Oracle Advanced Security Administrator's Guide*.

Action 7.25.3

SEVERITY LEVEL: 2
O/S VERSION: All
ORACLE VERSIONS: 9i & higher

Limiting users who can access iSQL*Plus can be done using the following techniques. Authentication on the OHS is required for AS SYSDBA and AS SYSOPER connections, but not for normal user connections by default. Authentication should be added for normal user connections. This can be done as follows:

Edit the *isqlplus.conf* file. Change the lines:

```
<Location /isqlplus>
SetHandler iplus-handler
Order deny, allow
Allow from all
</Location>
```

To

```
<Location /isqlplus>
SetHandler iplus-handler
Order deny, allow
AuthType Basic
AuthName 'iSQL*Plus'
AuthUserFile %ORACLE_HOME%\sqlplus\admin\iplus.pw
Require valid-user
</Location>
```

The file *iplus.pw* is the file that would include the OHS authentication usernames and passwords for user connections. Now, when a user connects, they are required to supply their Oracle database username and password as well as Oracle HTTP Server username and password.

Phase 7 ~ Application Development

Action 7.25.4

SEVERITY LEVEL: 2
O/S VERSION: All
ORACLE VERSIONS: 9i & higher

The default authentication file for connections is created at installation time with no entries at %ORACLE_HOME%\sqlplus\admin\iplusdba.pw. To connect with SYSDBA or SYSOPER privileges, the username and password need to be added to this file. This username and password are independent of the database username and password. Usernames and passwords for user connections are added to the separate file described in *Action 7.25.3* above.

Note: Remember password crackers are available for HTTP password files

Users are added for Oracle HTTP Server authentication by using the *htpasswd* utility. To add users for SYSDBA or SYSOPER connections do:

```
htpasswd %ORACLE_HOME%\sqlplus\admin\iplusdba.pw username
```

For user connections assuming the password file is called *iplus.pw* do:

```
htpasswd %ORACLE_HOME%\sqlplus\admin\iplus.pw username
```

In both cases the user is prompted to supply a password.

Action 7.25.5

SEVERITY LEVEL: 3
O/S VERSION: All
ORACLE VERSIONS: 9i & higher

The Product User Profile functionality available for normal client server installations is also available on a user / database basis for this tool.

Phase 7 ~ Application Development

Action 7.25.6

SEVERITY LEVEL: 2
O/S VERSION: All
ORACLE VERSIONS: 9i & higher

The *tnsnames.ora* file of the Oracle 9i database is a problem for access with iSQL*Plus. It is possible by default to access every database in the *tnsnames.ora* file of the 9i database.

Enable restricted database access. When enabled, a drop down list of available databases is displayed in place of the connection identifier field in the login screen. The configuration file *isqlplus.conf* can be modified to restrict databases accessed. The syntax of the line to change is:

```
FastCgiServer ... -initial-env "iSQLPlusConnectIdList=SID1, SID2,..."
```

Where SID1, SID2 is a comma-separated list of Oracle Network connection identifiers, for example:

```
FastCgiServer ... -initial-env "iSQLPlusConnectIdList=DEV2, TEST1, PROD3"
```

Note the placing of the quotes.

Action 7.25.7

SEVERITY LEVEL: 1
O/S VERSION: All
ORACLE VERSIONS: 9i & higher

Disable iSQL*Plus if it is not needed. On a production server, this tool should not be enabled. To disable iSQL*Plus, do the following:

- Stop the Oracle HTTP Server.
- Find the *oracle_apache.conf* file. This should be in %ORACLE_HOME%/Apache/Apache/conf for Windows and $ORACLE_HOME/Apache/Apache/conf for Unix.
- Comment out the line, including *isqlplus.conf* by adding a comment character (#). Example for Unix:

  ```
  # include "ORACLE_HOME/sqlplus/admin/isqlplus.conf"
  ```

  Where ORACLE_HOME is the path of the Oracle home directory.
- Save the file and restart the Oracle HTTP Server. *iSQL*Plus* should not be available.

Phase 7 ~ Application Development

Step 7.26 Oracle Features

SEVERITY LEVEL: 2
O/S VERSION: All
ORACLE VERSIONS: All

Feature	Description	How to Deactivate	Dependencies	Version	Default Status
Internet File System	DB-Filesystem with many APIs				Disabled
Oracle Oracle ConText (formally Intermedia)					Disabled
Oracle Text	Indexing of Text-Files		needs extproc(< 8.1.6, 9.0.1)		Enabled
Oracle XML-DB		init.ora-entry		9i Rel2	Enabled
Oracle Apache Listener		stop service *Apache*		8i, 9i, iAS	Enabled
Ultrasearch	Search Engine for Text and database		needs Oracle Text	8i, 9i, iAS	Disabled
Java functionality in the database		DocID 202914.1 How to cleanup the JVM in 9.0.1 DocID 159801.1 Full JVM Removal 8.1.7 DocID 126029.1 How to remove Jserver(JVM) in 8.1.5 and 8.1.6 of rdbms DocID 171658.1 How to Install and Uninstall the XDK for Java & PL/SQL		8i, 9i	Enabled
Extproc	calling external dlls/libs	delete extproc in tnsnames.ora		8i, 9i, iAS	Enabled
Extproc	calling external dlls/libs	delete extproc in tnsnames.ora		iAS	Enabled
Mod_fastcgi		remove entry Addmodule from httpd.conf			Enabled
Mod_plsql		remove entry Addmodule from httpd.conf			Enabled
Mod_ose		remove entry from oracle_apache.conf			Enabled
Xml		remove entry from oracle_apache.conf			Disabled
portal30		remove entry from oracle_apache.conf	need mod_plsql		Enabled
Ojsp		remove entry from oracle_apache.conf			Disabled
Oem		remove entry from oracle_apache.conf			Disabled

Step 7.27 — Debuggers

PROBLEM: If an attacker has access to one of the debugging interfaces within the database engine itself, then potentially a PL/SQL package, for instance, could be run and changes made that could lead to reading data that should not be read.

Action 7.27.1

SEVERITY LEVEL: 2
O/S VERSION: All
ORACLE VERSIONS: All

There are a number of debugging options available within Oracle:

- PL/SQL: offers the DBMS_DEBUG interface to the probe debugger.
- Orabdebug: This is the undocumented interface to the Oracle kernel debugger. This product was previously available as *oradbx* and is now built into *Server manager* and also *SQL*Plus* in later versions.
- sun.tools.debug.Agent can also be used for debugging.
- JDeveloper can be used to debug Java applications. JDeveloper utilizes JServers debugging facilities. It is possible to successfully debug an object loaded into the database with JDeveloper debugger.
- It is possible to use a pre-published Debug Agent object for debugging CORBA objects executing on a server.
- It is possible to perform standalone ORB debugging using one machine and ORB tracing by placing the client and server in one address space in one process.
- Oracle tracing. The output on System.out.println() goes to the screen for a client, but in Oracle8 and higher ORB, it goes to the server. The output is written to a trace file in the *bdump* directory under $ORACLE_HOME.
- The *printback* example in demo/examples/corba/basic/printback shows how to redirect the output on System.out.println().

Note: Oracle is working on a new PL/SQL debugging interface that is not public yet. Currently only developers of debuggers are being provided with its features. It should be part of JDeveloper in 9iR2

Protecting against users or attackers using a debugger or trace mechanisms on a production database server can be difficult with so many options available.

Various freeware and commercial PL/SQL debuggers are available. These include:

- http://pluto.dbnet.com.au/piper
- http://www.globecom.se/tora

Some simple guidelines can be followed:

- Check access to dbms_debug.
- Check access to dbms_java both for the debugger access and also for the debug agent.
- Check access to debug agents, remove access to bin/debugproxy and also check Java code in production for oracle.aurora.debug.DebugAgent to stop the agent being started.
- Check trace access.

Developers will insist debuggers are needed in production, test environments should be used to replicate errors, and debuggers can allow better enumeration of errors for a hacker and can allow access in some cases.

Step 7.28 — Divulging Database Information

PROBLEM: *Securing the database is one thing, but what if an organization published enough details on the Internet to allow an attacker to access their systems.*

Action 7.28.1

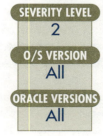

SEVERITY LEVEL: 2
O/S VERSION: All
ORACLE VERSIONS: All

A simple google search for information about the organization's production, development and test databases can sometime reveal too much. A simple check can show the following types of information:

- Oracle Sid – Production and non production
- Upgrade schedules (time of vulnerability)
- Data standards
- Reporting Information
- Data warehouse
- Oracle versions, Node names, host names, IP addresses and even file names on Unix hosts with sensitive information and read / write privileges.

All Oracle information that needs to be published for an audience should be kept on the Intranet, and be protected by a web login that includes authentication and authorization.

Employees with access to any of the above information or more should be made aware of the risks of casually posting it on the internet, in newsgroups, and mailing lists and any other media.

Ideally, none of this type of information should be made public, and if possible, should not be made available across the company. If it is not known throughout the company, it cannot be posted to a website or newsgroup.

PHASE 8
Application Servers and the Middle Tier

Information: This section is not intended to be an exhaustive summary of the application server security issues. The issues listed are a primer to this subject. Security for the application server is a newer area than security of the database server itself, which suggests that this section will change and grow rapidly. The tips and actions presented here are those that our reviewers have found the most effective in their use of Oracle 9iAS so far.

Step 8.1 Oracle Portal

PROBLEM: *Oracle Portal is administered through a web interface. By default this interface is accessible to anyone who knows the URL.*

Action 8.1.1

SEVERITY LEVEL: 2
O/S VERSION: All
ORACLE VERSIONS: 9iAS

Default URL Data Access Descriptor (DAD) admin page has a default URL that is accessible to anyone, and which makes it possible for people to alter, remove or add DADs. This URL has the form http://<hostname>:<portno>/pls/portal30_sso to edit user's account details and passwords. If possible, restrict user's logins to "end user" and not "full administrator". If the PORATL30 database user has been changed, then the password for the PORTAL30 DAD also needs to be changed. DAD information can be accessed by going to http://<hostname>:<portno>/pls/portal30/admin_/dadentries.htm . These two URL's need to have access to them restricted so that normal users cannot alter DAD security or portal configurations. Change the admin path in $ORACLE_HOME/Apache/modplsqlcfg/wdbsvr.env, and set a password if it is not set.

See Metalink note 108661.1 for details on restrictions. Another option is to create a DAD with a user that must have to log into the DAD security page.

Note: For Oracle application server 1.0.2.2.0 on Windows 2000, the Oracle Portal SSO kicks in automatically, restricting access to the DAD login page.

Phase 8 ~ Application Servers and the Middle Tier

Action 8.1.2

SEVERITY LEVEL: 1
O/S VERSION: All
ORACLE VERSIONS: 9iAS

Here is some useful information about *mod_plsql* (used in Portal). Most people think that their passwords are encrypted in the DAD. The DAD's are located in the file $ORACLE_HOME/iSuites/Apache/mod_plsql/cfg/wdbsvr.env file. This file contains the DAD usernames and passwords and the connect string needed to access the database. In earlier versions, these passwords were in clear text. In later versions, they are not encrypted. They are only BASE64 encoded with a leading "!". If the "!" is removed, unencrypted passwords can be used. More information can be found in Metalink note:

Doc ID: 182969.1 "How to Unencrypt the Portal Password in Wdbsvr.app".

Because the portal passwords are encoded and not encrypted the file, *wdbsvr.app* should be protected with 0700 permissions, not 0744 as the default installation. If other users can read the file and know the passwords are only encoded, then the passwords can be read. Access to "others" should be denied.

Note: If the HTTP server runs under a different account, then a group needs to be created and assigned to the above file and the permissions need to be 770 on Unix.

Action 8.1.3

SEVERITY LEVEL: 1
O/S VERSION: All
ORACLE VERSIONS: 9iAS

The Metalink note above also explains that the portal passwords are also visible in the table WWSEC_PERSON$. Access to this table should be revoked from all users except from the portal user and SYS.

Action 8.1.4

SEVERITY LEVEL: 2
O/S VERSION: All
ORACLE VERSIONS: 9iAS

By default, access to the mod_plsql Gateway administration URL

http://<hostname>:<port>/pls/admin /gateway.htm

is not protected. To prevent normal users from changing the configuration, some kind of authentication/protection should be set. See Note: 108661.1 on Metalink for details.

Note: See Action 1.9.2 for details of a new free tool from Oracle for monitoring all Oracle log files including 9iAS logs.

Phase 8 ~ Application Servers and the Middle Tier

Action 8.1.5

SEVERITY LEVEL 1
O/S VERSION All
ORACLE VERSIONS 9iAS

Remove all the example programs. Some programs allow dynamic SQL access to the database server.

Action 8.1.6

SEVERITY LEVEL 1
O/S VERSION All
ORACLE VERSIONS 9iAS

Revoke the DBA privilege from the portal30 accounts used as DAD accounts and admin accounts.

Action 8.1.7

SEVERITY LEVEL 1
O/S VERSION All
ORACLE VERSIONS 9iAS

Revoke public access from the PL/SQL package OWA_UTIL if it is installed. This package can be used from the web to show PL/SQL source and also to call arbitrary SQL. This package, along with any DBMS%, UTL% or any other packages, should be restricted by adding an entry to the exclusion list in the *wdbsvr.env* file.

You can also prevent authorization bypass by either ensuring that an on-line database application is in another schema to say the registration schema; or by adding packages to the exclusion list above for the on-line application. This will prevent users from substituting an on-line package in the DAD for the registration screen.

Also exclude the htp packages since they allow cross-site scripting attacks to take place because these packages allow generation of HTML tags.

Note: Some of the ideas in this section were taken from an excellent paper on 9iAS security by David Litchfield, which can be found at http://www.nextgenss.com/papers/hpoas.pdf.

Phase 8 ~ Application Servers and the Middle Tier

Step 8.2 Oracle Wireless Portal

PROBLEM: *Oracle wireless portal is created by default when installing Portal. This application has a username and password that should be secured. Wireless access is not renowned for its security.*

Action 8.2.1

Oracle Wireless Portal is created by default. During installation, a username and password and database SID are required. If this application is not to be used, then set a bogus username and secure password, and point the SID at a non critical database.

Step 8.3 Oracle Web Cache

PROBLEM: *It is possible to access the web cache administrator password in an O/S file where the password is not encrypted by default.*

Action 8.3.1

There are vulnerabilities associated with the Web Cache. The OEM website provided with Oracle Application server 9.0.2 provides an interface (HTML based) that allows the web cache administrator interface in 9iAS to be started. Because the web cache password is not encrypted by default, it is possible to obtain this password.

Since there is no patch available, the following steps to get around this are recommended:

- Edit $ORACLE_HOME/sysman/emd/targets.xml and replace the following line:
  `<property NAME="authpwd" VALUE="administrator"/>`
  With the line:
  `<property NAME="authpwd" VALUE="administrator" ENCRYPTED="FALSE"/>`
- Restart the OEM web site or issue the command:

  Note that restarting or reloading the web site changes the line $ emctl reload above to:
  `<property NAME="authpwd" VALUE="xxxx" ENCRYPTED="TRUE"/>`

Phase 8 ~ Application Servers and the Middle Tier

Action 8.3.2

SEVERITY LEVEL: 1
O/S VERSION: All
ORACLE VERSIONS: 9iAS

Remove world read permissions from the $ORACLE_HOME/webcache/webcache.xml file. This file contains the administrator password encrypted with a very weak encryption scheme.

Step 8.4 — Oracle iCache (Database Cache)

PROBLEM: *When creating the iCache database, the usernames and passwords of the database used as a template are left world readable.*

Action 8.4.1

SEVERITY LEVEL: 1
O/S VERSION: All
ORACLE VERSIONS: 9iAS

The default database created has default passwords set for SYS and SYSTEM. Many of the other issues that appear by default and are described in this guide are seen in this database.

Action 8.4.2

SEVERITY LEVEL: 2
O/S VERSION: All
ORACLE VERSIONS: 9iAS

The export files used to create this database should be deleted since they are created world readable, and left on both the 9iAS server and the server used as the source database. If the files cannot be deleted, then set the permissions to 0700.

Phase 8 ~ Application Servers and the Middle Tier

Step 8.5 — Apache

PROBLEM: *A number of problems with Apache have been well reported in various security forums. The main issue with Oracle's Version is that it tends to remain not as current as the main Apache release.*

Action 8.5.1

SEVERITY LEVEL: 2
O/S VERSION: All
ORACLE VERSIONS: 9iAS

Apache is Apache: it has to be secured. No information on how to do this is supplied in the IAS installation guides or read me files. Consider purchasing the O'Reilly book on Apache. Various Oracle-supplied Apache modules may have vulnerabilities. The versions used are usually not as current as the main Apache distribution.

Action 8.5.2

SEVERITY LEVEL: 3
O/S VERSION: All
ORACLE VERSIONS: 9iAS

While installing Apache on Windows, the system /<password> appear in the installer window's title bar. Be sure to change the system password during installation because of this, and then return it to its known value afterwards.

Action 8.5.3

SEVERITY LEVEL: 3
O/S VERSION: All
ORACLE VERSIONS: 9iAS

If the default HTTP server that comes with 8i, 9i and 9iAS is used, the port numbers for administration default to known values. See the values in the table in *Action 5.11.2*. Change these default values before use.

Phase 8 ~ Application Servers and the Middle Tier

Action 8.5.4

SEVERITY LEVEL: 1
O/S VERSION: All
ORACLE VERSIONS: 9iAS

Update the HTTP Server with patches: 2128936, 2209455, 2154563, 2424256

These will cover just Security Alerts 1, 8, 25, 28, and 36, solving all the problems with both the Server and MOD PL/SQL that are in the default configuration of the HTTP Server that installs with Oracle 8i and 9i.

Action 8.5.5

SEVERITY LEVEL: 4
O/S VERSION: All
ORACLE VERSIONS: 9iAS

Nessus includes some Oracle 9iAS plug-ins for some of the common 9iAS vulnerabilities.

O'Reilly's guide to Apache suggests that Oracle 9iAS should **not** be used on Win32 since it is extremely difficult to secure. Therefore the same should apply to 9iAS.

> **Note:** The default installation of 9iAS up to Oracle 9iR2 on Windows defaults everyone full control and access. This has been fixed by Oracle in 9iR2. The fix is implemented as a "tool" that is run after the universal installer, and is slated to be integrated in Version 9.0.3.
>
> The fix states the following: "members of the Administrator group are granted full control of the Oracle home directory and all subdirectories. Other users have no access to these directories at all." This unfortunately assumes that the Oracle software owner is also a Windows administrator. This solution does not appear to be the best for security!

Action 8.5.6

SEVERITY LEVEL: 1
O/S VERSION: All
ORACLE VERSIONS: 9iAS

Secure the file httpd.conf and the JServ zone properties and web application configuration files.

Phase 8 ~ Application Servers and the Middle Tier

Action 8.5.7

SEVERITY LEVEL: 1
O/S VERSION: All
ORACLE VERSIONS: 9iAS

OJSP: Remove the demo programs in the following JSP files:

```
Ora9ias/j2ee/OC4J_Demos/applications/ojspdemos/osjpdemos-web/basic/simple
Ora9ias/j2ee/OC4J_Demos/applications/ojspdemos/osjpdemos-web/basic/helouser
```

Action 8.5.8

SEVERITY LEVEL: 1
O/S VERSION: All
ORACLE VERSIONS: 9iAS

To protect against an attacker accessing compiled Java class files used for JSP, add the following to the *httpd.conf* file:

<Location/dirname/_pages>
Order deny, allow
Deny from all
</Location>

Where dirname is an alias pointing to a directory, and if the JSP pages are not held in a sub directory of htdocs, then add dirname as above. If they are in the sub directory, then leave out dirname.

If the JSP is using a *globals.jsa* file, then add the following to the *httpd.conf* file to prevent the file from being read.

<Files ~ "^\globals.jsa">
Order deny, allow
Deny from all
</Files>

Action 8.5.9

SEVERITY LEVEL: 1
O/S VERSION: All
ORACLE VERSIONS: 9iAS

Modify the *httpd.conf* file to stop remote anonymous users from accessing many of the monitoring services. Prevent access to the following URL's:

http://oracleserver/dms0
http://oracleserver/dms/DMSDump
http://oracleserver/servlet/DMSDump
http://oracleserver/servlet/Spy
http://oracleserver/soap/servlet/Spy
http://oracleserver/dms/AggreSpy
http://oracleserver/oprocmgr-status
http://oracleserver/oprocmgr-service

Step 8.6 — Oracle Internet File Server (iFS)

PROBLEM: *There is a known default password installed by default.*

Action 8.6.1

SEVERITY LEVEL
1

O/S VERSION
All

ORACLE VERSIONS
9iAS

Change the IFS guest password "welcome" in database AND in file:

```
$ORACLE_HOME\ifs1.1\settings\oracle\ifs\protocols\dav\impl\properties\IfsDavServletParameters.properties
#
# IfsDavServlet properties
#
ifs.dav.servicename=HttpServer
ifs.dav.servicepassword=
#Default=guest
ifs.dav.guestusername=guest
#Default=welcome
ifs.dav.guestpassword=welcome
```

Note: A Windows specific issue with 9iAS are the Windows services that Oracle Installs. These all run under the context of the local system account. It is fairly rare that *any* service really needs to run in this context. It is almost always possible to create a lower privileged account. This would eliminate the possibility of the privilege elevation in some cases, and generally 'harden' an installation from unknown future attacks (or at least limit the severity).

Phase 8 ~ Application Servers and the Middle Tier

Step 8.7 — Oracle Reports Server

PROBLEM: *There are a number of known issues with security of a reports server after a default installation.*

Action 8.7.1

SEVERITY LEVEL: 1
O/S VERSION: All
ORACLE VERSIONS: 9iAS

To secure Oracle reports server:

1. Start your reports service as a separate user.
2. Protect your *repserver.ora-file*. It contains (under 6i) the unencrypted schema password i.e.:
   `(REPOSITORYCONN=scott/tiger@oracl)`.
   With Reports 9i, this password will be encrypted after the first start of the reports service.
3. Upgrade to Developer Patch set 10. If you are using the Reports-Server-Queue, the password is stored unencrypted in table *rw_server_queue* (Fixed in Patch set 10, 6.0.8.19).
4. For better Security (User Management with cookies), use Oracle Portal (see Metalink for more information).
5. Set Environment-Variable/Registry REPORTS60_CGINODIAG to protect your *cgicmd.dat*. This file contains often the full connect strings (userid=SCOTT/TIGER@ORCL). Otherwise everyone can read this file (and the unencrypted passwords) with the following URL:
   http://myias/dev60cgi/rwcgi60/showmap?server=repserver

   (For more information see Metalink Note 133957.1).
6. Check the apache-listener log for unencrypted Oracle-passwords. If utl_http.request is used to submit new jobs and the *cgicmd.dat* is not used, the passwords will be sent to Apache unencrypted (and logged to *access_log*). Protect your *access_log* file.
7. Setting the environment variable REPORTS60_CGINODIAG will disable all debugging and diagnostic output from *rwcgi60*. This can be used to help prevent SQL Injection. Using utl_http.request to control submitting reports to the queue will give programmatic control of the handling of the error page generation without returning it to the browser.

Action 8.7.2

SEVERITY LEVEL: 2
O/S VERSION: All
ORACLE VERSIONS: 9iAS

Don't use ".RDF" files on reports server (in internet). These files contain the "source-code" of your report.
Always compile these reports into ".REP" files with rwcon60.

ORACLE SECURITY Step-by-Step

Phase 8 ~ Application Servers and the Middle Tier

Action 8.7.3

SEVERITY LEVEL: 3
O/S VERSION: All
ORACLE VERSIONS: 9iAS

Rename the rwcgi60 (.exe) executable to another name, e.g. petecgi. It is very easy to search google or other search engines with the search string "rwcgi60" or "rwcgi60.exe" within links and URLS (google advance option) and find the name of a reports server.

> **Note:** A good new white paper about Oracle reports security can be found at
> http://otn.oracle.com/products/reports/pdf/securing9i.pdf

Step 8.8 — XML/XSL and the XSQL Servlet

PROBLEM: *The XSQL servlet allows quick and easy development of XML/XSL based websites, but using this technology without care can allow an attacker access to the servers.*

> **Note:** This functionality is available as part of the 9iAS middle tier, and is delivered with the 9iAS product. The XSQL Servlet is based on the XML Java framework from Oracle. The XDK can be installed as part of Oracle 9iAS, or the whole XDK framework can be downloaded from technet.oracle.com

Action 8.8.1

SEVERITY LEVEL: 3
O/S VERSION: All
ORACLE VERSIONS: 9iAS

The username and password are available in XSQLConfig.xml. This file is located in the $ORACLE_HOME tree and can be in oracore/admin or /xdk/lib, but should be searched for in the source tree. An example of the file contents follows:

```xml
<connectiondefs>
    <connection name="myapp">
        <username>system</username>
        <password>manager</password>
        <dburl>jdbc:oracle:thin:@localhost:1521:ORCL</dburl>
        <driver>oracle.jdbc.driver.OracleDriver</driver>
    </connection>
</connectiondefs>
```

Phase 8 ~ Application Servers and the Middle Tier

Some solutions to this issue:

- You can set the location for this file as a wrapper classpath property in the *jserv.properties* or the zone.properties files. In $ORACLE_HOME/Apache/Jserv/jserv.properties. An example is:

```
...
# XSQLConfig.xml File location
wrapper.classpath=D:\oracle\oraias\oracore\admin
...
```

- Protect the file at the Operating system level, ensure that only the account that runs the servlet can read and write the file.

In some circumstances it is possible to use ../.. syntax to access this file from the web

Action 8.8.2

SEVERITY LEVEL: 2
O/S VERSION: All
ORACLE VERSIONS: 9iAS

To get HTML output from the generated XML from an Oracle XSQL page, an XSL stylesheet can be used.

Test the path to execute a servlet with the following:

<http://mytestserver/servlet/IsItWorking>
<http://mytestserver/servlets/IsItWorking>

The XSQL Class can be called with the browser as follows:

<http://mytestserver/servlet/oracle.xml.xsql.XSLQServlet>

Or

<http://mytestserver/servlets/oracle.xml.xsql.XSLQServlet>

If the Servlet Class exists, the version will be shown. If the version is => 1.0.0.0, then a backdoor to the system is available. Search on the web for information about Georgi Guninski and XSQL Servlet. He has a good example to call programs on a remote system with a stylesheet from another server.

This issue can be fixed as follows:

- Delete all of the class files in the default servlet directory such as the IsItWorking.class.
- Change the servlet URL /servlet and /servlets in the jserv.conf file.

Note: If the newer JServ Cartridge with Apache 1.3.19 is used, be careful to change ALL occurrences of the URL's in this file.

Phase 8 ~ Application Servers and the Middle Tier

Action 8.8.3

SEVERITY LEVEL: 3
O/S VERSION: All
ORACLE VERSIONS: 9iAS

The default URL's below should be restricted to stop any abuse:

>   /dms0
>   /dms/DMSDump
>   /servlet/DMSDump
>   /servlet/Spy
>   /dms/AgreeSpy

The solution is to:
- Disable the URL /servlet if possible.
- Deny the access to the dms0 URL and only allow to localhost.

Action 8.8.4

SEVERITY LEVEL: 3
O/S VERSION: All
ORACLE VERSIONS: 9iAS

The demos supplied with the XDK should be removed. Access to some of them allows *any* SQL to be run against the database.

If the URL below can be found, any SQL can be sent to the server:

`/xsql/demo/adhocsql/query.xsql?sql=<what ever you want>`

If this URL can be found, then it is like a *SQL*Plus* prompt for the Web.

To escape the ' ' use the + or %20:

`/xsql/demo/adhocsql/query.xsql?sql=select%20*%20from%20user_objects`

The only reliable way to secure this is to delete all of the samples.

Action 8.8.5

SEVERITY LEVEL 3
O/S VERSION All
ORACLE VERSIONS 9iAS

SQL Injection is a problem with the XSL servlet and XML pages. An example follows:

The placeholders in the SQL statement @USER or @PWD will be replaced with the value of the parameter in the following:

```
<?xml version="1.0" >
<xsql:query connection="myapp" xmlns:xsql="urn:oracle-xsql">
   select id,account,name from user where username='{@USER}' and pwd='{@PWD}'
</xsl:query>
```

The URL is normally called in this way:

http://mywebserver/mydemo/myApp.xsql?USER=jue&PWD=my

To poison the URL, the parameter PWD can be changed as follows:

```
http://mywebserver/mydemo/myApp.xsql?USER=jue&PWD=my'%20union%20select%20id,
account,name%20from%20user%20where%20'A'='A'
```

The statement in the XSQL page will now be transformed into:

```
select id,account,name from user where username='jue' and pwd='my' union select id,
account, name from user where 'A'='A'
```

If the SQL Statement is written in one single line, it is possible to disable the last parameter with a comment as follows:

```
http://mywebserver/mydemo/myApp.xsql?USER='admin'%20--
```

The statement in the XSQL page will be now transformed into:

```
select id,account,name from user where username='admin' -- and pwd=''
```

And now, it is possible to connect! The solution is to use *bind variables*. This also has the effect of speeding up performance if the page is accessed many times.

An example:

```
<?xml version="1.0" >
<xsql:query connection="myapp"
      xmlns:xsql="urn:oracle-xsql" bind-variable="USER PWD">
   select id,account,name from user where username=? and pwd=?
</xsl:query>
```

Action 8.8.6

SEVERITY LEVEL: 3
O/S VERSION: All
ORACLE VERSIONS: 9iAS

The Parameter *xml-stylesheet=none* in the URL will disable the style sheet process. While this is fine to debug, it should not be allowed in a production environment. Normally, the actual SQL being used would not be visible to the user of the web page, but if the above is possible, then the XML output is visible.

It is also possible to create your own stylesheet, access it remotely using the URL, and load the stylesheet from your own server. This can be used to call a program remotely.

This feature can be disabled as follows:

Edit the XMLConfig.xml file and set the Value **allow-client-style** to no

```
<defaults>
    <allow-client-style>no</allow-client-style>
</defaults>
```

Again, it is better to use *bind variables* so that SQL Injection cannot be done.

Action 8.8.7

SEVERITY LEVEL: 2
O/S VERSION: All
ORACLE VERSIONS: 9iAS

If it is possible to get an account on the server, then it is possible to use a command line utility to get XML data exports from the database.

If read access to the configuration file is possible, then the password can be read from there. The class to do this is:

`oracle.xml.xsql.XSQLCommandLine.`

An example follows:

```
java -cp
/opt/oracle/ora9i/lib/oraclexsql.jar:/opt/oracle/ora9i/lib/xmlparserv2.jar:/opt/oracle/ora9i/xdk/ad
min:/opt/oracle/ora9i/jdbc/lib/classes12.jar:/opt/oracle/ora9i/rdbms/jlib/xsu12.jar
oracle.xml.xsql.XSQLCommandLine bad.xsql
```

Pay attention to the right classpath! The path to the configuration file must be in the *classpath*.
Next install the Oracle XDX locally on a server, and use only the path to the original configuration file!

In the XML file, call the connection descriptor used to connect to the right database.

```
Example bad.xsql
<?xml version="1.0"?>
<page connection="demo" xmlns:xsql="urn:oracle-xsql">
<xsql:include-request-params/>
<xsql:query>
        SELECT * from user_objects
</xsql:query>
</page>
```

This tool and all classes needed can be downloaded from http://technet.oracle.com. With Oracle XSQL, it is possible to insert or change data. A very powerful SQL loader utility can be built with these techniques.

To secure against this issue:
- Delete the XML configuration file XMLConfig.xml in a production environment.
- Do not install the XDK, if it is not needed in production. If it must be used, then see the solutions in *Action 7.28.1*.

Action 8.8.8

SEVERITY LEVEL: 3
O/S VERSION: All
ORACLE VERSIONS: 9iAS

The URL http://mytestserver/oprocmger-status will display the status of the process manager of the *Jserv cartridge*. It is not possible to disable this URL because this URL is used internally.

One solution would be to allow only the local IP Address of the web server to call the URL. An example could be:

```
<IfModule mod_oprocmgr.c>
   ProcNode bhgvki 7780
   <Location /oprocmgr-service>
     SetHandler oprocmgr-service
      order deny,allow
      deny from all
      allow from  192.168.10.99
   </Location>
   <Location /oprocmgr-status>
     SetHandler oprocmgr-status
      order deny,allow
      deny from all
      allow from  192.168.10.99
   </Location>
</IfModule>
```

Action 8.8.9

SEVERITY LEVEL: 3
O/S VERSION: All
ORACLE VERSIONS: 9iAS

If the default URL /servlet or /servlets is used, it is possible to call every servlet in the *classpath* of the Jserv cartridge. Examples:

/servlet/DMSDump or /servlet/Spy

The solution is as follows:
- Change the mapping to the URL servlet. If it is possible with the application, change the URL to maybe xservlets or something else.
- If Apache > 1.3.19 is used, the Jserv configuration file and xml.conf file must be configured. In the Jserv configuration file, change ALL occurrences of /servlet to the new URL.
- If an application handler has been defined elsewhere to use a servlet over a file extension, like the XSQL servlet in xml.conf, change the URL's.

A Final Word

The data in a corporate database should be the most valuable asset that an organization owns. Even following all of the actions in this guide and more cannot protect against a malicious employee, whether he or she is a normal user or an administrator. A malicious employee with a password or two cannot be stopped. Do not assume all staff members are honest and stable. Check the background of staff, especially in sensitive organizations such as the military, financial services and law. Keep policies and plans up to date, and establish contingency plans if an administrator or user causes malicious damage.

Appendixes

Useful Resources For Oracle Security Professionals

Newsgroups and mailing lists to watch for database issues:

alt.2600
alt.2600.hackers
alt.2600.magazine
comp.database.oracle
comp.databases.oracle

comp.database.oracle.server
comp.databases.oracle.server
comp.sys.sun.*
The bugtraq mailing list on security focus
The pen-test mailing list on security focus

For history of the Oracle server newsgroup, see

http://groups.google.com/groups?hl=en&lr=&safe=off&group=comp.databases.oracle.server

(Click the radio button, "Search only in comp.databases.oracle.server")

The web sites that our contributors most often watch:

http://www.securityfocus.com
http://www.cert.org
http://www.sans.org
http://www.treachery.net
http://sunsolve.Sun.COM
http://www.enteract.com/~lspitz
http://csrc.ncsl.nist.gov

http://technet.oracle.com
http://www.sunhelp.org
http://www.sun.com/bigadmin/home/index.html
http://rootprompt.org
http://www.oracle.com
http://otn.oracle.com/deploy/security/alerts.htm

General Oracle web sites:

http://technet.oracle.com/index.html
http://tahiti.oracle.com/pls/tahiti/tahiti.homepage
http://www.jlcomp.demon.co.uk/faq/ind_faq.html
http://www.dbresources.com
http://www.ixora.com.au

http://www.dba-village.com
http://www.oracle.com/oramag/code/asktom
http://metalink.oracle.com
http://www.orapub.com

Cross-Reference Check List

This checklist cross-reference, which could be used to define a company standard for securing Oracle, lists every action in the guide, cross-referenced by severity level and by Operating system. Each action that applies only to an initial installation has also been highlighted.

This cross-reference will allow the database administrator and security manager to secure an Oracle database to a desired security level. It will also allow all of the actions necessary to secure a default installation.

Action	Description	Severity Level	O/S	Oracle Version	Default Install
0.1	Known Vulnerabilities	1	ALL	ALL	YES
0.2	Identify and record software versions and patch levels on the System	1	ALL	ALL	YES
0.3	Record database configuration	2	ALL	ALL	YES
0.4	Record security configuration	2	ALL	ALL	YES
0.5	Review database security procedures	2	ALL	ALL	YES
0.6	Store copies of the media off site	3	ALL	ALL	YES
0.7	Location of servers	2	ALL	ALL	YES
0.8	Architecture	3	ALL	ALL	YES
1.1.1	Owner of Oracle software	1	ALL	ALL	YES
1.1.2	Lock software owner account	1	ALL	ALL	YES
1.1.3	Name of the Oracle software owner	2	ALL	ALL	YES
1.1.4	Limit access to software owner account	2	Unix	ALL	YES
1.1.5	Separate owners for different components	2	ALL	ALL	YES
1.2.1	Check permissions of $ORACLE_HOME/bin	1	Unix	ALL	YES
1.2.2	Check *umask* value	1	Unix	ALL	YES
1.2.3	Check owner and group for all files in $ORACLE_HOME	1	Unix	ALL	YES
1.2.4	File permission issues for Windows	1	Windows	ALL	YES
1.2.5	Location of temp directories	1	Unix	ALL	YES
1.2.6	Windows group issues	1	Windows	ALL	YES
1.3.1	Review membership of OSDBA	1	ALL	ALL	YES
1.3.2	Ensure Oracle is not in root group	1	Unix	ALL	YES
1.3.3	O/S name of OSDBA group	1	Unix	ALL	YES
1.3.4	O/S name of OSDBA group on Windows	2	Windows	ALL	YES
1.4.1	Check trace file permissions	3	ALL	ALL	
1.4.2	Remove *tkprof* from production database	3	ALL	ALL	YES
1.4.3	Check permissions of the datafiles	1	ALL	ALL	YES

Cross-Reference Check List CONTINUED

Action	Description	Severity Level	O/S	Oracle Version	Default Install
1.4.4	Monitor Oracle log files	3	ALL	ALL	
1.4.5	Check for temporary files	2	ALL	ALL	
1.4.6	Check for tertiary trace files	2	ALL	ALL	
1.4.7	Check for remote data access files (RDA)	3	ALL	ALL	
1.4.8	Raw device permissions	1	Unix	ALL	YES
1.5.1	Usernames and passwords in process list	1	Unix	ALL	
1.5.2	Restrict the *ps* command	2	Unix	ALL	YES
1.5.3	Search history files for usernames and passwords	2	Unix	ALL	
1.6.1	Secure network transmissions	3	ALL	ALL	
1.6.2	Encrypt data transmissions	3	ALL	ALL	
1.6.3	Secure password transmission on the server	1	ALL	ALL	YES
1.6.4	Secure password transmission on the client	1	ALL	ALL	YES
1.6.5	JDBC thin driver transmissions	1	ALL	ALL	YES
1.7.1	Permissions on Oracle SUID and SGID files	3	Unix	ALL	YES
1.7.2	Non Oracle SUID and SGID files	3	Unix	ALL	
1.8.1	Audit environment variables for usernames and password	3	ALL	ALL	
1.8.2	Audit the machine for scripts containing usernames and passwords	2	ALL	ALL	
1.8.3	Audit *cron* for usernames and passwords	2	Unix	ALL	
1.8.4	Audit client configuration files for usernames and passwords	2	ALL	ALL	
1.8.5	Remove database creation scripts	2	ALL	ALL	YES
1.9.1	O/S auditing	2	ALL	ALL	YES
1.9.2	Save log files to a separate server using *Syslog* or Windows event viewer	2	ALL	ALL	YES
1.9.3	Integrity check O/S files used by Oracle	2	Unix	ALL	YES
1.9.4	Use host based IDS	3	ALL	ALL	
1.9.5	Review expected processes	2	ALL	ALL	
1.10.1	Control file permissions	2	ALL	ALL	YES
1.11.1	Confirm who is creating trace files	3	ALL	ALL	
1.11.2	Audit trace files for attempts to read passwords	3	ALL	ALL	
1.11.3	Ensure no user has ALTER SESSION and ALTER SYSTEM privileges	1	ALL	ALL	YES
1.12.1	Audit export file existence	1	ALL	ALL	
1.12.2	Changing database passwords after full import	1	ALL	ALL	
1.13.1	Locate archive log files	2	ALL	ALL	

Cross-Reference Check List CONTINUED

Action	Description	Severity Level	O/S	Oracle Version	Default Install
1.13.2	Save archivelog files to disk	2	ALL	ALL	
1.14.1	Audit external tables used	2	ALL	9i	
1.15.1	Restrict access to native PL/SQL compilation	1	ALL	9i	YES
1.16	Be aware of key files containing hashes or passwords	3	ALL	ALL	YES
1.17.1	Password protected listener can be shut down	3	Windows	ALL	
2.1.1	Audit database users activities	3	ALL	ALL	
2.1.2	Audit application database logins	3	ALL	ALL	
2.1.3	Audit users database passwords	2	ALL	8 and above	YES
2.1.4	Ensure users do not share account ID's	2	ALL	ALL	
2.1.5	Use proxy authentication	3	ALL	8 and above	
2.2.1	Audit default database accounts	1	ALL	ALL	YES
2.2.2	Add password management for default accounts	1	ALL	ALL	YES
2.2.3	Audit *internal* alias login	2	ALL	8i and lower	YES
2.2.4	Audit non database Oracle passwords	2	ALL	ALL	YES
2.2.5	Change *sys* password	1	ALL	ALL	YES
2.2.6	Change system password	1	ALL	ALL	YES
2.2.7	Create business process to audit default accounts regularly	2	ALL	ALL	
2.2.8	Disable remote login password file	2	ALL	ALL	YES
2.2.9	Use of *system* tablespace as default	3	ALL	ALL	YES
2.2.10	Modify Oracle scripts for default accounts that are used	1	ALL	ALL	YES
2.2.11	Audit known default role passwords	1	ALL	ALL	YES
2.3.1	Audit users accounts for passwords same as username	2	ALL	ALL	
2.3.2	Audit users accounts for weak passwords	2	ALL	ALL	
2.3.3	Lock dormant database accounts	3	ALL	ALL	
2.3.4	Data exposure on users	5	ALL	ALL	
2.3.5	Naming convention for users accounts	5	ALL	ALL	
2.3.6	Use LDAP for external authentication	4	ALL	9i and above	
2.3.7	Review database accounts, ensuring they belong to business users.	2	ALL	ALL	
2.4.1	Secure remote password login file	3	ALL	ALL	YES
2.5.1	Change SID and service name for third-party applications	4	ALL	ALL	YES
2.6.1	Applications authentication systems	3	ALL	ALL	
3.1.1	Audit *utl_file_dir* parameter	3	ALL	ALL	YES

Cross-Reference Check List CONTINUED

Action	Description	Severity Level	O/S	Oracle Version	Default Install
3.1.2	Audit *dbms_backup_restore* package permissions	3	ALL	ALL	YES
3.1.3	Java access to the O/S	2	ALL	8 and above	YES
3.1.4	Java and Oracle interaction	2	ALL	8 and above	YES
3.1.5	Secure Oracle Con Text	3	ALL	8 and above	YES
3.2.1	Secure ALL_USERS view	3	ALL	ALL	YES
3.2.2	Secure all ALL_% views	4	ALL	ALL	YES
3.3.1	Make *extproc* secure	2	ALL	8 and above	YES
3.4.1	Data Access Descriptors	4	ALL	9iAS	YES
3.5.1	Access to catalog roles	3	ALL	ALL	YES
3.5.2	Access to dba role views	3	ALL	ALL	YES
3.5.3	Password protect admin roles	4	ALL	ALL	YES
3.5.4	Role hierarchy	4	ALL	ALL	
3.5.5	Role naming conventions	5	ALL	ALL	
3.5.6	Create a role to manage users accounts	5	ALL	ALL	YES
3.6.1	Check database in archivelog mode	3	ALL	ALL	
3.6.2	*user_dump_dest* is valid	4	ALL	ALL	YES
3.6.3	*background_dump_dest* is valid	4	ALL	ALL	YES
3.6.4	*core_dump_dest* is valid	4	ALL	ALL	YES
3.6.5	Global_names is true	3	ALL	ALL	YES
3.6.6	Log_archive_start is set to true	4	ALL	ALL	YES
3.6.7	Max_enabled_roles is set correctly	3	ALL	ALL	YES
3.6.8	Os_authent_prefix is set to "" (null string).	2	ALL	ALL	YES
3.6.9	Os_roles is set to false	4	ALL	ALL	YES
3.6.10	O7_dictionary_accessibility is set to false	1	ALL	ALL	YES
3.6.11	Remote_os_authent is set to false	3	ALL	ALL	YES
3.6.12	Remote_os_roles is set to false	1	ALL	ALL	YES
3.6.13	Confirm parameters in database are the same as the configuration file	3	ALL	ALL	
3.6.14	Audit use of IFILE and the contents of files pointed to by IFILE	3	ALL	9i and above	
3.6.15	Remote_listener is null	3	ALL	9i and above	YES
3.6.16	Pfile and spfile can only be written to and read by the software owner.	2	ALL	ALL	YES
3.6.17	Exempt access policy privilege is revoked	2	ALL	9i and higher	YES
3.6.18	Check record locking parameters	2	ALL	ALL	YES

Cross-Reference Check List CONTINUED

Action	Description	Severity Level	O/S	Oracle Version	Default Install
3.7.1	Non *sys* objects in system tablespace	1	ALL	ALL	YES
3.8.1	Users who have *dba* privilege	1	ALL	ALL	YES
3.8.2	Users or roles granted ALL PRIVILEGES	1	ALL	ALL	YES
3.8.3	Privileges with ANY keyword granted	1	ALL	ALL	YES
3.8.4	Privileges granted "WITH ADMIN"	2	ALL	ALL	YES
3.8.5	Privileges granted "WITH GRANT"	2	ALL	ALL	YES
3.8.6	Review system privileges granted	1	ALL	ALL	YES
3.8.7	Application objects owned by privileged users	2	ALL	ALL	YES
3.8.8	Direct access granted to tables and objects	2	ALL	ALL	YES
3.8.9	"CREATE LIBRARY" privilege	1	ALL	ALL	YES
3.8.10	Advice on role use	3	ALL	ALL	YES
3.8.11	Audit access privileges on objects	2	ALL	ALL	YES
3.8.12	Integrity constraints	3	ALL	ALL	
3.8.13	Use triggers to insert critical data	3	ALL	ALL	
3.8.14	Restrict users to one role at once	2	ALL	ALL	
3.8.15	"BECOME USER" privilege	2	ALL	ALL	YES
3.9.1	Audit EXTERNAL users	2	ALL	ALL	YES
3.9.2	External users who are *dba*	1	ALL	ALL	YES
3.9.3	External users who have "ALL PRIVILEGES"	1	ALL	ALL	YES
3.9.4	Ensure external users have the least privileges possible	2	ALL	ALL	
3.9.5	Remote host based authentication	2	ALL	ALL	YES
3.9.6	No external users have SYSDBA or SYSOPER	1	ALL	ALL	YES
3.10.1	Revoke public execute privilege on *utl_file*	1	ALL	8 and higher	YES
3.10.2	Revoke public execute privilege on *utl_tcp*	1	ALL	8.1.7 and above	YES
3.10.3	Revoke public execute privilege on *utl_http*	1	ALL	8.1.7 and above	YES
3.10.4	Revoke public privilege on *utl_smtp*	1	ALL	8.1.7 and above	YES
3.10.5	Audit public execute privileges on *sys* owned packages.	1	ALL	ALL	YES
3.10.6	Revoke the public execute privilege on dbms_random.	2	ALL	ALL	YES
3.10.7	Revoke public execute privilege on *dbms_lob*	1	ALL	8i and above	YES
3.10.8	Revoke privileges on *dbms_sql* and *dbms_sys_sql*.	1	ALL	ALL	YES
3.10.9	Audit packages available via a database link	1	ALL	ALL	
3.10.10	Invokers rights PL/SQL procedures	2	ALL	ALL	

Cross-Reference Check List CONTINUED

Action	Description	Severity Level	O/S	Oracle Version	Default Install
3.10.11	Audit DIRECTORY objects	2	ALL	8 and higher	YES
3.11.1	Audit directly granted privileges	2	ALL	ALL	
3.11.2	Access tables through packages or roles.	4	ALL	ALL	
3.12.1	Change *system* users default tablespace.	1	ALL	ALL	YES
3.12.2	Change users default and temporary tablespaces	2	ALL	ALL	YES
3.13.1	Revoke the RESOURCE role from users	1	ALL	ALL	YES
3.13.2	Revoke the CONNECT role from all users	2	ALL	ALL	YES
3.13.3	Add passwords to critical and administrative roles	3	ALL	ALL	
3.13.4	Revoke all rights from PUBLIC	3	ALL	ALL	
3.14.1	Set password lifetime in profile	3	ALL	8 and above	
3.14.2	Set password grace time	3	ALL	8 and above	
3.14.3	Set password reuse max	2	ALL	8 and above	
3.14.4	Set failed login attempts	3	ALL	8 and above	
3.14.5	Set up profiles for each class of database user	3	ALL	ALL	
3.14.6	Set up general profile parameters	2	ALL	ALL	
3.15.1	Set _trace_files_public to false	3	ALL	ALL	
3.15.2	Review hidden initialisation parameters	3	ALL	ALL	
3.16.1	Objects in application tablespaces not owned by schema owner should be dropped	3	ALL	ALL	
3.17.1	Audit quota use per user	3	ALL	ALL	YES
3.17.2	Establish different users for schema management and data management	3	ALL	ALL	YES
3.18.1	Set up naming conventions for schema owners and administrators and users	5	ALL	ALL	
3.19.1	Audit users database triggers	2	ALL	ALL	YES
3.20.1	Audit access to critical *sys* owned views like user$	1	ALL	ALL	YES
3.20.2	Audit access to all dba and *sys* owned views	1	ALL	ALL	YES
3.21.1	Revoke object creation privileges from all but schema owners	2	ALL	ALL	YES
3.21.2	Ensure users can only see the objects they need	2	ALL	ALL	YES
3.22.1	Audit views to ensure only select access is allowed	2	ALL	ALL	YES
3.23.1	Reduce the chance of brute force attacks	2	ALL	ALL	
3.24.1	Prevent the dba reading system tables	2	ALL	ALL	YES
3.25.1	Prevent the dba from reading application data	4	ALL	ALL	
3.26.1	Integration and server to sever communications	2	ALL	ALL	
3.27.1	Internet access to the Oracle database	2	ALL	9iR2 and higher	YES

Cross-Reference Check List CONTINUED

Action	Description	Severity Level	O/S	Oracle Version	Default Install
3.28.1	Secure *statspack*	2	ALL	8i and higher	YES
4.1.1	Configure audit and storage.	2	ALL	ALL	
4.2.1	Audit insert failures on critical objects	2	ALL	ALL	
4.2.2	Use triggers to capture login events	2	ALL	ALL	YES
4.3.1	Audit create session	2	ALL	ALL	YES
4.3.2	Audit use of all grant privileges.	2	ALL	ALL	YES
4.3.3	Audit the use of all drop statements	3	ALL	ALL	
4.3.4	Audit the use of all alter statements	2	ALL	ALL	
4.3.5	Audit the use of create user	3	ALL	ALL	YES
4.3.6	Audit create role	3	ALL	ALL	
4.3.7	Audit all create statements	3	ALL	ALL	
4.3.8	Establish procedures to review audit logs	3	ALL	ALL	YES
4.3.9	Use Log Miner to audit certain activities	4	ALL	ALL	
4.4.1	Configure basic audit	2	ALL	ALL	
4.4.2	Limit users who can change the audit trail	2	ALL	ALL	YES
4.4.3	Protect the audit trail	2	ALL	ALL	YES
4.4.4	Backup the audit trail	3	ALL	ALL	YES
4.4.5	Purge the audit trail	4	ALL	ALL	YES
4.5.1	Check date / time stamps on database objects	3	ALL	ALL	
4.6.1	Ensure reports and alerts are in place to deal with irregularities found through audit	3	ALL	ALL	YES
4.7.1	Use triggers for row level auditing	3	ALL	ALL	
4.7.2	Use VPD, RLS and label security.	3	ALL	8 and above	
4.8.1	Failure to be alerted of suspicious activities	2	ALL	ALL	YES
4.9.1	Failure to audit the security profile.	2	ALL	ALL	
4.10.1	Audit the Oracle generated log files	2	ALL	ALL	
5.1.1	Prevent set commands on the listener	1	ALL	ALL	YES
5.1.2	Prevent remote dba access on sql*net v1	4	ALL	ALL	
5.1.3	Audit the *listener.ora* file	5	ALL	ALL	
5.1.4	Enable shared sockets	3	ALL	Windows	
5.1.5	Force the MTS dispatcher to use specific ports	4	ALL	ALL	
5.1.6	Do not use the standard listener ports	2	ALL	ALL	YES
5.1.7	Do not use known SID or service name	2	ALL	ALL	YES

Cross-Reference Check List CONTINUED

Action	Description	Severity Level	O/S	Oracle Version	Default Install
5.1.8	In small environments do not use hostnames in listener.ora.	2	ALL	ALL	
5.1.9	Use a personal firewall on database administrator computers	2	ALL	ALL	YES
5.1.10	Secure *listener.ora* at the O/S level	2	ALL	ALL	YES
5.2.1	Restrict sources of database connections	3	ALL	ALL	
5.2.2	Use connection manager and Oracle names to restrict connections by source	2	ALL	ALL	
5.3.1	Set the listener password	1	ALL	ALL	YES
5.4.1	Restrict listener banner information	3	ALL	ALL	
5.5.1	Use a firewall to protect the Oracle server.	2	ALL	ALL	
5.6.1	Audit Oracle client file permissions	4	ALL	ALL	
5.6.2	Audit client configuration file contents	5	ALL	ALL	
5.6.3	Audit the listener	2	ALL	ALL	YES
5.7.1	Audit database links for hard clear text passwords	1	ALL	ALL	YES
5.7.2	Discover what objects can be seen in the linked database	2	ALL	ALL	YES
5.7.3	Create a policy to manage database links	1	ALL	ALL	YES
5.7.4	Database link user should not be a dba	1	ALL	ALL	YES
5.7.5	Audit what links exist into and from the database	1	ALL	ALL	YES
5.8.1	Confirm the file permissions in the network admin directory	2	ALL	ALL	YES
5.8.2	Add only minimum configuration files to all clients	2	ALL	ALL	
5.9.1	Keep up to date with Oracle listener vulnerabilities	2	ALL	ALL	
5.10.1	Secure remote dba access to the server	1	ALL	ALL	
5.10.2	Use an application gateway firewall	2	ALL	ALL	
5.11.1	Set server to dedicated in the tnsnames.ora file	1	ALL	ALL	YES
5.11.2	Disable Oracle ports that are not needed.	3	ALL	ALL	YES
5.12.1	Audit the intelligent agent	2	ALL	ALL	YES
5.12.2	Protect clear text passwords for snmp	2	ALL	ALL	YES
5.13.1	Use Oracle advance security to encrypt data transfer	3	ALL	ALL	
5.13.2	Enable SSL to protect client transmissions	3	ALL	ALL	
6.1.1	Review and document backup and restore procedures	3	ALL	ALL	YES
6.1.2	Review and document recovery procedures	3	ALL	ALL	YES
6.1.3	Store backup media off site	3	ALL	ALL	YES
6.1.4	Schedule cold backups	3	ALL	ALL	YES
6.1.5	Validate the backup media regularly	3	ALL	ALL	YES

Cross-Reference Check List CONTINUED

Action	Description	Severity Level	O/S	Oracle Version	Default Install
6.1.6	Do not allow backups to be available on-line	2	ALL	ALL	
6.1.7	Create and use media retrieval procedures	2	ALL	ALL	
6.2.1	Mirror the on line redo logs	2	ALL	ALL	YES
6.3.1	Ensure the database is in archive log mode	2	ALL	ALL	YES
6.3.2	Ensure archive log directories exist and are protected	2	ALL	ALL	YES
6.3.3	Ensure archive logs are written to backup and are purged	3	ALL	ALL	YES
6.4.1	Separate the Oracle software from data and from on-line redo and archive	3	ALL	ALL	YES
6.4.2	Keep Oracle data files on separate disks	3	ALL	ALL	YES
6.4.3	Use OFA	5	ALL	ALL	
6.4.4	Use striping and mirroring or RAID for Oracle data	4	ALL	ALL	
6.5.1	Magnetically wipe old disks that have contained database data.	2	ALL	ALL	
6.6.1	Document and review disaster recovery procedures	4	ALL	ALL	YES
6.6.2	Include business users in disaster recovery planning	4	ALL	ALL	YES
7.1.1	Identify and *wrap* all PL/SQL code in the database	2	ALL	ALL	YES
7.1.2	Checksum all PL./SQL objects in the database	3	ALL	ALL	
7.1.3	Audit PL/SQL code for hard coded usernames and passwords	3	ALL	ALL	
7.1.4	Audit PL/SQL code for possible SQL injection attacks	2	ALL	ALL	
7.1.5	Ensure as little information as possible about schema structure is available from the code	3	ALL	ALL	
7.1.6	Pre-compile Java code before loading into the database.	3	ALL	ALL	YES
7.2.1	Review which applications access the database and how and from where.	2	ALL	ALL	
7.2.2	Implement procedures to limit which applications can access the database and from where	2	ALL	ALL	
7.2.3	Limit administration tools from accessing the database.	3	ALL	ALL	
7.3.1	When decommissioning old applications remove all binaries and files	4	ALL	ALL	
7.4.1	Review procedures for adding new applications	4	ALL	ALL	
7.5.1	Movers, leavers and joiners	2	ALL	ALL	
7.6.1	Audit application file permissions	3	ALL	ALL	
7.7.1	Check for evidence of development on production databases	3	ALL	ALL	
7.8.1	Restrict ad-hoc queries	3	ALL	ALL	
7.9.1	Review users permissions in test and development databases	2	ALL	ALL	
7.9.2	Check for database links with access to production databases	2	ALL	ALL	
7.9.3	Ensure "live" data held in test or development is mangled or obfusticated.	2	ALL	ALL	
7.9.4	Do not locate test and development databases on the same server as production	2	ALL	ALL	

Cross-Reference Check List CONTINUED

Action	Description	Severity Level	O/S	Oracle Version	Default Install
7.9.5	No access from test and development to production	2	ALL	ALL	
7.9.6	No developer access to production	1	ALL	ALL	YES
7.9.7	No developer database accounts on production	2	ALL	ALL	
7.9.8	Backups and exports copy passwords to test and development	2	ALL	ALL	
7.9.9	Place development and test on different network segment to production	2	ALL	ALL	
7.10.1	Move all non application objects from application tablespaces	2	ALL	ALL	
7.10.2	Ensure no privileged user owns application objects	2	ALL	ALL	
7.11.1	Audit resources used by the database	2	ALL	ALL	
7.12.1	Do not duplicate Oracle authentication	1	ALL	ALL	
7.12.2	Do not use one database login to authenticate all other users	2	ALL	ALL	
7.13.1	Do not use schema owners for administration tasks	2	ALL	ALL	
7.13.2	Ensure the schema owner is not a dba	2	ALL	ALL	
7.13.3	Lock schema owner accounts	2	ALL	ALL	
7.14.1	Audit public synonyms	5	ALL	ALL	
7.15.1	Do not hard code usernames and passwords in application source code	2	ALL	ALL	
7.15.2	Do not use Java	2	ALL	8 and above	
7.15.3	Do not allow applications to change the schema	2	ALL	ALL	
7.16.1	Batch processes should access the database through one designed account	1	ALL	ALL	
7.16.2	Do not use external accounts for batch processes	1	ALL	ALL	
7.16.3	Consider password retrieval and use in schedulers	1	ALL	ALL	
7.16.4	Enable batch database accounts only when needed	1	ALL	ALL	
7.17.1	Use product user profile to secure SQL*Plus	4	ALL	ALL	
7.17.2	Audit query tool privileges	3	ALL	ALL	
7.18.1	Encrypt critical data	2	ALL	ALL	
7.19.1	Audit generated applications for known weaknesses	2	ALL	ALL	
7.19.2	Audit public libraries used for know vulnerabilities	2	ALL	ALL	
7.20.1	Use change control	2	ALL	ALL	
7.21.1	Audit advance queues used	2	ALL	ALL	
7.22.1	Audit tools used for password leakage	2	ALL	ALL	
7.23.1	Ensure no tool offers better access to the database than the application	2	ALL	ALL	
7.24.1	Checksum application files for Trojans	2	ALL	ALL	
7.25.1	Start the Oracle HTTP Server as a non privileged user	1	ALL	9i and higher	YES

ORACLE SECURITY Step-by-Step

Cross-Reference Check List CONTINUED

Action	Description	Severity Level	O/S	Oracle Version	Default Install
7.25.2	Configure HTTPS and secure the listener	3	ALL	9i and higher	YES
7.25.3	Add authentication for users	2	ALL	9i and higher	YES
7.25.4	Set HTTP passwords	2	ALL	9i and higher	YES
7.25.5	Configure product user profile	3	ALL	9i and higher	YES
7.25.6	Restrict databases that can be accessed	2	ALL	9i and higher	YES
7.25.7	Disable iSQL*Plus on production servers	1	ALL	9i and higher	YES
7.26.1	Enable and disable various database features	2	ALL	ALL	
7.27.1	Protect debugger interfaces	2	ALL	ALL	
7.28.1	Do not divulge system information to the public	2	ALL	ALL	YES
8.1.1	Secure the portal DAD admin page	2	ALL	9iAS	YES
8.1.2	Encryption of the DAD password	1	ALL	9iAS	YES
8.1.3	Secure the portal users passwords in the database	1	ALL	9iAS	YES
8.1.4	Restrict the portal gateway URL	2	ALL	9iAS	YES
8.1.5	Remove the portal example programs	1	ALL	9iAS	YES
8.1.6	Revoke DBA from portal admin database users	1	ALL	9iAS	YES
8.1.7	Restrict access to OWA_UTL and other PL/SQL packages	1	ALL	9iAS	YES
8.2.1	Create secure wireless user and password	3	ALL	9iAS	YES
8.3.1	Permissions on file containing Webcache admin password	1	ALL	9iAS	YES
8.3.2	Permissions on Webcache.xml	1	ALL	9iAS	YES
8.4.1	Reset default account passwords in database cache database	1	ALL	9iAS	YES
8.4.2	Permissions for export files used to create database cache	2	ALL	9iAS	YES
8.5.1	Protect Apache	2	ALL	9iAS	YES
8.5.2	SYSTEM password appears in Apache install window title	3	ALL	9iAS	YES
8.5.3	Change default port numbers	3	ALL	9iAS	YES
8.5.4	Apply patches to web server	1	ALL	9iAS	YES
8.5.5	Run *nessus* against 9iAS	4	ALL	9iAS	YES
8.5.6	Protect *httpd.conf* file	1	ALL	9iAS	YES
8.5.7	Remove OJSP example programs	1	ALL	9iAS	YES
8.5.8	Protect against an attacker reading JSP class files	1	ALL	9iAS	YES
8.5.9	Restrict dynamic monitoiring services	1	ALL	9iAS	YES
8.6.1	Change IFS password	1	ALL	9iAS	YES
8.7.1	Secure the reports sever	1	ALL	9iAS	YES

Cross-Reference Check List CONTINUED

Action	Description	Severity Level	O/S	Oracle Version	Default Install
8.7.2	Use only compiled reports	2	ALL	9iAS	YES
8.7.3	Rename *rwcgi60* executable	3	ALL	9iAS	YES
8.8.1	Protect XMLConfig.xml	3	ALL	9iAS	YES
8.8.2	Delete servlet class files	2	ALL	9iAS	YES
8.8.3	Disable servlet URL	3	ALL	9iAS	YES
8.8.4	Delete XSQL examples	3	ALL	9iAS	YES
8.8.5	In XSQL use bind variables	3	ALL	9iAS	YES
8.8.6	Set allow-client-style=no	3	ALL	9iAS	YES
8.8.7	Delete the XSQL XDK from production databases	2	ALL	9iAS	YES
8.8.8	Restrict the XSQL status URL	3	ALL	9iAS	YES
8.8.9	Change the mapping for the servlet URL	3	ALL	9iAS	YES

Notes